SO-BIP-409

OLD age in a CHanGInG SOCIeTY

OLD AGE in a CHANGING SOCIETY

ZENA SMITH BLAU

New Viewpoints
A Division of Franklin Watts, Inc.
New York   1973

cover and interior design by Nicholas Krenitsky

Library of Congress Cataloging in Publication Data

Blau, Zena Smith, 1922–
    Old age in a changing society.

    Includes bibliographical references.
    1. Ages–United States.   2. United States–
Social conditions—1960—   I. Title.
HQ1064.U5B43   301.43'5'0973   74-190126
ISBN 0-531-06354-2
ISBN 0-531-06480-8 (pbk.)

To my mother, Lena Kreczmer Smith,
and my father, Joseph Smith (1894–1962),
with love, gratitude, and respect

O heavens,
If you do love old men, if your sweet sway
Allow obedience, if you yourselves are old,
Make it your cause. Send down and take my part!
King Lear
Act II, Scene 4

CONTENTS

Preface   xi

I   Old Age in a Changing Society   1

II   Aging, Widowhood, and Retirement:
A Sociological Perspective   21

III   Parents and Children   37

IV   The Significance of Friendship   59

V   Structural Constraints on Friendship   77

VI   Changes in Identity   99

VII   Influence of Intimates on Identity Change   115

VIII   Illness and Work Alienation in Old Age   133

IX   Patterns of Response to Aging   147

X   New Roles for Later Life   175

XI   Role Exit: A Theoretical Essay   209

Notes   247

Index   277

PReFaCe

Many people try to imagine what their life will be like when they retire or are widowed, particularly as they approach the stage in life when these things happen to acquaintances and associates. But they can rarely foresee the full range of consequences set off by later exits from long-held roles—partly because they lack a knowledgeable perspective on other possible roles in their repertory. The present work, by providing such a perspective, can help the reader gain not only a more realistic assessment of the changes that may follow widowhood and retirement but a greater understanding of how to prepare for and cope with these changes when they occur.

In the present era, vastly increased numbers of people survive middle age and face the prospect of living for a long time in a society that as yet has found no ways to use the qualities, talents, and skills of its aging citizens. Since most of us view life as an ultimate value, we hail any act or artifact that extends it as a boon to humanity. Perhaps some day that will be true. For the present, however, I question the wisdom of a society that allocates considerable resources and talent to prolonging human life but fails to provide meaningful social roles for older people. That, I submit, is the critical problem of aging in modern society.

I do not deny the importance of the other problems that beset older people. Poverty, illness, inadequate and inappropriate housing are more widespread among the old than any other age group—but they are not unique to old age. The solutions to these problems are known and understood. They persist because America, although the most affluent nation in the world, is not willing to allocate the resources necessary to provide decent incomes, decent housing, and decent health care to all its citizens, including the old.

An additional and equally pressing need of people in all stages and walks of life, including the old, is to be useful. For it is the sustained experience of being necessary to others that gives meaning and purpose to the life of all human beings. Opportunities to remain useful members of the society are severely undermined by the exits from adult social roles that are typical of old age.

True, older people do receive some *financial* restitution after widowhood and retirement, but our society has failed as yet to assume any significant degree of responsibility for creating new and meaningful forms of *social* restitution for them. As a result, enforced idleness and uselessness have become the fate of many older people in American society. Only an affluent society can maintain a considerable segment of its population in nonproductive idleness. To do so, however, is a waste of human resources and human spirit that could be used to benefit both the society and its older members. If human life is precious, then it is folly to waste it. If it is not, then why extend it? This is the dilemma that old age poses for a post-industrial society.

Several people helped in various ways to make this book possible, and I take this occasion to acknowledge their contributions.

I am indebted to Professors Milton Barron of the City University of New York, Gordon Streib of Cornell University, Bernard Kutner of Albert Einstein College of Medicine. The late John Dean and the late Edward A.

Suchman, directors of a series of studies on aging at Cornell University in the late forties and early fifties (funded by the Rockefeller and Lilly foundations), invited me to join them as a research fellow to help design three of their studies and analyze data from them: the Elmira study of older people; the Kips-Bay study of the health needs of older people in New York City; and the study of associates of Kips-Bay respondents. The original data that appear in the present book are from these sources.

Bernard Rosenberg, Professor of Sociology at CCNY, my close friend and fellow sociologist, was instrumental in my decision to write this book and in arranging for its publication. I do not know what would have been its fate had I not had his continuing encouragement and support.

Robert F. Merton, Professor of Sociology at Columbia University, as teacher, dissertation adviser, and friend, had an important influence on my development as a sociologist. Being his student was an exciting adventure, and I shall always remember him with great fondness.

Paul F. Lazarsfeld, Professor of Sociology Emeritus at Columbia University, introduced me to the logic and methods of survey analysis. His zest and imagination in teaching his craft led me to first appreciate the value and possibilities of quantitative data.

Joyce Starr and Helen Miller, while graduate students of sociology at Northwestern University, served as dedicated and creative research assistants in the preparation of the present volume. Joyce Starr, in particular, greatly expedited the preparation of the first draft of the manuscript.

Linda Tomal Papp and Nancy Morris had the demanding task of typing various drafts of the manuscript. I greatly appreciate the efficiency and good humor with which each of them discharged their responsibilities.

Merton Krause, William Simon, and the late Noël Jenkin, my colleagues at the Institute for Juvenile Research, provided time, resources, and encouragement.

Ivan Dee, former editor of Quadrangle Books, and Mary Elinore Smith, were skillful and understanding editors of the manuscript. I appreciate the care they exercised *not* to sacrifice meaning for form.

Last, although not least, I am indebted to my seventeen-year-old daughter Pamela, who has been a continuing source of joy and growth to me. During our countless conversations on the subject, she led me to see that her resistance to "growing up" in the conventional meaning of the term is, in reality, a struggle against the same forces in contemporary society that lead to the impoverishment of life and spirit in old age.

OLD aGe
In a
CHanGInG
SOCIeTY

OLD aGe
in a
CHanGinG
SOCieTY

"Promise me—promise me I won't get old."
—DOROTHY PARKER

How an individual deals with his own old age is very much conditioned by the social order that exists during his lifetime. The far-reaching and rapid changes of modern society have profoundly affected the position of old people and their ability to deal with their own problems. They face new problems, specifically social as distinct from physical or economic, and the solution of these problems requires new forms of social action.

Until now the study of old age has produced a large body of facts and figures. To be sure, such work is necessary and useful in shaping public policy designed to help the old. But what is largely missing in this work is an interpretation of the facts, infused with sociological imagination and human compassion. One is dismayed, for example, by the tendency of many writers either to deny or to gloss over the useless and meaningless lives of many older people in our affluent society. Some observers have even rationalized the isolation of the old in modern society by arguing that "disengagement" is a normal and inevitable accompaniment of aging. As evidence for this argument, they point out that *some* inactive and relatively isolated people express satisfaction with life.[1] No doubt there are old people vegetating in mental institutions (which care for a disproportionate number of the aged) who might also indicate a satisfaction with life if they were asked. But most evidence does not support the disengagement theory. For, as a rule, if they have any option, older people prefer significant social roles in which they are able to feel that they are as they were, that there is a sense of meaning and purpose in their lives.

While older persons in modern society, particularly those with adequate economic resources, have a freedom and personal discretion not available in more traditional societies, their freedom is a mixed blessing. As Erich Fromm so cogently points out, there is a critical break between "freedom from" and the existential dilemma of "freedom for what?" [2] Without cultural guidelines, the freedom to choose is a burden, not an opportunity. This kind of cultural ambiguity helps explain why old age cannot be viewed merely as an economic, physical, or psychological problem, or even as a combination of these, but must be understood as an existential problem for the older person and as a critical social problem for the larger society.

The emergence of old age as a social problem has its roots in modern society's technological and social innovations. Because of them, life expectancy has dramatically increased in the United States and in other industrial nations since the turn of the century. Between 1900 and 1960 the American population was multiplied two and a half times. In that same period, however, the proportion of the population sixty-five years and older increased five times. Thus in 1900 there were only 3.1 million people in this age group. By 1960 there were 16.7 million older people in the United States, and by 1990 the figure is expected to reach 2.7 million. In short, within twenty years older people will constitute at least 10 per cent of the American population. [3]

It has been estimated that the average lifetime of an individual in ancient Rome and in medieval society was between twenty and thirty years, and in mid-nineteenth-century America about forty years. At the turn of the century it was forty-nine years. By 1964, over the short period of about sixty years, the average lifetime had increased by two decades, to seventy years. [4]

3

To a large extent these dramatic gains are due to a sharp decline in infant and child mortality rates, age categories in which death rates were normally highest in premodern societies. In the United States, for example, the sharpest decline in the death rate has occurred in the one-to-four age group; a more moderate decline has occurred among the five-to-fifty-five age group, and the smallest decline is found in the age group beyond fifty-five.[5]

As women live longer than men, the disparity in the sex composition of the older population increases. In 1900, for example, among people sixty-five and older there were 102 males for every 100 females. By 1966 the ratio of males to females in this age group had dropped to 76.6.[6] Among people seventy-five and older, the excess of women over men is even more marked: 73 men to every 100 women. Thus the imbalance in sex composition, which in the general population is slight (49 percent males and 51 percent females), increases markedly in successively older age groups; and estimates for the future indicate a further decline in the sex ratio. By 1985, in the group beyond seventy-five, the ratio of men to women is expected to be 61.1.[7]

Other demographic changes, as well, have led to new problems connected with aging. Earlier marriage, fewer children, and children's leaving the home sooner—all combine to end the duties of parenthood earlier than in former times. Sons go into the armed services; children in the middle classes leave home to attend college. With greater affluence, young people in large cities, when they begin work, live separately from their parents, either alone or with their peers, until they marry and establish their own homes.

4

Table 1 documents these demographic changes. In 1959 the number of years between the age of marriage of spouses and the marriage of their last child had declined to twenty-seven years, as compared to thirty-three in 1890. In the earlier period, the husband or wife often died before the marriage of the couple's youngest child. By 1959, however, the median age of the wife at the marriage of her last child was forty-seven years; that of her husband, forty-nine years. Thus today a couple can expect to live together without the presence of children for another sixteen years or so before the death of one of the partners.[8]

Commonly in the past one child would remain at home to help the widowed parent during the period of bereavement and to maintain some continuity of family life. When the youngest offspring did marry, the young couple often lived in the home of the widowed mother. In her own house the mother maintained a position that a woman does not enjoy today if she goes to live with a married son or daughter; it is not her home and belongings but theirs, and she lives *with them*. Moreover, because men live longer and children marry earlier, many years pass between the time her children move away and the time her husband dies. During these years her children have grown accustomed to living in their own nuclear family, without the presence of "outsiders." An older parent moving into a long-established household can easily create new strains in the family life of the younger couple. Now it is the parent who is the dependent, and her child and the latter's spouse occupy a superior position, at least in the management of household affairs.

As a result of modernization, the productive functions of the urban family have dwindled; it has become a unit of

5

TABLE 1
Median Age of Husband and Wife
at Successive Events in the Family Cycle

Stage	1890	1940	1950	1959
Median age of wife at—				
First marriage	22.0	21.5	20.1	20.2
Birth of last child *	31.9	27.1	26.1	25.8
Marriage of last child	55.3	50.0	47.6	47.1
Death of husband	53.3	60.9	61.4	63.6
Median age of husband at—				
First marriage	26.1	24.3	22.8	22.3
Birth of last child	36.0	29.9	28.8	27.9
Marriage of last child	59.4	52.8	50.3	49.2
Death of wife	57.4	63.6	64.1	65.7

* The authors suggest that these ages are probably too young by a year or two for all dates, according to data from cohorts of women collected in August, 1959, by the Bureau of the Census.

Source: Paul C. Glick, David M. Heer, and John C. Beresford, "Family Formation and Family Composition: Trends and Prospects," paper read at the annual meeting of the American Association for the Advancement of Science, Chicago, December, 1959, p. 12.

consumption with no direct role in the production process. In agricultural societies children and older people are an asset to the family. They help in the household and on the farm. In an urban society, on the other hand, large families are a liability. With progressive industrialization, children and old people are excluded from the labor force. The adult male who is the head of the household usually must support the family. While they have small children to rear and socialize, white women in the United States have not, as a rule, been gainfully employed. Among Negroes the proportion of employed women is far greater, since discrimination against black people, particularly black men, has made it impossible for black women to follow the pattern of whites. Thus the role of older women in rearing grandchildren is far more significant than among whites.

Living space is more costly in urban areas, especially in and around larger cities, and the costs of rearing and educating children are generally higher. People have fewer children and smaller living quarters, and it is therefore difficult to accommodate aged relatives. Added to this is the need for privacy, and both adult children and their aged parents strongly prefer separate residences.[9]

Although men and women remain fathers and mothers even after the dispersal of their children, their roles are not the same. They lose all formal authority over the children, though not all influence—or affection or respect. Certainly the parents whose children continue to depend on them for money or services can maintain a measure of authority, or at least can claim the right to participate in, and to some extent influence, the lives of their children.[10] But the right of adult children to be independent from parents is firmly established in American society, and is usually adhered to by both generations. Furthermore, adult children decide how much participation and influence parents may have in their lives. It is not unheard of for children to cut virtually all ties with a parent who insists on preempting these rights.

All these changes have substantially diminished the ties between grown children and their parents. By the time parents reach their sixties, the likelihood is that separate residence is well established and strongly preferred by both generations. True, they maintain friendly relations, and parents often extend various forms of help, such as financial

7

aid and services, to their children or grandchildren, but they are in no way considered members of their children's families. Their status, when they visit the children, is not much different from that of old family friends. Their unsolicited advice or interference in the affairs of the children's family life is discouraged, and a source of conflict if it occurs. Thus parents occupy only a marginal position in the lives of their children, especially when the children reach a higher social class, with corresponding changes in their style of life, associations, and interests.[11] There are few actual parental rights or obligations left, except in times of crisis. If a son or son-in-law, a daughter or daughter-in-law dies, for example, parents may step in as surrogates for a time. Or they may do so for short periods under happier circumstances, as when the young couple vacations without their children. But aside from these special occasions, older parents are outsiders in the family life of their children.

The evidence suggests that this process is probably typical for middle-class Americans. But among recent migrants, black and white, from rural areas to the city, three generations more frequently live under one roof. Particularly in fatherless homes, the grandmother may be the effective head of a household composed of one or more daughters and the daughters' children. As the economic lot of the working class improves, and mobility into the middle class continues, the middle-class pattern can be expected in time to become more widespread throughout society.

These changes in the nature of family life become especially important for older people after they are widowed. It is then, for the first time in their lives, that they find themselves no longer members of a nuclear family—that is,

8

without the rights and responsibilities that normally define family membership.

CHANGES IN THE ECONOMY

Among economic changes, the relatively recent institution of job retirement has had a tremendous effect on old people. The mechanization and automation of production has brought a steady decline in the need for unskilled and semi-skilled labor. In the past thirty years there has been less demand for people with the qualifications of the typical worker before the depression of the 1930's: a grade-school education, a pair of willing hands, and a strong back.

As economic life becomes more industrialized and bureaucratic, the self-employed become a diminishing proportion of the labor force at all occupational levels. More and more people become employees, with less and less opportunity to decide on the matter of retirement. Today only the urban self-employed, who constitute a small percentage of the labor force (9.7 percent),[12] can still choose when to retire.[13] For the vast majority of the gainfully employed, management makes the rules for retirement, often with the assent of unions. Indeed, the unions—for example, in the oil, steel, and automobile industries—have actually exerted pressure to lower the eligibility age for pension rights.[14] Pressure on employees to retire before the age of sixty-five is bound to increase among younger workers, too, because the exit of a company's oldest employees improves the seniority status of the younger ones.

Many workers, to be sure, readily accept compulsory retirement, particularly the less skilled. But the evidence shows that the higher a man's occupational status, the less

9

willing he is, as a rule, to retire.[15] People who enjoy their work are naturally more reluctant to retire than those who view their jobs principally as a means of earning a living.

Before bureaucracy entered industry, farmers and small entrepreneurs could retire gradually. Today an employee must retire at sixty-five or sixty-eight regardless of his ability, need, or desire. Once retired, he is rarely able to return to gainful employment, except for marginal jobs that do not attract younger personnel because of low pay and prestige, or undesirable working conditions. Moreover, social security laws are designed to encourage minimal earnings. At best, then, the retired person ordinarily can return to the labor market only at a lower level than the one he previously occupied. He is thus subject to the "ego threat" that generally accompanies any downward occupational mobility—an experience most older people prefer to avoid.

The accumulated experience of older employees is no longer the asset it was in traditional, slowly changing societies. Innovations in modern industry demand younger personnel familiar with new knowledge and techniques. Skills become obsolete relatively quickly, and the desire to increase profits requires change and growth. Older workers at the higher levels of the occupational hierarchy not only block the younger employees' chances for promotion, but they may also resist innovation, particularly if it represents a threat to their job security or status. The rate of promotion is more rapid today; there is reason to believe that this generation is reaching high executive positions at a younger age than ever before.

On the other hand, in factories the lot of older workers has improved as a result of wide unionization. The application of the seniority principle has given them advantages over younger workers in such matters as the distribution of overtime, promotions, desirable transfers, and daytime shift assignments. Then, too, older men almost always hold top union positions, resisting younger workers' attempts to assume leadership. In political parties and reform agencies as well, older men maintain control over institutions that might otherwise serve as agencies of protest.[16]

Still on the positive side, the economic position of older workers is better than that of younger ones. Their children are grown; their wives often have jobs; and they are at the peak of their earning power. Younger workers, in contrast, have heavy expenses, particularly in a period of inflation. They marry, buy homes, have families, and assume debts in order to share in the high standard of living that all Americans are taught to want and expect. They resent contributing to the pension and social security systems that benefit older, better-off workers. Some countries (for example, Sweden, Great Britain, and Japan) have programs of family allowances, housing assistance, and other services to help younger people, but young American families rely heavily on the "buy now, pay later" principle.

Because the present generation did not experience the depression of the 1930's, the terrible vulnerability of workers before the emergence of large-scale unions and the introduction of the seniority principle into industry are remote to them. From their standpoint, it seems unjust to protect the status of older workers with less formal education and less knowledge of technical innovations than they themselves have. From time to time one comes across accounts of informal pressures by younger against older

11

workers, particularly when jobs become scarce. For example, a steel worker says, "Everyone over sixty-five should be chased out of these mills. Make retirement compulsory. There aren't enough jobs to go around and these old codgers have had theirs. Get 'em out." [17]

The Great Depression introduced compulsory retirement. Social security laws and pension systems were a response to the plight of older workers, many of whom, after a period of prolonged unemployment, found themselves barred from reentering the labor force.[18] With amazing speed over a twenty-five-year period, occupational retirement has become institutionalized in America. In a rapidly expanding economy, this system, which encourages older workers to retire, also gives more opportunities to better-educated younger workers. As higher education spreads among the poor and among minority groups such as women and blacks, these groups will compete for jobs requiring technical skills that did not exist when older workers entered the labor force, so the age of retirement can be expected to be pushed back from sixty-five to sixty or even younger.[19]

To understand how the structural changes caused by industrialization and urbanization can affect older persons, one needs a perspective on the unique characteristics of the old. The linear model of individual growth and development, while providing some comfort to those who prefer to view the life cycle as a great "unfolding," does not do much to illuminate the significance of old age in our society. Old age is not merely another turning point in the life cycle— a transition from one social status to another, as is the case in all earlier stages of life. It is a time of life when the individual becomes permanently detached from the two institutional structures—the nuclear family and the occupational system—that give form and meaning to adult existence in modern times.

The marginal position of the aged in American society had already become visible by the 1950's. Even earlier, in the late 1940's, Talcott Parsons called attention to the problems of the old in the United States, the most industrially advanced society in the world:

> By comparison with other societies the United States assumes the extreme position in the isolation of old age from participation in the most important social structures and interests. Structurally speaking, there seem to be two primary bases of this situation: in the first place . . . the isolation of the individual conjugal family. . . . When the children of a couple have become independent through marriage and occupational status the parental couple is left without attachment to any continuous kinship group. . . . The second basis of the situation lies in the occupational structure. So far . . . as an individual's occupational status centers in a specific "job" he either holds the job or does not and the tendency is to maintain the the full level of functions up to a given point, and then abruptly to retire. . . . In view of the very great significance of occupational status . . . retirement leaves the older man in a peculiarly functionless situation. . . .[20]

Widowhood and retirement are two statuses typical of old age and *only* at this stage of the life cycle. Although they are two quite different experiences, they have some important properties in common. They both denote a "roleless" status; that is to say, it does not carry with it, as status ordinarily does, any culturally prescribed rights and duties

13

toward others in the social system. Rather, widowhood and retirement designate an *exit* from a major social role.

Some older people, to be sure—widowers in particular —do remarry.[21] And some men return to the labor force after retirement.[22] For these fortunate individuals, old age need not mean the end of active life. But they constitute a distinct minority.

Most people over sixty-five lose significant roles. Widowhood, of course, is more prevalent among women, owing to the shorter life expectancy of men and to women's custom of marrying men somewhat older than themselves. Thus, in 1962, 43 percent of the women aged sixty-five to seventy-four were widowed, but only 12 percent of the men. In the seventy-five-and-over category, 72 percent of the women, compared with 32 percent of the men, were without partners.[23] For men, on the other hand, retirement is the typical form of "role exit," since they, far more often than women, have been in the labor force throughout their adult lives. In 1963, 71 percent of the men sixty-five and over were retired.[24] In that same period, the *total* proportion of women in the labor force was only 37 percent.

The concept of role exit enables us to compare and analyze what the two different experiences of retirement and widowhood have in common, thereby enlarging our understanding of how role changes affect the self-conceptions and behavior of older people. Many problems of old age are not in themselves direct concomitants of aging but are rather consequences of the role exits that typically occur in old age. This distinction is important, for while it may not be possible to prevent people from aging or to safeguard them from widowhood and occupational retirement,   **14** it is possible to devise new social strategies that will give older people opportunities for new and meaningful roles and thereby serve to counteract, or at least to lessen, the negative effects of role exit.

The study of role exit in old age can further help to extend our theoretical knowledge about the significance of social roles in human behavior. An individual achieves a personal and social identity during his performance of roles. His self-attitudes are subject to change because as he matures his roles change: he enters new groups, learns new activities, and acquires new relationships. But since his time and resources are limited, he must also relinquish earlier roles and the activities and relationships that defined them. Indeed, an important condition of psychological and social growth is the individual's ability and readiness to give up roles that he has already mastered and to learn new ones that are more complex, more demanding—and more rewarding.

Thus role exit is not an experience unique to old age but a recurring process that every individual undergoes all through life in his passage from childhood to youth to adulthood to old age.

There are, however, several important differences between earlier role exits and those that occur in old age. In earlier life a person usually follows a prescribed route of role entrances and role exits. Exit from one social group is followed in an orderly way by entry into a new group, with new activities and new role partners. Various social mechanisms help prepare a person to relinquish old roles and provide opportunities for him to enter new ones. Some strain, however, accompanies any status change, particularly one that means the end of a valued social role. As Gregory Rochlin observes, ". . . in the dissolution of a meaningful relationship, a satisfying image of the self tends in part to be given up and the experience of loss becomes intensified. It is no less true, however, that loss is always followed by attempts at restitution." [25] In the stages of life prior to old age, these attempts are aided by the ordered, sequential character of institutional roles.

This sequential ordering of roles assures the individual new roles in return for those he must relinquish, and thereby alleviates the strains of role exit. Moreover, while he enacts one role, other opportunities and mechanisms prepare him for the next sequence of roles he is expected to play. A high school youth about to graduate may regret the prospect of leaving enjoyable activities with his classmates, but at the same time he can look forward either to college or a job. Each will give him a chance to put into practice the skills he has mastered in order to earn his livelihood and thereby achieve independence from his parents—an important promise that adulthood holds out to youth.

Besides the promise of new, socially valued roles, other preparatory mechanisms are at work to induce an individual to relinquish the security of old roles and to look forward to the challenge of new ones. Very early in the socialization process, a child learns that adults ought to marry and have children, that women ought to cook, keep house, and raise children, and that men ought to work and make a living for their families. And the overwhelmingly large majority of adults do enact these core roles, despite wide variations in the attractiveness and ability of adults in the general population.[26]

16

There are, however, many other groups to which adults may belong and social roles they may play, though they do not feel the same obligation toward them, nor are they as readily available. Women with young children become acquainted with the mothers of their children's playmates; they join PTA's and other organizations related to their needs and interests as parents, often forming enduring friendships. Similarly, men may join organizations connected with their jobs, such as labor unions and professional associations. They may become friendly with co-workers on the job and spend leisure time with them. A night out with the "boys" to bowl or play cards becomes an established, recurrent social event during their working life. Finally, part of the ordinary social life of married people is visiting back and forth with other married couples with whom they share common interests.

Usually the importance of marital and occupational status as conditions for belonging to voluntary associations and for forming and maintaining friendships is overlooked, simply because most adults are married and most men have jobs. Yet when a person must relinquish either of these core social roles, his opportunities to engage in optional roles decline if he is no longer married or employed. Thus one of the ironies of old age is that just when an individual needs substitute roles most, to replace the loss of institutional roles, such alternatives become less available to him than earlier in life.

While role exit recurs constantly prior to old age, the role exits typical in old age are in some ways different from those formerly experienced. Retirement and widowhood terminate a person's participation in the principal institutional structures of society—the nuclear family and the occupational structure. As a rule, they are not followed by entry into any other institutionally significant groups—that is, by new roles that he can look forward to and prepare himself for. Augustine long ago recognized this when he observed:

> As boys we can look forward to being youths; as youths to being grown up; and as young men to reaching our prime and, in our prime, to growing old. Whether this will happen is uncertain; but there is always something to look forward to. But an old man has no further stage before him. Now I have grown old.[27]

This fact—that role exits in old age typically end one's participation in the two principal institutional systems—makes possible, in a relatively pure form, a systematic exploration of role exit without regard to the effects of subsequent entry into other roles. Thus old age leads itself to a study of the processes and effects of role exit in a way that other periods of life do not. The strains that attend divorce, unemployment, migration, promotion, and social mobility have all been studied. Each represents unique and different experiences, but they all take place earlier in the life cycle and, as a rule, are temporary role exits. Divorced people usually remarry; the unemployed usually find jobs after a period of time; emigrants resettle in a new community or a new country; upwardly mobile people acquire the style of life of members of their class of destination; and so forth.

All the experiences named above are roleless statuses. Like widowhood and retirement, they do not entail group

memberships and do not carry with them culturally prescribed rights and duties. Quite the contrary; they merely
designate the loss of a formerly enacted social role. But unlike retirement and widowhood in old age, roleless statuses
earlier in life always set the individual apart, place him in
a deviant position from his age and sex peers. That is to
say, only the occasional adult man or woman is divorced or
unemployed; the large majority in his sex and age category
are married and employed.

In modern society, people who are widowed or retired
are also different from the majority of their age-sex group
before the age of sixty, but beyond that age they come to
occupy the same roleless position as the majority of their
generation. It is therefore possible to look for similarities in
the effects of these two quite different types of role exit,
to compare their effects on persons whose contemporaries are still engaged in their recently relinquished role,
and on persons whose contemporaries have, for the most
part, experienced the same status change. It seems reason-
able to suppose that the meaning and the consequences of
any type of significant role change for the individual depends on the social context in which it occurs. Thus, while
the disruption of a marriage by divorce, separation, or
death of one of the marital partners is ordinarily a personal
tragedy, the individual's ability to deal with his pain and to
restore his sense of "wholeness" is not simply a matter of
the resources of his own personality. It is also influenced by
the status of his intimates and contemporaries, for they
represent the social resources of solace, activity, and companionship—which, if they are available, can to some degree provide gratification to the individual who has had a   19

major role loss. To be widowed or divorced, for example, has different consequences for the individual if his friends and acquaintances are still married or if they are not. Here again, old age offers possibilities for study of a problem that is not readily available for study in younger age groups, because exit from a core institutional role is the exception rather than the rule for anyone under sixty.

Finally, the study of role exit in old age can contribute to role theory by enlarging our general understanding of institutional roles in human behavior. Adults become so fully accustomed to enacting the core social roles of spouse, parent, and breadwinner that they seldom realize the extent to which their self-identity, their pattern of social relationships, and the meaning of their daily existence are shaped by these few major roles. Only in retrospect, following permanent exit from a major social role, does a person fully realize the influence of that role.

aging,
WIDOWHOOD,
and
RETIREMENT:

A SOCIOLOGICAL PERSPECTIVE

The first signs of old age are seldom solely physiological. For most people, old age approaches when their children leave home, signifying the end of their parental responsibilities. Parenthood in the literal sense does not end until the progenitors or offspring die. But until a child reaches maturity and leaves home, parenthood is also a social role, with culturally prescribed rights and duties. The distinctive responsibilities of parenthood are physical and emotional nurturing, socialization, and economic support. Once these are accomplished, the children are considered ready to marry and establish families of their own. Common residence is one of the principal cultural definitions of the family. When a young person leaves home and starts his own family, the term "my family" no longer refers to parents or siblings.[1]

In effect, then, reciprocal role exit takes place for both parents and children when the latter grow up and leave home. Once active parenthood ends, the accompanying strains are not very different from the strains of other role exits. The "tears of happiness" a mother sheds at a son's or daughter's wedding connote, on one level, joy that her child is wed and entering into a significant role. But on another level, "tears of happiness" is also a euphemism for the mother's sadness as the substance of her relationship to her child ends.

The term "empty-nest syndrome" refers to a woman's depression after all her children have left home. In a sense, the menopause and the conclusion of child-rearing activities have the same meaning for women that occupational retirement has for men. Each role is closely related to sex identity—motherhood with femaleness and work with maleness—and the irrevocable exit from these roles psychologically

22

signifies the onset of barrenness and impotence, both signs of old age.

The end of active parenthood may cause emotional strains, particularly for the mother, but certain social practices and opportunities ease the adjustment to the new situation. Because people are marrying younger, having fewer children, and *their* children are also marrying younger, most parents are still middle-aged when their children leave them.[2] At this stage in life, men are still working and at the peak of their earning power, while women have opportunities for numerous new activities. In the past few decades, more and more middle-aged women have entered or re-entered the labor market. In 1968, 53 percent of women forty-five to fifty-four years old were employed, compared with only 25 percent in the same age group in 1940. Also in recent years, more middle-aged women have furthered their education as preparation for a career in the post-maternal phase of their lives.[3]

Moreover, at least two conditions postpone the time when parents must finally adjust to their children's departure. If parents have many children, as is more often the case in the working class than in the middle class, the youngest are likely to leave them only later in life. Thus in large families separation from children occurs in gradual stages, easing adjustment to the loss of the parental role. Although middle-class parents have fewer children, the practice of sending children away to college, even while prolonging their economic dependency, allows parents to get accustomed to living without them. With less contact with, and responsibility for, their children, middle-aged parents may once again turn to each other for companion-   23 ship and support. Indeed, a number of studies report that in many cases post-parental married relationships become richer and more intimate than during the active years of child-rearing, when women, especially, experience conflict between their obligations toward their children and toward their spouse.[4]

Despite the strong cultural emphasis on the independence of married children, middle-aged parents often find a role in their children's lives. Several studies report that most middle-class parents provide some form of material help to their married children, while working-class parents offer services of various kinds. One author observes that "parents . . . are aware that their assistance to their child's family, if given discreetly, produces the desired response they seek, namely, increased appreciation and affection for themselves, and participation in some of their child's activities." [5]

Grandparenthood, which has traditionally evoked an image of the kindly, white-haired elder citizen, is increasingly becoming a middle-age phenomenon. Grandparenthood entails no clear-cut rights or obligations, but it symbolically represents the family's continuity. Couples have the satisfaction of visiting and doing things with their young grandchildren—the same things they did with their own children, except, of course, that grandparents have neither the responsibilities nor the authority of parents. Grandchildren, at least while they are young, help to ease the strains of having lost the active parental role.

In contrast, widowhood and retirement, the typical role exits in later life, occur abruptly. For the most part, individuals or institutional agencies can provide only economic help in such events. Social security benefits, retire-

24

ment pensions, annuities, and life insurance reduce some of the economic problems of widowhood and retirement, but other than these no social practices exist to ease the strains of these two role exits.

Igor Stravinsky has summed up the discontinuity of old age:

> Of the two hardest problems of age the first is simply the lack of preparation, the lack of a natural or acquired provision of experience. We observe other people in the condition all our lives but fail to learn biologically from the spectacle, and somehow even fail to believe that the same can and will happen to us.[6]

Not surprisingly, all studies of aging report a decline in morale. It is not always recognized, however, that demoralization is not an inevitable part of aging, but that it is often the result of an individual's exit from the core social roles of adulthood. If, for example, the morale of people under seventy is compared with that of those over seventy, at the same time taking into account whether or not they are still married or employed, it turns out that role exit, particularly retirement, is a far more significant cause of demoralization than chronological age *per se*. Table 2 presents the findings from the Elmira study of older people, which were later repeated in the Kips Bay study of older people in New York City.[7]

Through systematic comparisons of many older people we can determine typical responses to specific events. To gain an understanding of the subjective meaning of widowhood and retirement, however, we must go beyond abstractions to the personal accounts of older people in which they

TABLE 2

Percentages of Persons
with Low Morale Scores—
by Age and Employment Status (Elmira)

	Under 70		70 and Over	
Employed	17	(129)	21	(33)
Retired	39	(38) *	57	(53) †
Housewives	28	(96)	56	(81)

Percentages of Persons
with Low Morale Scores—
by Age and Marital Status ‡

	Under 70		70 and Over	
Married	17	(152)	45	(57)
Widowed	34	(74)	54	(87)
Single	43	(28)	53	(19)

* Difference significant at the 0.05 level.
† Difference significant at the 0.01 level.
‡ Divorced and separated respondents have been excluded from the analysis owing to the small number of cases (16) in the sample.

Note: Numbers in parentheses in this table and all subsequent tables indicate the number of cases on which percentages are based.

describe the impact of their experiences. The two statements that follow, the first by a retired man and the second by a widower, lend immediacy to the meaning of role exit.

What am I doing on this earth? What good am I here? . . .
Not having learned how to play or having formed any kind of hobby in almost fifty years of hard work, I now find myself at a loss to know what to do with the life I must continue to live.   **26**

. . . Since I retired, it seems I am living in a different world. My old business associates don't know that I am still in this world. My social acquaintances seem also to have forgotten that I am still here. . . . I know there is something wrong with me —in fact all the trouble is of my own making, but I can't seem to solve my problem. . . .

My wife died sixteen years ago. . . . I was lost for a time afterward: felt like it was the end of the world. For a while I went on thinking she was still there. I could imagine what she would be doing at a certain time, or what she would have said [in answer] to something. Well, that went on for quite a while, but in the last few years I haven't thought about it so much. . . . I don't know what I'm doing still living . . . all I have to do now is live out my years. But when you get to be my age you can't expect to live much longer. . . . I don't have anything to keep living for.[8]

These accounts illustrate important similarities, as well as dissimilarities, in the ways two very different kinds of role exit are experienced. They are similar insofar as both events mean significant changes in the daily existence of the individuals, and both convey the sense of desolation following the loss of important social relationships. Equally notable, however, are the differences these two experiences evoke. The widower during his bereavement finds solace in recalling his wife's companionship. His comment "all I have to do now is live out my years" indicates an attitude of passive resignation to the inactivity and loneliness of old age. The retired man, on the other hand, experiences not only loneliness but also self-denigration. The loss of work and social relationships leads him to question the very meaning of his existence, as indicated by his query: "What am I doing on this earth? What good am I here?" More-over, unlike the widower, he feels regret—regret that in the past he had failed to cultivate other interests besides his work. Thus, he has neither resigned himself to his difficulties nor has he been able to resolve them. And his inability to do so gives him a sense of inadequacy—"there is something wrong with me"—that is not evidenced by the widower.

One would expect that of the two forms of role exit, widowhood would have the more serious effect on morale in old age, for marriage represents a relationship based on bonds of love and enduring solidarity over a long period of years. Losing a spouse causes grief, as is usual at the end of any love relationship. And since people generally have stronger sentiments about love than about work, retirement—though it may evoke sadness and regret—evokes less pain than widowhood. But these two experiences, when compared systematically, reveal that the emotional affect attached to a role is only one of several variables determining its significance. While a job does not as a rule carry with it the emotional and sexual attachments of a marital relationship, it does have other properties that protect morale in old age more effectively.

Many people think of work primarily as a means of earning a livelihood, in contrast to the intrinsic value placed on marriage. But a man's occupational position has other functions for him; and though he may be less aware of them, they are no less significant for his sense of efficacy and self-worth.

To be sure, men work to earn a living, but in doing so they conform to one of the major cultural definitions of the   **28** male role in adult society. Adult males are expected to work. The social disapproval that occurs when this norm is violated—as expressed, for example, in the epithet "playboy"—indicates that men who do not work are regarded as less manly and less adult.[9] Thus work is an integral part of the male's personal *and* social identity. Regardless of the satisfaction derived from work, employment in itself is likely to have great emotional significance for men reared in this society. Consequently, even though men are now expected to retire when they reach a certain age, many of them find this requirement to be inconsistent with their image of masculinity. This is exemplified in the following comment:

> Some men are lazy. I can't sit around and do nothing. Who stays home? Women stay home, and children stay home. It makes me mad. . . . It used to be different. I'd bring home sixty or seventy dollars on a payday and the kids would jump with excitement. The old man has brought home a good pay.[10]

Retirement, as this comment implies, deprives a man of the respect accorded the breadwinner in the American family and constrains him to assume a role similar to that of women. In this respect, retirement is a more demoralizing experience for men than for women.[11] Women may choose to work, but according to cultural prescription they are not obliged to do so. Even when wives do work, it is not their occupational status, but their husband's, that determines the social status of the family.

The social expectation that older people must give up their jobs at some fixed age, therefore, often represents a marked and sudden discontinuity for the individuals, particularly for men, whether they themselves accept this norm or not. Thus one retired man asks sarcastically: "What am I supposed to do? Read some, listen to the radio, eat, sleep, go to the movies? Isn't that a useful way to spend your life! I don't know how long I'm supposed to go on living this way." [12]

While this man does not question the legitimacy of retirement, he, like many others in the same position, does not know what is expected of him in retirement. This suggests that one of the strains of retirement arises not so much from the required relinquishment of the occupational role as from the absence of any clear-cut set of social expectations that might support a man in this new and unfamiliar position. The sharp discontinuity between the clearly defined activities and social relationships of the work role and the relative absence of these in retirement often results in serious difficulties for the older person.

Employment conditions in industrial urban societies impose a fairly rigid pattern on the individual's daily existence. The unequivocal specification of work tasks, as well as of the time and place in which they are to be performed, forces the individual to organize his life to conform to these requirements. A large portion of the worker's daily existence is structured by specified work activities, and the amount of free time for other activities is relatively limited. Retirement disrupts his daily life pattern. The eight hours he devoted to his work now become free time, which he may use as he pleases. For the rare person who has many interests outside his job, and the resources to pursue them, it may be relatively easy to develop a new and satisfying way of life, especially if he has friends who share his interests. But most older persons are thrust into a normless, un-structured situation. Inactivity is a recurrent theme among retired men.[13] One of them says: "Do you know what my biggest problem is? Finding something to keep me busy two or three hours every day. Not a damned thing to do. What am I supposed to do?" [14]

Moreover, not all older people accept the norm of retirement, as the following account shows:

> Mr. S. believes that a man should work until he is not able to. He firmly believes that people should work until they die. He does not think that there is a "best" age for retirement . . . people should keep on working. When asked to explain why, he thought a while and said that working was good. He had no more to say.[15]

The rejection of the retirement norm expressed by this man is shared by many older people, even though it has become a firmly established practice in contemporary society. For example, 70 percent of the respondents in Elmira expressed disagreement with the statement "workers ought to be encouraged to retire at sixty-five," and a more recent study reports that seven out of every ten men who continue to have jobs past sixty-five do not plan to retire at all.[16]

Retirement poses a true dilemma for older people who believe, like Mr. S., that work is a lifelong obligation; their exclusion from the occupational structure denies them the opportunity to act according to their beliefs. Retirants who share this strong belief in work may be the ones most apt to express feelings of uselessness and even of self-hatred:

You know what they ought to do with old men like me? Take us out and shoot us. We're no good for anything. What the hell am I   31 alive for? I'm no good to myself, no good to anybody else. Rest? What the hell have I got to rest from—I never do anything. . . .[17]

Though widowhood, like retirement, signifies the involuntary loss of a significant role, it does not have the invidious implications for the social position of older people that retirement does. This is due to the basic difference in the manner in which these two events occur. Widowhood is a natural event, and is therefore fixed by uncontrollable forces. Retirement, in contrast, rests ultimately on a social judgment that the interests of the society are better served by excluding older people from work. It therefore threatens the individual's self-esteem, whereas no similar threat is inherent in widowhood. Retirement, more so than widowhood, lessens opportunities for daily social contacts and is therefore more demoralizing.

The formal work role carries with it numerous informal relations and affiliations. While the death of the marital partner disrupts a single, though highly significant, social relationship, retirement is likely to destroy many relationships: with co-workers, with customers, with clients, and with other occupational contacts. Moreover, retirement may signify the loss of several group affiliations, such as the work group, the union or occupational association, work-connected recreational groups, and the like. To be sure, none of these relationships, taken singly, has the significance of the marital relationship for an individual, but taken together they often represent a substantial part of his social relationships. One older employee facing the prospect of retirement explicitly recognized its social implications when he said, "I missed my wife when she died; I guess I'll miss my friends when I retire." [18]

Retirement can end work-connected friendships for two reasons. First, loss of a job curtails the opportunities for contact between friends, as this comment indicates: "Most of the friends I had I made on the job or as customers. I don't see them any more." [19] Second, and perhaps more important, retirement destroys the basis of such friendships—the common interests and experiences that had been shared on the job. The shoptalk that provides enjoyment and release for those who work together only serves to remind the retired man of his exclusion from these activities. As one expresses it, "They get together to talk business, and since I'm out of that they don't want me around." [20] The retirant no longer shares the common experiences of his former colleagues, and therefore becomes estranged from them, even though the need for friends appears to be great in retirement.

Widowhood also has isolating effects on the individual in old age, although not to the same degree, it appears, as retirement. In the Elmira study, a comparison (shown in Table 3) of the social participation of retired and employed older people, on the one hand, and of widowed and married people, on the other, shows that differences in social participation are greater among the former than among the latter —an indication that exit from employment affects the participation of people more than does exit from marriage.[21]

Widowed people, besides losing a companion, often also lose contact with those who had been primarily their spouses's friends or associates. For example, a woman may

TABLE 3
Percentages of Persons with High Social Participation Scores— by Employment and Marital Status

Employment Status			Marital Status		
Employed	61	(173)	Married	60	(225)
Retired	47 *	(98)	Widowed	53	(179)

* Significant at 0.05 level.

have some association with her husband's business friends or co-workers as long as he is alive, but after he dies she probably will cease meeting them, since she herself has no close friendship ties with them.

The death of one marital partner may also destroy the basis of the relationship between the surviving partner and those married couples with whom man and wife had jointly associated. When two married couples come together socially, it often happens, for part of the time at least, that the men talk about subjects of interest to them, and the women do the same.[22] This pattern must change when one of the partners dies. Simultaneously, the balance between the sexes is destroyed. One of two patterns of interaction is likely to develop in this new social situation. The two women (or men) may feel obliged to talk about matters of a more general nature to permit the "odd" person to participate in the conversation, which requires some modifications in their behavior. Or the two friends of the same sex may lapse into their customary topics of conversation, and the

34

"odd" person is apt to feel excluded. Neither alternative can be expected to be as gratifying to the participants as the relationship that existed between them before the death of one of the spouses. Consequently the social contacts between the widowed person and his or her married friends tend to become less frequent and, in some cases, may cease altogether.

It should also be pointed out that an unattached woman—whether she is widowed, divorced, or single—is sometimes considered a potential rival by married women, particularly in those age groups in which women outnumber men. In such cases friendships between women of dissimilar marital status often wane, and the unattached woman may either become more isolated or cultivate friendships with other unattached women or men. It is interesting to note that in the Elmira study single women had more extensive friendship relations than widows, which tends to confirm that it is the change in marital status that reduces the social participation of the widowed, not the fact that they are unattached.[23]

Needless to say, the detrimental effects of widowhood or retirement on the morale and the social life of older people are cumulative. Persons who have experienced both forms of role exit are more isolated socially and more prone to demoralization than those who are either widowed or retired.[24]

In short, the fact that people grow old does not in itself account for many of the changes in mood and behavior observed in old age. The role changes that signify permanent detachment from society's two principal institutional systems—the nuclear family and the occupational system

—are far more important factors than physical changes. As long as people continue to perform roles within these systems—whether they are sixty or seventy or even eighty— they do not differ either socially or psychologically from people still in their forties or fifties.[25]

parents
and
CHILDReN

After retirement or widowhood, older people first turn to their children—the "nearest and dearest" of all their social ties—for solace and companionship. But these parents are soon disappointed. Although studies show that the aged do maintain contact with their children,[1] evidence also indicates—but is often overlooked by sociologists—that the relationship between the generations is not as satisfying as it might appear. Perhaps as a function of the deep-rooted belief that children ought to aid and comfort their parents, it is often assumed that regular contacts between parents and their adult offspring will prevent loneliness and demoralization. Unfortunately this does not happen very often, and reluctance to speak candidly about these issues only compounds the problems of older people.

The transformation of the relationship between parents and their children as they grow old is an enduring problem. For in all societies and in all periods, old people share two common experiences: the waning of physical powers and the death of contemporaries. Both affect their motivation and their capacity to carry on customary social roles, altering the balance of power between them and the younger generation. Unless customs exist to protect the power and authority of the old, these will be seized by younger, more vigorous adults. Although societies vary in the status they accord the old, one can say that in traditional, slowly changing societies the experience of the old represents knowledge and judgment valuable to society; for it helps to preserve the institutional system's stability in the face of recurrent problems that arise, despite the "turnover" in personnel that takes place from generation to generation.

In such societies, as a rule, the continuity between adulthood and old age is greater. The extended family, the principal social unit of the society, not only carries out the procreation and socialization of the young but is also society's principal producer of goods and services. Thus the individual's ties to his kinship group are varied and complex. Although differentiated according to sex and generation, each age-sex subgroup is an integral part of the kinship structure, with clearly defined rights and with responsibilities to others in the same system. A spouse's death may terminate a marriage without seriously affecting one's customary pattern of kinship relationships and activities, because the conjugal pair is not a separate, self-sustained unit to the same degree as it has increasingly become in modern Western societies. Throughout his married life, and even during widowhood, the individual in such a society maintains strong bonds of interdependence, reinforced by spatial proximity, with other kin.

Retirement has no exact counterpart in simple societies. Productive work is carried on within the extended kinship system. The work routine changes somewhat as the aging person's vigor decreases, but even then he continues to perform tasks, although less arduous ones. Work is not merely productive but also involves caring for and instructing the young and participating in ceremonial and decision-making conclaves. Then, too, old people in traditional societies have to be active because almost everyone lives close to the margin of subsistence. The enforced idleness of the old is possible only in affluent societies, or in small affluent strata of traditional societies.

Although the potential for conflict between the elder

39

and younger adults exists in all societies, the status and power of the old in traditional societies can be protected in different ways and made legitimate by religious and magical means. Stability is important, for the outbreak of severe conflicts between the generations would seriously jeopardize the kinship group, which is the principal bulwark of the social order in these societies.

As social systems become more complex, various tasks formerly performed within the kinship system are transferred to outside institutional bodies. This development opens the way for younger adult members to escape the elders' domination and control. Once society's elder members lose their monopoly over the positions that confer wealth, prestige, or power, their authority wanes, although they fight to maintain it. Ultimately, however, the old will be the losers, if only because the young will outlive them.

In essence, the old face a dilemma in their relations with the younger generation. A society's continuity, or a family's, requires adults to prepare the younger generation to carry out the core institutional roles. But the young reach their full powers, and are eager to exercise them, before their elders are willing to relinquish those roles. Conflict will occur if the younger generation's claims on adult roles are ignored. Under some conditions—such as the breakdown of norms that allow the hegemony of older people—the young will forcibly displace the old. Power, of course, is often assumed without struggle; either way, role reversal follows, and the old become the subjects of their children's authority.

Role reversal, and its consequences for old people, is the subject of Shakespeare's tragedy *King Lear*. Shakespeare   **40** understood the two conflicting needs of old people: they seek their children's love and support, and yet wish to preserve their own independence. He dramatically portrays the incompatibility of these needs and shows how friendships with peers can help an older person avoid this dilemma— issues of interest to sociologists.

Commentaries on *Lear* focus attention on one central theme: the betrayal of the old king by his two elder daughters, Goneril and Regan, who have become prototypes of the perfidy of the young in their relations with the old. But what is often overlooked is that Lear's tragedy is caused not by his old age or the decline of his powers, but by his decision to retire and invest his daughters with the powers of his office.

The drama begins without prologue or preliminaries. Lear simply announces his decision to retire and divide his kingdom among his three daughters.

> . . . Know we have divided
> In three our kingdom; and 'tis our fast intent
> To shake all cares and business from our age,
> Conferring them on younger strengths while we,
> Unburthen'd, crawl toward death.

This abrupt beginning effectively conveys the sharp discontinuity between one's past life and the existence following a major role exit.[2]

After he decides to abdicate, Lear stages a "trial of love" for his three daughters, and wants to be reassured about the wisdom of his decision. He eagerly accepts the declaration of enduring and undivided love that his two elder daughters well understand he is seeking from them.   41

Only Cordelia, his youngest daughter, refuses to tell him
what he most wants to hear, and insists on speaking the
truth:

> You have begot me, bred me, lov'd me. I
> Return those duties back as are right fit,
> Obey you, love you, and most honor you.
> Why have my sisters husbands, if they say
> They love you all? Haply, when I shall wed,
> That lord whose hand must take my plight shall carry
> Half my love with him, half my care and duty.
> Sure I shall never marry like my sisters
> To love my father all.

But Lear is too committed to his plan to heed Cordelia's warning, another indication that the "trial of love"
was not a genuine effort at a rational decision, but only a
pathetic attempt to allay any doubts about the wisdom of
giving way to his own weariness and loneliness. When a human being becomes old and must recognize his own mortality, his wish for independence, which preserves human dignity but often at the cost of loneliness, is often overwhelmed
by his need for love. Lear rewards Cordelia's candor by dis-
inheriting and banishing her from his kingdom, and pro-
ceeds to invest his two elder daughters with his

> power, pre-eminence, and all the large effects
> that troop with majesty

asking only in return that,

> Ourself, by monthly course,
> with reservation of an hundred knights
> By you to be sustain'd, shall our abode
> make you with by due turns.

The action reveals the transformation in Lear's social relationships after his retirement and the painful effects these changes have, in turn, on his own identity. Lear's presence in his eldest daughter's household soon irritates Goneril, and conflict develops. Goneril's comment on the situation has a curiously contemporary quality:

> How, in one house
> Should many people, under two commands
> Hold amity? 'Tis hard; almost impossible.

She and her household have ceased to view Lear as a figure of authority. He is perceived as an

> Idle old man, that still would manage those authorities
> that he hath given away.

Lear struggles to maintain his former conception of himself as a royal and respected personage by ignoring the disrespect and neglect shown him by his daughters and their contemporaries. His surrender to reality begins as one of his knightly companions observes with resentment that "There's a great abatement of kindness" shown Lear by his daughter and her household. Poor Lear then says,

> Thou but remember'st me of mine own conception. I have perceived a most faint neglect of late, which I have rather blamed as mine own jealous curiosity than as a very pretense and purpose of kindness. I will look further into't. . . .

From this point on, a subtle change in Lear begins to take place. He acknowledges that he no longer commands the respect he once did. This acknowledgment constitutes Lear's first courageous act. He finally begins to understand the folly he has committed, and is at last prepared to confront the truth that others perceive a man by the roles he plays. Thus, when he asks Goneril's steward, "Who am I, Sir?" the steward answers him without title or ceremony— "My lady's father." The Fool, whom Lear loves and who loves him, tells him:

> . . . thou mad'st thy daughters thy mother; . . . when thou gav'st them the rod and put'st down thine own breeches.

And the Fool goes on to say:

> . . . Now thou art an 0 without a figure. I am better than thou art now: I am a fool, thou art nothing.

These lines express the essence of the tragedy that Lear has brought upon himself. Retirement and the gift of his wealth and office to his children have led to a reversal in their roles. This phenomenon is common after retirement and widowhood, particularly when old people have no other economic or social resources and must depend upon their children for economic support or companionship.[3] Added to this is the "rolelessness" of retirement and widowhood. A king, a husband, or a fool have culturally designated rights and responsibilities to others, and the latter have reciprocal rights and responsibilities to them. A retirant or a widower, in contrast, enters a roleless status; each term merely designates a former status but does not confer any new rights or obligations upon the individual or upon others.

Old people, therefore, need the affection, loyalty, and support of friends more than ever before. Sharing memories and experiences with friends helps to preserve one's identity following significant role exits. Lear's daughters and their households consider him an "idle old man" and a "has-been," but to his loyal company of men and to the Fool,   **44** who is also his most intimate friend, Lear remains the same worthy man that he had been when he ruled his kingdom. So long as his knights surround him, Lear is not altogether dependent on his children and on others not of his own generation. With this issue, Shakespeare brings the drama to a climax, which is further evidence of his understanding of old age.

For Lear, as for others in his position, the degradation gets worse day by day. In the face of all the indignities, Lear has maintained the demeanor of a man and a king. But when Goneril, his eldest daughter, orders half his company sent away, Lear, deeply hurt and weeping, rages at his daughter:

> Life and death! I am asham'd
> That thou hast power to shake my manhood thus,
> That these hot tears, which break from me perforce,
> Should make thee worth them. Blasts and fogs upon thee!

Lear and his retinue leave Goneril and settle in his second daughter's household. But Regan, even more ruthless than her sister, demands that her father reduce his company further. Lear—no longer the proud, dignified sovereign but only a broken old man—pleads with his daughters to be merciful and to understand his need for his friends. Goneril cunningly asks him, "What need you five and twenty? ten, or five, to follow in a house, where twice so many have a command to tend you?" Whereupon Regan winds up the ghastly haggling with the query, "What need one?" Lear gives this memorable reply:

> O, reason not the need! Our basest beggars
> Are in the poorest thing superfluous.   **45**

Allow not nature more than nature needs,
Man's life is cheap as beast's. Thou art a lady.
If only to go warm were gorgeous,
Why, nature needs not what thou gorgeous wear'st,
Which scarcely keeps thee warm. But, for true need—
You heavens, give me that patience, patience I need!
You see me here, you gods, a poor old man,
As full of grief as age, wretched in both!
If it be you that stirs these daughters' hearts
Against their father, fool me not so much
To bear it tamely; touch me with noble anger,
And let not woman's weapons, water drops,
Stain my man's cheeks! No, you unnatural hags,
I will have such revenges on you both
That all the world shall—I will do such things—
What they are yet, I know not; but they shall be
The terrors of the earth! You think I'll weep?
No, I'll not weep.
I have full cause of weeping, but this heart
Shall break into a hundred thousand flaws
Or ere I'll weep. O fool, I shall go mad.

Lear and his last three loyal companions go into the storm,
to wander over the land in madness and beggary; yet the
sinister forces of nature do not hurt him as much as his
daughters' perfidy.

Rumble thy bellyful! Spit, fire! Spout, rain!
Nor rain, wind, thunder, fire, are my daughters.
I tax not you, you elements, with unkindness.
I never gave you kingdom, call'd you children,
You owe me no subscription. Then let fall
Your horrible pleasure. . . .   **46**

Goneril and Regan inspire repugnance and horror because they violate a basic and pervasive social norm. The norm of reciprocity is deeply ingrained in our lives. When others perform services for us, particularly when those services are voluntary and unsolicited, we experience gratitude and will want to reciprocate when the giver needs our help. This norm is especially strong in filial relationships. Indeed, the parent-child interaction first establishes the capacity for gratitude. Children are indebted to their parents for the ultimate gift—life itself—and for the time devoted to their nurture and socialization. The bond of gratitude is such, Georg Simmel writes, that:

. . . Once we have received something good from another person, once he has preceded us with his action, we no longer can make up for it completely, no matter how much our own return gift or service may objectively or legally surpass his own. The reason is that his gift, because it was the first, has a voluntary character which no return gift can have. For, to return the benefit we are obliged ethically; we operate under a coercion which, though neither social nor legal but moral, is still a coercion. The first gift is given in full spontaneity; it has a freedom without any duty, even without the duty of gratitude. . . . Only when we give first are we free, and this is the reason why, in the first gift, which is not occasioned by any gratitude, there lies a beauty, a spontaneous devotion to the other, an opening up and flowering from the "virgin soil" of the soul, as it were, which cannot be matched by any subsequent gift, no matter how superior its content. The difference involved here finds expression in the feeling (apparently often unjustified in regard to the concrete *content* of the gift) that we *cannot* return a gift; for it has a freedom which the return gift, because it is *that,* cannot possibly possess.[4]   47

Children feel an irredeemable obligation toward parents, which gives force to the biblical commandment, "Honor thy father and thy mother."

But the expectation that the individual should marry and produce progeny often conflicts with filial obligations. Indeed, as a rule, just when parents become widowed and retired—that is, when they most need their children's solace and companionship—their offspring are deeply involved in their own marital, parental, and occupational obligations.

The cultural norms, supported by a person's sense of gratitude, demand that adult children honor their filial obligations in their parents' time of need. But time and energy are scarce resources. When an individual has several role obligations, he must have priorities. Ties to spouse and children have greater immediacy and urgency, for at the very least his children have a future, whereas his obligations to parents are retroactive, and his affection far less intense than before. This is likely to be the case in contemporary societies, in which nuclear family ties have primacy over the extended family. Americans, for example, think it important to loosen the strong emotional bonds formed by the parent-child relationship in the small, enclosed, modern nuclear family.[5] Independence for adolescents is promoted in many ways: by stressing romantic love, by urging self-reliance, by emphasizing popularity with peers, and by sending middle-class children away to summer camp and to college. When children marry, emotional involvement between the generations diminishes further.

But persons reared in a love-oriented, democratic family environment will, when they become adults, remain grateful and obligated to their parents. Thus a conflict arises **48** as the individual's love and emotional involvement with his parents decline but his sense of obligation does not.

At issue, in short, in the parent and child relationship, as in other love relationships, is the question of faithfulness. On this Simmel writes:

. . . Perhaps the greatest tragedy of human conditions springs from (among other things) the utterly unrationalizable and constantly shifting mixture of the stable and variable elements of our nature. Even when we have entered a binding relationship with our whole being, we may yet remain in the same mood and inclination as before with some of our aspects—perhaps with those that are turned outward, but possibly even with some internal ones. But other aspects develop into entirely new interests, aims, capacities, and thus come to throw our total existence into new directions. In doing so, they turn us away from earlier conditions (by conditions, of course, only purely internal ones are understood here, not those of external duty) with a sort of unfaithfulness, which is neither quite innocent, since there still exist some bonds which must now be broken, nor quite guilty, since we are no longer the persons we were when we entered the relationship; the subject to whom the unfaithfulness could be imputed has disappeared.[6]

By cultural definition, familial relationships, particularly those between parents and children, differ from all other social relationships. According to David Schneider, the familial relationship is characterized by

. . . enduring diffuse solidarity . . . solidarity because the relationship is supportive, helpful, and cooperative, it rests on trust and the other can be trusted. Diffuse because it is not narrowly confined to a specific goal or a specific kind of behavior.[7]   **49**

Children have an enduring sense of diffuse obligation as long as their parents live; but enduring solidarity, if solidarity means close bonds of affection and intimacy, will probably not last long because modern society emphasizes independence between the generations.

The maintenance of separate households protects each generation's independence and privacy, and minimizes the kind of conflict between parents and children portrayed in *Lear*. By not living with married children, parents can avoid becoming subject to their children's authority. But the old pay heavily for this independence. Separate residence between the generations is made possible by industrial society's greater economic resources [8] and by public programs that provide at least minimal economic security and some health care and housing for old people.[9] As the state increases its support for the old, their independence from their children increases even more.[10]

In turn, adult children have been relieved, to a considerable extent, of the responsibility of caring for their aging parents. As long as parental couples remain intact and can rely on their own resources—economic and occupational—and provide each other with companionship, they will not make heavy demands on their grown children's time and resources. From all indications, parental couples, especially during middle age, maintain friendly contact and exchange services with their children and their grandchildren.[11]

But as parents grow old, even limited contacts decline. Parents have fewer resources to give, particularly after retirement or widowhood, and the younger generation by this time has less need of help, because they have reached their 50 peak earning power and their own children are in adolescence or beyond. Adult children, as a rule, fulfill their material obligations and dutifully maintain some contact with aging parents, but their separate existence, interests, and daily experiences lessen intimacy between the generations, and estrangement, carefully hidden on both sides, begins. Such estrangement goes counter to the norm of permanent "enduring diffuse solidarity" and is thus kept secret. People feel guilty or ashamed about deviant behavior and usually do not discuss it, except anonymously, as in a recent letter to a newspaper:

> I do not believe my husband and I are so different from most old folks. . . . I am sure our children would be shocked and would insist that we are dreaming things up if they recognized the writer of this item. No matter that it is many months since we have seen them . . . we still love them and want to protect them from humiliation.

Was it only yesterday that they played on the kitchen floor, looked up into my contented face and blew me kisses? When was it that they wept because Mama had to go back to work? They pleaded with me to stay with them; I explained that times were hard and Daddy couldn't get work. Many were hungry, but Mommy was lucky. She could teach school and bring home enough money so her little ones would not go hungry.

So began the hard years, the struggle to survive, to provide food and clothing and education and adequate housing for five children. The daily trek from the blackboard to the sink and back to the blackboard. Arms laden with groceries, Mama trudged home each evening to be greeted with hugs and kisses and a warm welcome from her little ones. Twenty-five years of this, twenty-five years of listening to school bells, marking papers and worrying about maids and sitters who did not always come on time. But eventually the little ones grew into young men and women, educated, well-fed and self-assured. Now Mama could take it easy. Depression years had passed; no more lean times, only fat, happy times. Or so she thought! In place of her deserved rest she was busy caring for the grandchildren. Times had changed and all young mothers went to work. No matter that they could not afford maids—Mama was home. She now had the dubious joy of providing sitting service, cleaning other people's houses—for love, of course! She even had the pleasure of carting groceries and cooked foods to the children's homes. Papa didn't mind too much, for he loved his children and their children, too. He sat back and told stories of their exploits—he was so proud of all of them. But the years took their toll of Mama and of Papa, too. They grew old and lonely. The children moved far away. The grandchildren grew up, grew away from the old folks and lost interest in people who were too tired to visit them and play with them. If you should meet Mama or Papa, be sure to ask how the family is; they will put on quite a show. They will tell all about the darling grandchildren who come to stay for days on end, the jokes they tell, the love they show. Oh, yes, Mama and Papa are proud! Proud of their flesh and blood? Are you kidding? They have forgotten what their offspring look like and often resort to looking at pictures to refresh their memories, for their children are too busy to write, to call or to visit—except perhaps on Mother's Day or Father's Day if it is convenient. Yes, the old folks are proud—so proud that they have learned to dissemble, to pretend. If you should meet them and know the truth, please help them stay proud; play the game, too, won't you? [12]   **52**

This poignant account of the estrangement between the generations during the years when they live apart helps to explain why relations with children seldom help to counteract the desolating effects of retirement or widowhood.

After widowhood, a person living alone no longer has a clearly designated role in any family system. He does not call his children's family "my family"; they are, instead, referred to as his son's family or his daughter's family—an indication that he is not regarded as a member of their families.[13] The old have neither the prerogatives nor the responsibilities of full-fledged nuclear unit membership. They cannot disturb their children's families, or offer advice, or get involved in disputes. They may, upon request, perform such services as baby-sitting. The old, in short, are "outsiders" who visit and are visited by their children. They are expected to be pleasant and undemanding, to have their own interests, and generally to avoid being a burden on their children, except when illness or some emergency arises. It is obvious that these expectations are quite different from relationships within the immediate nuclear family and that they have the same limitations that are imposed upon other outsiders. Yet there seems to be a mutual interest among parents and children, even in the face of these restrictions, to preserve the fiction that parents are "insiders" and not "outsiders." [14] This effort to camouflage the marginality of older parents, particularly of the widowed, in the family life of their children often gives their relationship a pseudo-intimate character.

One can understand the motivation of parents and of children to pretend that intimacy exists, but it is more difficult to understand why researchers should help to perpetuate such myths. Thus the phrase "intimacy at a distance," coined by Leopold Rosenmayr and Eva Köckeis [15] to describe filial relationships in various Western countries, has been widely adopted by other sociologists, even though it is merely a euphemism for pseudo-intimacy. Such concepts do not clarify, but merely obfuscate, the problems of filial relationships.

To be integrated into any social system, an individual must have qualities or services to offer that another member needs or wants. When no "demand" exists, a person, as a rule, either feels useless or develops psychological defenses against the pain of this knowledge. Just as Lear sought to remain oblivious of "a most faint neglect," so older people will not admit their marginal status in the lives of adult children and their families.

Survey researchers report that parents have frequent contact with their children. Although not false, these reports possibly might be exaggerated. Such bare reports convey nothing about the actual nature of filial relationships. Irving Rosow, one of the very few sociologists who have attempted to do just this, reports:

> Apparently in our sample, relations to children are by far the most emotionally charged area of life, one fraught with anxiety, subject to distortion and denial, about which respondents constantly try to reassure themselves. . . . The distinction between formal responsibility for old parents and the emotional tie between generations is crucial. The quality of intergenerational relations warrants much more intensive attention than it has been accorded in existing studies of the family.[16]

Filial relations give little comfort to the widowed and   **54** the retired. Although most of them have children and see them regularly, widowed people, more than the married *and* the single, suffer from loneliness.[17] To be sure, loneliness is caused by the "desolation" of having lost a formerly valued social role.[18] But it is also evident that filial relationships do not help greatly to alleviate the strains of desolation following the normal role exits of old age. The Kips Bay and Elmira studies revealed no significant differences in the morale of widowed and retired people who had regular contact with their children compared with those who did not.[19] More recently, Ethel Shanas and others found that newly widowed people who had frequent contact with their children complained of loneliness somewhat less often than people without such contacts. But among the widowed as a whole, loneliness is felt as frequently by those who see their children regularly as by those without regular contacts.[20]

The inconsistent findings about the role of filial relationships in forestalling loneliness and demoralization in old age contrast markedly with the empirical evidence showing that friendships effectively safeguard morale in old age.

Pseudo-intimacy is not an effective substitute for intimacy in any social relationship, including filial relationships. Parents, especially after major role exits like widowhood and retirement, require role substitutes in which others appreciate their qualities and services. If they seek restitution for their losses in relationships with their children, as many older people do, they are likely to be disappointed. More than that, if they make demands that their children cannot meet, they will alienate them.[21] Children feel obli-

gated and guilty toward their parents, but adult children do
not, as a rule, need their parents because they have other
"resources"—the core social roles of spouse, parent, and
breadwinner—that absorb most of their time and energy.
King Lear points this out so well.

"Generativity," [22] not "reciprocity," must be the norm
in relations between parents and adult children. Formal obligations can be legislated, but faithfulness cannot. Enduring obligations for goods and services in institutionalized
relationships can be prescribed and socially enforced, but
not the persistence of diffuse emotional commitment. That is
why it is better not to cling to past bonds—even the unique
bonds of filiality. Instead, the individual in old age must
seek restitution for work, for marriage, and for his children
among contemporaries who share his needs, his interests,
and his attitudes. Some people like to recall the days when
it was commonplace for the old to live in the households
of their children, as one older widow observed:

> In the past I think that families were more united. The young
> and old lived together in the same house. I remember that my
> grandmothers lived with us at one time and everyone thought
> it was the right thing. Now, they don't seem to want old people
> around, they want them to live by themselves or live in a nursing
> home.

Nostalgia obscures the costs when the old live with
their children. But independence from children, by living
alone, is also costly, as this comment of another elderly
widow illustrates:

> . . . Being lonely is hard. But I can do what I want to do and

> what they [her children] don't know won't hurt them. I'm my
> own boss. I like it better even though its' lonely.

An enduring dilemma confronts the widowed individual in old age—to submit to his children's authority or to confront life's loneliness as a person living alone, no longer a member of any family groups. Friendships represent one way to deal with this dilemma.

THE
SIGNIFICANCE
OF FRIENDSHIP

Marriage, parenthood, and work are obligatory social roles —they add meaning and purpose to adulthood. Friendship, in contrast, constitutes an optional social role. It is good to have friends; but it is not necessary, or even considered appropriate, to devote the amount of time and energy to friendships that one devotes to family responsibilities and to work. People are expected to fulfill the demands of work and family life, and the judgment of their success or failure as adults rests primarily on the attainment and maintenance of these roles, not on the number of friends they have or on the quality of their friendships.[1]

David Schneider describes how friendship is perceived in American society:

> In the contrast between home and work, there is that interstitial area, that peculiar domain that combines the best parts of each, but is neither, called the vacation, a commercial undertaking which provides a home away from home. Friendship, like a vacation, provides the best parts of the two distinct domains, and is of the same interstitial quality.

> Where one is born with one's relatives, and one's diffuse solidarity is with them "for life," one can pick and choose one's friends at will and with certain clear purposes in mind.[2]

One especially needs close friends during adolescence, because it is a time of uncertainty and ambiguity. The individual is loosening his emotional ties to his parents and acquiring skills that will enable him to take on adult responsibilities.

In adulthood, the time once given to friendships is transferred to the nuclear family. Other social relationships   **60** become secondary and are often transitory. The neighborhood and the job provide regular opportunities for daily contacts with others. People exchange pleasantries and visits with couples with whom they become acquainted in their different contexts. But as a rule such relationships shift and change with the changes in job and residence that adults make over the course of years. Each new residence and each change of job ends and begins friendships.

Consequently, urban dwellers in contemporary society form many acquaintances over a lifetime. But they have few of the close and enduring friendships that are found in traditional societies in which people carry on a variety of activities with the same set of peers over a lifetime.[3]

Simmel characterizes the superficial friendships in contemporary urban life as "acquaintance."

> . . . There is the sociologically highly peculiar relation which in our times . . . is designated simply as "acquaintance." Mutual "acquaintance" by no means is *knowledge* of one another; it involves no actual insight into the individual nature of the personality . . . "acquaintance" depends upon the knowledge of the *that* of the personality, not of its *what*. . . . By saying that one is acquainted, even well acquainted, with a particular person, one characterizes quite clearly the lack of really intimate relations. . . . One knows of the other only what he is toward the outside, either in the purely social-representative sense, or in the sense of that which he shows us. The degree of knowledge covered by "being well acquainted with one another" refers . . . not to what is essential in him intrinsically but only to what is significant for that aspect of him which is turned toward others and the world.[4]

The friends of most adults are, in fact, acquaintances.

The lack of genuine intimacy and commitment in such relationships makes little difference to people *as long as they continue to perform their major institutional roles.* Even among people in their sixties and older, acquaintances are not essential to the maintenance of high morale. Among the employed and the married in the Elmira and Kips Bay studies, for example, low morale was only slightly more common among people with low social participation scores than among those with high scores. This simply means that an active social life adds little to the power of the core social roles to forestall the demoralization of the aging individual.

Many friendships connected with a role are maintained only as long as a person enacts that particular role—for example, only as long as he works at a job or only as long as a person is married to someone. Such relationships, because they are not truly intimate, end when role exit diminishes the occasions for contact and the bond of common interest upon which the friendship has depended.[5] Illustrative of the fate of this kind of relationship is the remark of the retirant quoted in a previous chapter:

> . . . Since I retired it seems I am living in a different world. My old business associates don't know that I am still in the world. My social acquaintances seem also to have forgotten that I am still here. . . .[6]

Core social roles are critical because they integrate the individual into groups outside the immediate kinship group. Exit from a social role, on the other hand, diminishes a person's social participation with peers, as the retirant's complaint verifies. The lower social participation scores of retired and widowed older people, compared with those of their age peers who still have institutional roles, reflect the process just described. The old person's dilemma is this: he needs friends to lessen the demoralizing effects of major role exit; *but just when friendship becomes most important, friendship opportunities are fewer than ever before.*

As long as people are married, or working, morale in old age remains high, regardless of the extent of social participation. That is, work and the social contact afforded by the job effectively sustain morale even in cases of older employees who otherwise are relatively isolated. Marriage, although to a lesser degree, also protects morale in old age, including that of people who have few social resources outside the marital relationship.

The extent of social participation thus becomes critical for morale only after widowhood or retirement. If people can sustain an active social life, either with old friends or by finding new ones, neither retirement nor widowhood, as a rule, have the demoralizing effects noted in cases where older people do not have such alternative social resources. Tables 4 and 5 offer evidence that extensive social activity with age peers constitutes an effective *alternative* for either the marital or occupational role.[7]

It can be seen that the incidence of low morale is not significantly higher among either the employed or the married with low participation scores when compared with those with high scores. But among the retired and the widowed, a very substantial difference in morale is apparent between people with low and high participation scores. Low morale is typical among retired (69 percent) and widowed people (61 percent) who have low participation scores. But the incidence of low morale is not significantly higher

63

TABLE 4
Incidence of Low Morale
by Employment Status and Participation

Extent of Participation	Employed		Retired		Housewives	
Low	25	(63)	69	(49)	52	(73)
High	14	(101)	27	(42)	34	(103)
Difference	11		42 †		18 *	

TABLE 5
Incidence of Low Morale
by Marital Status and Participation

Extent of Participation	Married		Widowed		Single	
Low	33	(83)	61	(76)	65	(26)
High	20	(126)	31	(84)	24	(24)
Difference	13		30 †		41 *	

* Difference significant at the 0.05 level.
† Difference significant at the 0.01 level.

among retirants with extensive social participation than among the employed, and the same is true of the widowed with the high participation scores compared with the still-married. In short, *low morale is the exception, rather than the rule, among older people who maintain an active social life after widowhood or retirement.*

An important principle of general significance is revealed by this finding concerning the significance of extensive social participation in old age.

The *number* of social roles that a person plays can be taken as a crude measure of his social resources—that is, of his socially shared activities, as distinct from his solitary ones. The more social roles a person engages in at any given time, the greater the likelihood that there are people who need him, either because he has services to offer that they want, or because he possesses personal qualities of intrinsic significance to them.[8] In this sense, a person who plays many roles, unlike those with fewer ones, enjoys more power not only to influence others but also to manage his own destiny; for then he is not so dependent on any single role to sustain a sense of well-being.

An important difference between a young child and an adult, when considered from this perspective, is that the former has only a single set of people—his family—to depend on, whereas an adult is engaged in a number of different role sets that give him a sense of usefulness and well being.[9]

The institutional roles of marriage, parenthood, and work represent the minimal social resources that adults normally possess—a *pool* of resources that add meaning and purpose to their lives. I am not suggesting that all people derive equal satisfaction from performing these core social roles. Some people are happy in their marriages, while others are not. Some people greatly enjoy their jobs; others find their work boring and routine. Some people derive a great deal of gratification from rearing children; others find it frustrating or tedious. Moreover, the satisfaction gained from these roles varies from one day to the next. There are days when everything goes wrong at work. But people can gain relief at home from the strains of the job, while some people find relief from tensions at home in their job relationships.

The processes described above help to explain why exit from any significant social role depletes a person's social resources, in much the same way that the loss of a considerable sum of money depletes a person's economic resources. One of the paradoxes of old age is that the role exits of old age free the individual from the demands of adulthood, giving him greater freedom than he enjoyed as an adult. But at the same time, each role exit signifies a reduction of his social resources, thereby constricting his freedom to control his own destiny and to influence others. If this were not true, then the most socially isolated people would also be the freest.

But exactly the opposite is the case. Precisely those older people with extensive social ties do best after role exit. In short, though friendships are of minor significance in adulthood, compared to work and marriage, they are an effective restitution for the loss of the work and marital roles in old age. At this point in life, therefore, friendships with one's peers again become, as in youth, a vital need of the individual. For just as peer relationships in youth loosen the emotional bonds to parents, and thereby facilitate the transition from childhood to adulthood because they constitute independent social resources not subject to parental control, so relationships with peers can soothe the shock of role exit. But this is true only if a person's adult social life was not confined solely to his co-workers and to the friendships in which he and his spouse had jointly participated as a couple. As we have already pointed out, friendships that are contingent on having a job and being married are the ones most likely to be disrupted by exit from these major roles. In this respect, middle-class people are often at a   **66** greater advantage than those in the working class, because, as many studies have shown, middle-class adults participate in more organizations and special-interest groups than do working-class adults. Consequently, their friendships that are not connected with their marital and occupational roles become alternative sources of activity after widowhood and retirement.

Friendships with peers are more effective alternatives to marriage and work roles than are relationships with children, though only the latter are defined as institutionally significant. Indeed, because friendship rests on mutual choice and mutual need and involves a voluntary exchange of sociability between *equals,* it sustains a person's sense of usefulness and self-esteem more effectively than filial relationships.

Children and parents, by definition, cannot be equals or contemporaries. Children do not choose their parents, and their relation to them is not based on present needs or interests but on normative obligations incurred in the past. They have duties toward their parents that they are expected to fulfill, regardless of whether they like them or value them as persons; and they are also expected to continue to accord their parents deference and respect. The maintenance of some degree of psychological distance, therefore, is implied in filial relationships, forbidding the same degree of spontaneity and reciprocity that governs the relationships of equals. Although they no longer have any real authority over their children, parents continue to take a proprietary interest in them; the habit of offering advice and guidance dies hard, and parents think of adult children as *their* children. At times they must exercise the greatest restraint not to correct or advise them as they had done over the many years during which they had invoked these parental prerogatives. Moreover, parents have, as a rule, a great emotional investment in their children and are strongly identified with them. They "take to heart" their children's troubles and worry about them. Parental concern can be a burden. Often children will not freely share their troubles with their parents, but withhold information that they believe will cause them pain or worry. It is difficult enough in times of trouble to manage one's own depression and anxiety without also having to assume the burden of allaying those of another. For all these reasons there cannot be in filial relations the same freedom and reciprocal sharing of intimacy that take place in friendship relations.

Bonds of friendship, as a rule, develop only between people who view each other as equals and who have interests and experiences in common that they can freely share with one another. For these reasons, friendships are usually confined to people of the same generation and at a similar stage in life.

Since parents and adult children are of different generations and the latter have social resources—spouse, children, work—no longer available to their aged parents, intimacy and understanding are difficult to maintain between the generations in all societies and in all eras.[10] It is probably safe to say that differences between the old, the middle-aged, and the young are probably greater now than ever before. Most people today in their seventies and eighties grew up in rural areas and small towns. Many of them, especially those in the cities, are foreign-born and thus products of different cultures. As a rule, this generation has had   **68** limited formal education—most men were manual workers and the women, housewives. Trying to maintain their ethnic identity, many of them lived in ethnic neighborhoods most of their lives. Today's older people struggled to improve their material lot, whereas their children, for the most part native-born and now middle-aged, have more formal education. The number of white-collar workers has increased, as well as the number of women working before marriage and returning to the labor force in middle age. The interests and outlook on life of adults today, therefore, are not the same as those of their aging parents. The grandchildren—the post-depression, post–World War II generation—are, of course, even further removed from their families in their interests and life styles.

Because of the gulf between the generations in rapidly changing societies, older people need opportunities to meet and associate with members of their own generation. The evidence indicates that peer friendships, not filial relationships, determine morale in old age. This does not mean that children stop being important to older people, but that filial ties should not be thought of as upholding older people's morale.[11] In the Elmira study, for example, no relationship could be found between frequency of contact with children and morale. And at least two other studies report that people who see their children less have higher morale scores than other older people.[12] Amiable and satisfying filial relationships are more likely to exist when older people have their own independent social resources and are not compelled to make emotional demands on their children.[13]

The intimacy that older people want, but do not generally find, in relations with their children do occur in some

69

friendships. I am not speaking here of the common run of friendships discussed earlier in this chapter, but of the rarer variety of friendship, in which the partners accept and confide in each other, and trust that their confidences will not be betrayed.

Again, Simmel is the sociologist par excellence when it comes to understanding the diversity and subtleties of human relationships:

> We now come to a totally different configuration. It is found in those relationships which . . . do not center around clearly circumscribed interests that must be fixed objectively, if only because of their "superficiality." Instead, they are built, at least in their idea, upon the person in its totality. The principal types here are friendship and marriage. . . .
>
> The ideal of friendship . . . aims at an absolute psychological intimacy. . . . This entering of the whole undivided ego into the relationship may be more plausible in friendship than in love for the reason that friendship lacks the specific concentration upon one element which love derives from its sensuousness. . . . Undoubtedly, for most people, sexual love opens the doors of the total personality more widely than does anything else. For not a few, in fact, love is the only form in which they can give their ego in its totality. . . . Probably this observation can be made especially often of women. . . . Yet where the feeling of love is not sufficiently expansive . . . the preponderance of the erotic bond may suppress . . . the opening-up of those reservoirs of the personality that lie outside the erotic sphere.
>
> Friendship lacks this vehemence, but also the frequent unevenness, of this abandon. It may be, therefore, more apt than love to connect a whole person with another person in its entirety; it may melt reserves more easily than love does—if not

as stormily, yet on a larger scale and in a more enduring sequence. Yet such complete intimacy becomes probably more and more difficult as differentiation among men increases. Modern man, possibly, has too much to hide to sustain a friendship in the ancient sense. Besides, except for their earliest years, personalities are perhaps too uniquely individualized to allow full reciprocity of understanding and receptivity. . . . The modern way of feeling tends more heavily toward differentiated friendships, which cover only one side of the personality, without playing into other aspects of it.[14]

As in the study of filial relationships, so also in the study of friendships contemporary sociologists have been concerned more with the quantity of older people's friendships than with their qualitative aspects.

An important exception is the excellent study by Marjorie Fisk Lowenthal and Clayton Haven on the significance of intimate friendships in old age. It contains new information and serves to confirm and extend the general proposition being advanced in this chapter—that friendship is an effective alternative for forestalling the demoralization that results from role exit.[15]

Lowenthal and Haven show that a single intimate friendship is an effective "buffer" against demoralization produced by the three major kinds of social losses that beset older people: widowhood, retirement, and diminished social participation. Indeed, the morale of people who are more isolated in old age, *but who have one intimate friendship,* is as high as that of people with increased social participation. Only for those *without* a confidant does more social participation help to forestall demoralization in old age. One intimate friendship, in short, is as effective as several

71

less intimate ones for safeguarding morale after role exit. Finding an intimate friend, however, depends on opportunities as well as on one's capacity for intimacy. The older a person becomes, the greater the probability that a friendship, like a marriage, will be disrupted by the death of one of the partners. The person who has extensive social relations is much more apt to find a replacement than is the person who has had no other friends. And since individuals vary in their capacity for intimacy, this also influences the likelihood of close friendships.

Simmel, in the passage quoted earlier, called attention to the specialization of roles that is characteristic of life in urban societies: one person shares different activities and interests with different sets of people. Thus most adult friendships have a role-contingent character and therefore lack intimacy.

Evidence suggests, interestingly enough, that in modern society women have a greater need and a greater capacity for intimate friendships than do men, at least in old age, and probably also earlier in life.[16]

Lowenthal and Haven found, for example, that more women than men have intimate friendships, and that this sex difference persists regardless of variations in age, marital status, occupational status, educational and socio-economic level, and the extent of social participation of the older people they studied. Also revealing is their finding that in general the wife is the man's only confidante whereas the woman's closest confidante is most likely to be a woman friend. This suggests that men satisfy their needs for intimacy largely within the marriage, but women seek gratification for such needs in close friendships with their own sex. If this is the case, then the prevailing assumption that women "need" marriage more than men because they are more emotionally dependent may very well be wrong. There is some evidence, in fact, that just the opposite may be the case, that the maintenance of both major institutional roles is more important for the morale of older men than it is for women, who resort more to friendships to sustain their morale.

With increasing age, for example, male suicide rates, which in all age groups exceed those of women, increase markedly, while those of women do not.[17] The trauma of retirement, and all the discontinuities it implies, is undoubtedly an important factor in the rise in the suicide rates among older men. But widowed men also show a far greater proneness to suicide than do widowed women, though widowhood is far less common among them than among women and their opportunities for remarriage are much greater. Some recent evidence shows that widowed older men complain more of loneliness than do widowed women, at least in the United States. But among older married people, loneliness is more frequently reported by women than by men.[18]

Why do men fulfill their intimacy needs primarily in marriage, whereas women find it in close friendships with other women? The answer lies in the different ways the two sexes are socialized. A boy is taught to suppress, and to feel ashamed about, gentleness, tenderness, and feeling. Men are taught to cultivate coolness and toughness, to hide their need for response, and to suppress overt expressions of affection toward other men. Suppressing his feelings weakens a person's ability to form intimate social relationships, and disuse weakens any ability. Men achieve more emotional independence than women, but at the cost of a reduced capacity for intimacy. Indeed this difference between men and women often causes friction between them. Women feel deprived at meager expressions of affection, while men feel pressured and uncomfortable when these are demanded. This seems to be particularly true among working-class males,[19] but such suppression of feeling is truer for men than for women in American society as a whole.

The way in which men are socialized may be functional for carrying on bureaucratic occupations in a calm, detached manner, and for maintaining easy, harmonious (albeit more superficial) relationships with co-workers. Less involvement with co-workers and friends also facilitates geographical and social mobility, and success in the occupational world is enhanced by a person's readiness to go "where the opportunities are." As a result, many men in contemporary urban societies form relatively superficial social relations on the job and in leisure activities, and therefore rely more heavily on their wives as their principal source of affection and intimacy.

But women also need solace and emotional support. And often they have a greater capacity for intimate relationships because society permits them, far more than it permits men, to express emotional dependency and affectionate exchanges with members of their own sex. Traditionally, the specifically feminine emotional task has been to give support and sustenance, and to be sensitive to the needs of others. This is the culturally assigned task for married women.[20] The same quality applies to intimate friendships. But in order to give affection and support, women must receive them too. Women's dependency-needs motivate them to seek intimacy first in their marriage; but if it is not forthcoming there—and often it is not—they turn to female friends for the free give-and-take of confidences that is missing in their married life.

The dependency-needs of women and their greater capability for forming close intimate friendships prepare them for widowhood. Although the probabilities are that women, more than men, will not remarry, and that they will spend a part of their later lives alone and unattached to any family unit, the greater prevalence of widowhood among women seems to increase the pool of potential friends. Thus their widowhood need not, theoretically at least, promote isolation. Nevertheless, under existing conditions it often does.

STRUCTURAL
CONSTRAINTS
ON FRIENDSHIP

. . . Some difficulties and some qualities are not so much
attached to this or that individual or to this or that
moment of existence, considered from the social point
of view. They are, as it were, exterior to the individual,
who passes through their beam of light as through
various pre-existent, general and inevitable solstices.
                                    —MARCEL PROUST

Social participation—friendship in particular—helps to sustain morale in widowhood and retirement. People differ not only in their social needs and motivation but also in the opportunities available to implement those needs. This is no less true in old age than in other periods. The older person's opportunities to maintain old friendships and to form new ones therefore deserve close attention.

After role exit, the older person needs alternative social roles, in which he can meet others and exchange services with them, so he may feel that his existence matters to someone besides himself. Men and women become human through association with others, and social intercourse and social response remain psychological necessities as long as they live.

As shown in chapter 2, retirement and widowhood generally have an adverse effect on older people's social participation. But when analyzing different categories of retired and widowed people, we discover that the effects of role exit on friendships vary in a consistent and interesting manner.

Obviously, people beyond sixty are not homogeneous. The disparity is as wide, for example, between sixty- and eighty-year-old people as between forty- and sixty-year-old people. At age sixty, the proportion of retired and widowed people is far smaller than at age eighty. Similarly, among the different age-sex categories of the older population, different proportions of men and women have experienced each form of role exit; the proportion of those who have retired thus rises more sharply among men past seventy than the proportion of the widowed. Among women, the proportion of the widowed rises more steeply with advancing age than the proportion of retired, because fewer women than men hold jobs in earlier adulthood. Finally, among people sixty and over, just as in the younger age categories, socio-economic differences, based on income and education, affect one's style of living and interests. In short, there are considerable variations in age, sex, and class positions of the married and the widowed and of employed and retired older people.

To an important degree, these three attributes—age, sex, and class position—condition an individual's and his friends' location in the social structure. That is to say, throughout life, all other things being equal, age, sex, and class position determine which friendships are formed and maintained. All societies consider age and sex as the basic categories for grouping people and for assigning them social roles. Therefore the opportunities for interaction and communality of interest and perspective, as a rule, are greater among members of the same age-sex categories than among those in different social categories. And in modern industrial societies, in which occupational and educational differences are greater than in traditional societies, class position is a third factor that conditions both the opportunities for interaction and for the sharing of common tastes and interests—the basis for any kind of intimate social relationship, including friendship.

Because age, sex, and class position govern friendship choices and friendship associations, the prevalence of retirement and widowhood among a person's age-sex-class peers affects older people's friendships.

In the Elmira study, dividing the widowed into two age categories—those in their sixties and those seventy and over—revealed different friendship patterns among the younger and older groups. The widowed of both sexes still in their sixties associate less with friends, but among people seventy and over it is the married people's social participation that declines, not that of the widowed.[1] The Kips Bay area study in New York City confirmed this.

Widowhood, in short, was found to have no detrimental effects on the friendship participation of people seventy and over, but it has detrimental effects on the friendships of those still in their sixties. How can one explain this unanticipated finding, that the same role exit has different consequences for the individual's social participation, depending on whether he is under or over seventy years old?

There are, of course, more widowed persons among older than among younger people, and this is important. Among men in their sixties, very few are widowed. In the Elmira sample, for example, this proportion is only 13 percent, and the social life of widowers in this age group suffers in comparison with that of the married. But among men over seventy, a greater proportion (33 percent) are widowed, and widowhood no longer has adverse effects on social participation. The same is true of women. As the proportion of widows increases with age (from 43 percent in the group under seventy to 65 percent in the group seventy and over), widowhood ceases to hinder friendships.[2]

Widowhood appears to have an adverse effect on social participation only when it places an individual in a different position from most of his age and sex peers. People tend to form friendships with others in their own age group; and to the extent that this occurs, the widowed individual under seventy is likely to be an "odd" person at social gatherings, since most of his associates are probably still married and participate with their spouses in social activities. His widowhood, then, may have a detrimental effect on his participation. But after seventy, married couples who continue to participate jointly in social activities become the deviants, since most of their friends in this age group are likely to be widowed. A social gathering of septuagenarians, for example, most of whom are by now widowed, will often be composed largely of people of the same sex, and the married couple does not quite fit in. Moreover, a widow's (or widower's) continued association with couples whose company she and her spouse used to enjoy together reminds her of the loss she has suffered, and this may discourage her from associating frequently with her married friends.

Sex also influences the formation of friendships, and consequently conditions the effect of widowhood on social participation.[3] Widowhood has a detrimental effect on the friendships of both men and women in their sixties; but, in this younger group, loss of spouse is likely to have a more adverse effect on the participation of men than on that of women. Thus among people in their sixties, the difference in the proportion of high participants between married and widowed *men* is markedly higher than that between married and widowed *women*. Married men associate more with friends than do married women; widowers, at least those under seventy, do so less than widows.

This difference can also be explained in structural terms. The under-seventy age group differs significantly in the proportion of widowers (13 percent) and widows (43 percent). Since loss of spouse is rare among younger men, the widower occupies a more deviant position within his 81 age-and-sex group than does the widow. This means that the overwhelming majority of the widower's male friends under seventy are still married and consequently tend to participate in social activities with other couples, since their wives prefer "get-togethers" in which other women are also present. To a wife, meeting other women is more enjoyable than visiting her husband's widower friend, with whom she, if not her husband, is likely to have few shared interests. To be sure, younger widows would encounter similar problems in their social relations with married friends. But widowhood is less detrimental to the participation of women under seventy than to that of men in the same age group, because widowhood is more prevalent among women and therefore the woman in her sixties is more likely to have more associates who are widowed too. The younger widow, therefore, is not in as deviant a position socially as the younger widower, although widowhood probably decreases her social contacts with married friends as much as it does that of men. Hence widowhood does not affect younger women's participation to the same extent as that of younger men.

Among people seventy and over, in whom there is a far larger proportion of widowers (33 percent), the difference in the participation of married and widowed men disappears. In other words, as this change in marital status becomes more prevalent among their age and sex peers, widowhood ceases to have an isolating effect upon widowers. By this time, a number of their friends have also become widowers, who can be relied on for social companionship. Indeed, older widowers associate more with friends (67 percent) than do younger ones (47 percent), whereas **82** older married men tend to do so less (65 percent) than younger ones (72 percent).

The social participation of women reveals the same pattern. The proportion of high participants among married women drops from 64 percent in the younger group to 44 percent in the older one, but there is no such drop among the widowed. Among women over seventy, two-thirds of whom are widowed, it is the married person who occupies a deviant position, and thus associates somewhat less with friends than the widow in the same age group.

These findings suggest the following generalization: the effect of major role exits on older people's friendships depends on the *prevalence* of these exits among their peers. An exit that places the individual in a deviant position in his age or sex group interferes with his opportunities to maintain old friendships. For an exit from a major role that places an individual in a minority position among his peers differentiates his interests and experiences from theirs, and thereby reduces the basis for the formation and persistence of friendships. But if the same status change becomes predominant in a social group, then the individual who retains his earlier role becomes the deviant one, and consequently it is his social participation that suffers.[4]

Up to this point, the discussion has been confined to a consideration of how age and sex affect friendship in widowhood. But class position is also important for the formation and maintenance of friendships. By and large, adults enter into friendships with people of similar social-class position not as a matter of principle, but because the opportunities for interaction—at work, in the neighborhood, and

in all voluntary groups and associations to which people belong—are typically far greater among people with a similar
class position than among those of widely different socio-
economic status. Moreover, because people of similar class
position have similar means and a similar living style, they
are more likely to have in common interests, tastes, and
general outlook upon which friendships are based.

Since class position, besides age and sex similarities,
influences friendship choices, one would expect that the frequency of widowhood on different socio-economic levels
would also affect older people's friendships. But this expectation was only partly borne out in the two communities
studied. The postulated effects of the prevalence of widowhood upon friendships followed the expected pattern consistently only in the middle class. Thus it can be seen in
Table 6 that in the age-sex-class groups in which a third or
less of the people are widowed, widowed people have less
association with friends than do married couples; but where
the widowed constitute over a third of the social category,
widowhood does not have a detrimental effect on friendships.

Among the working class, however, particularly in the
case of women, widowhood consistently has an isolating
effect on social life in old age—an indication that other factors that are unique to working-class people, and especially
women, prevent individuals from taking advantage of the
social opportunities created by the prevalence of widowhood
among their peers.

Different participation patterns among working-class
wives *before* the advent of old age probably explain their
different social position in widowhood. Evidence shows that **84**

the social life of the working-class adult woman is limited largely to neighbors and relatives. Even social activities with her spouse are often quite rare.[5] The higher-class woman's social life, on the other hand, is more likely to include extensive association with other women throughout her married life. As a result of more varied organizational activities and social pastimes that bring her into frequent contact with age-sex peers, she accumulates over the years a relatively wide circle of friends and acquaintances distributed over a wider geographical area. To be sure, her participation in these activities may become more limited as she grows older. She may see less of her old friends and acquaintances and devote herself more to activities that she can share with her husband. But her husband's death generates a need for alternative sources of companionship, and she is likely, after the first shock of grief, to welcome the solicitude of old friends and to take advantage of opportunities to reestablish closer ties with them, particularly with other widows who, like herself, also want social companionship. In other words, the middle-class widow is likely to reestablish, with some modifications of course, her earlier social activities—bridge, shopping, attendance at cultural events, visits, travel—with other women whom she had known before. Thus her activities with other women of like status prior to widowhood constitute a reservoir of social opportunities that the middle- and higher-class woman can draw on after the death of her husband, particularly if several of her old friends are also widows and equally disposed to strengthen old social ties. In contrast, the lower-class woman, who in middle age, while her husband was alive, probably did not share social activities with other women,   **85**

Class	Sex	Age
High	Men	Under 70
		Over 70
	Women	Under 70
		Over 70
Low	Men	Under 70
		Over 70
	Women	Under 70
		Over 70
Total		
High	Men	Under 70
		Over 70
	Women	Under 70
		Over 70
Low	Men	Under 70
		Over 70
	Women	Under 70
		Over 70
Total		

* A positive difference indicates that
cates that participation is higher among the

TABLE 6
Participation by Marital Status and Age-Sex Class Position in Elmira and Kips-Bay

Elmira

Per-centage Wid-owed	N	Married	N	Wid-owed	N	Differ-ence *
		Percentage of High Friendship Participation				
17	(58)	76	(41)	50	(10)	+26
36	(25)	77	(13)	78	(9)	− 1
42	(89)	62	(36)	88	(37)	−26
70	(59)	27	(11)	56	(41)	−29
10	(72)	69	(55)	43	(7)	+26
31	(47)	59	(27)	60	(15)	− 1
46	(61)	64	(28)	43	(28)	+21
60	(57)	57	(14)	47	(34)	+10
	(468)					
						Kips Bay
3	(38)	47	(30)	—	—	—
25	(19)	47	(15)	0	(5)	+47
51	(42)	60	(15)	76	(21)	−16
64	(39)	0	(7)	28	(25)	−28
10	(68)	21	(47)	43	(7)	−21
39	(63)	23	(26)	38	(24)	−15
56	(109)	44	(25)	43	(60)	+ 1
63	(122)	50	(8)	28	(76)	+22
	(500)					

friendship participation is higher among the married; a negative difference indi-
widowed.

outside of neighboring, is less apt to have this reservoir of social opportunities to draw upon in widowhood.

The economic deprivation caused by her husband's death, regardless of the prevalence of widowhood among her peers, also limits the lower-class woman's social opportunities. To be sure, for the middle-class woman, widowhood also often entails some reduction in income, particularly if her husband was still in the labor force; but her financial resources are generally greater than those of the lower-class widow, who must rely on Social Security payments or old-age assistance grants. No matter how modest her social activities are, they usually cost money—the carfare required to pay visits, the refreshments offered to a guest, the price of a movie ticket. This may be a barrier for the lower-class widow, but not for the one in a higher-class position.

The friendships of working-class men, while more limited than those of their middle-class counterparts, are not as locally centered as those of their wives, simply because they made friends on the job with men of their own age with whom social ties can be strengthened or renewed when they are left widowed. Besides, older widowed men, being in short supply, are often sought by widows as companions and potential marriage partners, and such friendships help, of course, to sustain or even to increase a widower's social life.

Analyzing the effect of retirement on friendships, which parallels that of widowhood, confirms this chapter's central proposition: the effects of retirement on the social life of the older person, like those of widowhood, vary according to the prevalence of this form of role exit [6] among his own age-sex-class peers.

The two communities studied revealed that in all three social categories in which retirement is infrequent, male retirants associate less with friends than do the employed, indicating that this change in status has adverse effects on participation. On the other hand, in most of the social categories in which retirement *is* prevalent, no adverse effects on friendships were noted (see Table 7). In short, the consequences of retirement among men depend on its prevalence among others of similar age, sex, and socio-economic position—just as with widowhood.

These findings can readily be explained. Retirement, whatever a man's age, reduces opportunities for contacts with co-workers. But early retirement also disturbs those social ties that the individual has established with age peers outside the work situation, since most men in their sixties are still employed. Even employed friends who are not co-workers often discuss their job experiences when they meet. They may exchange amusing stories that originated at work. They may relieve tensions that have arisen on the job by telling their friends about conflicts with co-workers and superiors, and, in turn, listen sympathetically to the work-connected problems of their friends. They may talk about their successful experiences on the job and thereby heighten the gratification derived from these achievements.

Retirement deprives the older person of the experiences shared by people who work. As a result, he can no longer fully participate in the conversational give-and-take of his employed friends.

89

Class	Sex	Age
High	Men	Under 70
		Over 70
	Women	Under 70
		Over 70
Low	Men	Under 70
		Over 70
	Women	Under 70
		Over 70
Total		
High	Men	Under 70
		Over 70
	Women	Under 70
		Over 70
Low	Men	Under 70
		Over 70
	Women	Under 70
		Over 70
Total		

* A positive difference indicates that
tive difference indicates that this is *not*

TABLE 7
Friendship Participation by Employment Status
and Age-Sex-Class Position in Elmira and Kips Bay

Percentage Retired	N	Percentage of High Friendship Participation				**Elmira**
		Employed	N	Retired	N	Difference *
30	(58)	75	(40)	59	(17)	+16
56	(25)	82	(11)	79	(14)	+ 3
9	(89)	65	(23)	63	(8)	+ 2
9	(59)	40	(5)	40	(5)	0
21	(72)	71	(58)	60	(15)	+11
63	(47)	78	(18)	50	(30)	+28
2	(61)	47	(17)	—	—	—
14	(57)	60	(5)	60	(8)	− 3
	(468)					**Kips Bay**
11	(38)	55	(33)	25	(5)	+30
50	(19)	30	(10)	40	(10)	−10
15	(42)	63	(16)	67	(6)	− 4
19	(39)	—	(3)	43	(7)	—
53	(68)	28	(32)	33	(36)	− 5
81	(63)	33	(12)	36	(50)	− 3
31	(109)	67	(33)	45	(33)	+22
46	(122)	47	(19)	29	(55)	+18
	(500)					

friendship participation is higher among the employed than among retirants; a nega-
the case.

The person who retires while most of his friends are still employed becomes a deviant in his social group, an "outsider." After retirement, he can no longer join in the conversations about business in which he participated as a worker. They become a sign of his no longer being in the in-group, and a barrier to continued association with his employed friends. In short, the pattern that integrated the individual who was in the same position as the majority of his friends excludes him when his position becomes different from theirs.

The retirant over seventy is less likely to encounter this problem. Most of his age peers are also retired, and thus he does not feel different from his friends. (In the two communities studied, at least half the men over seventy, at all class levels, were retired.) As a result, the older retirant ceases to be at a social disadvantage with men who are still employed. Indeed, in the Kips Bay area of New York City, where retirement is generally more prevalent than in Elmira, it is the *employed* man over seventy who deviates from his age and sex peers, and consequently associates less with friends than his retired counterpart. In short, the retirant is more than compensated for the loss of social contact with his co-workers if most of his peers experience a similar status change.

For women, however, the effects of retirement on their friendships follow no discernible pattern. Retirement is, of course, generally less prevalent among women than among men, since many women are not employed during their married life. Nevertheless, retired women associate with friends as much as, or more than, do employed women. Clearly, the prevalence of retirement among women does not influence friendships. These findings emphasize the profound difference in the significance of gainful employment for men and women in our society.

For the married woman, marital duties, rearing children, and managing the household are culturally defined as obligatory social roles. To be sure, there is a growing acceptance of employment for women, particularly after their children are grown; but the prevailing attitude still is that a job is a secondary role for women and must not be allowed to interfere with their primary responsibilities, those of wife and mother. As a result, friendship among women, whether they are gainfully employed or not, depends on their marital status and, in their child-rearing years, somewhat on their maternal status. Indeed, the married woman who seems unduly concerned with her job might be criticized not only by her own sex but by men as well.

Conversations at social gatherings reveal this attitude toward the female work role. Since most married women are housewives, the working wives must talk about matters of common interest to the other women—that is, engage in "woman talk." Although women may jokingly disparage this type of behavior, just as they exhort their husbands to stop "talking shop," they nevertheless tend to persist in it. The occasional working woman who deviates risks criticism from her housewife friends, who are typically in the majority and can effectively impose negative sanctions upon such deviants. But most working wives willingly give precedence to their feminine roles and rarely allow their jobs to destroy their association with others.

Since being a wife is the focus of a woman's social life, widowhood, not retirement, has the major impact. A man's   **93** social life, on the other hand, is strongly conditioned by his work role and, consequently, also by retirement.[7]

This chapter's finding—that the effects of widowhood and retirement on older people's friendships are not uniform but are governed by the prevalence of each role exit among their own age, sex, and class peers—has important implications for social policy. Since widowed and retired persons are a minority group, they are at a disadvantage socially. As has been shown, widowhood and retirement generally isolate those individuals who are a small minority, but not when they have contact with others who have experienced the same role changes.

Role exits in old age are inevitable, but the isolating effects—caused when a person is removed from the institutional structures that once provided him with regular social contacts—can be avoided. New social structures are needed through which older people, especially those who have experienced role exit, have opportunities for regular contact with others in a similar position and with similar needs.

The establishment of new communities and housing complexes within metropolitan centers, where older people constitute the majority group, is a relatively recent social innovation aimed at counteracting the marginality and social isolation of older people. Many people oppose housing for the elderly on the ground that it separates and isolates older people from the general population and thereby denies them the opportunity for integration into the life of the general community. Proponents of this position advocate housing communities that reflect the age distribution of any community as the solution to the isolation of the old.

94

They are wrong. They assume that residential balance will bring about social ties between different age groups. They do not recognize that age-integrated housing complexes solve nothing. It is the *dispersion* of older people in the general community that promotes their social isolation.

Rosow, whose recent comparative study of older people in dispersed and concentrated housing settings is the best empirical study on this subject, comes to a similar conclusion:

> Residential settings of statistically "normal" age composition may be excellent instruments for inadvertently alienating and demoralizing the elderly. With the attrition of ties with their family, friends, and other groups, the dispersal of their age peers in a normal neighborhood reduces the number of friends available to them. . . . Conversely, residential settings heavily weighted with older people concentrate rather than diffuse the field of potential friends and thereby maximize the prospect of friendship formation and group embeddedness. Indeed, this may be the basic reason for the success of so many retirement communities.[8]

Since the old are a minority group, not merely numerically but also because retirement and widowhood place them in a different social position from most adults, they require alternative social structures that provide them opportunities for contact with their peers. Age-concentrated housing and retirement communities do *not* curtail the social opportunities of older people. Instead they extend such opportunities in a way that proves, from all available evidence, to be highly effective, particularly for those older people who, as shown in the Elmira and Kips Bay studies, are most vulnerable to the isolating effects of widowhood and retirement.

Thus Rosow found that the social life of working-class people, the group that is most isolated following role exit, improved most in age-concentrated housing. In projects with a heavy concentration of older people, working-class people under seventy-five increased their active association with their neighbors by one-fourth; and those seventy-five and over increased this association by two-and-a-half times compared with the extent of neighboring that occurred among people of the same age group in "normal" settings. These findings make it clear that the provision of age-concentrated housing for older people in lower-status groups is especially beneficial.

The greater social resources of middle-class people, and the fact that they are not as locally centered as those of the working class, make them less responsive to variations in age concentration during their sixties. But as they grow older, even their more extensive social resources decrease through role exits and through the death of old friends; and they, like their working-class counterparts, fare considerably better socially in age-concentrated housing than in a normal residential milieu.[9] Unlike old people in lower-income groups, however, the middle- and upper-class elderly can afford to migrate to retirement communities in the West and Southwest, or to move to the growing number of apartment complexes constructed with private capital that are designed for the growing post-middle-aged population in metropolitan centers.

Not surprisingly, many people in a youth-oriented society will resist age-graded housing complexes or communities. This attitude, which is more characteristic of middle-class people than of the working class, represents a form of "false consciousness" that goes against the interests of the current generation of older people and of the adults who will become the next aged generation.

To deny that age constitutes a significant basis for association is to ignore reality. In all societies, age grading is a basic principle of social organization. One could argue that people ought not to be denied opportunities solely because they are old, or female, or black. But as long as these status attributes result in widespread discrimination, social action is needed to defend the interests of those with lower status attributes. Indeed, it is often in the interest of several different minority groups to join together to promote changes in the status quo that disadvantages them in a similar way.

Some sociologists deny that the old constitute a minority group.[10] I disagree. To the extent that they are barred from full and equal participation in the occupational structure, which in contemporary society is the principal determinant of status, wealth, and power, the old are in the same disadvantaged position as any other political minority, and they have the same right and responsibility to utilize the political process to improve their lot.

It may seem that the advocacy of age-concentrated housing complexes and communities contradicts the equality principle. But empirical evidence supports the opposite conclusion. For, as I have shown, age segregation in housing promotes the social opportunities of older people to gain access to others who have common social needs and common political interests. Dispersing older people in the general community not only isolates them socially but also undermines their capacity to join together to become a significant political force. Age-concentrated housing would promote and extend the social and political opportunities of older people who now constitute a disadvantaged minority. In this important sense it would promote democracy.[11]

CHANGES
IN IDENTITY

The sense of ego identity . . . is the accrued confidence
that one's ability to maintain inner sameness and continuity
(one's ego in the psychological sense) is matched by
the sameness and continuity of one's meaning for others.[1]
—ERIK ERIKSON

The social category, particularly in modern societies, to which a person is assigned on the basis of chronological age—young, middle-aged, or old—often does not correspond to what he himself considers his age identity. No one wants to grow old in a society in which youthfulness is so admired. While aging chronologically and physically, some people can sustain a sense of inner sameness; that is, they do not feel or think of themselves as old. Others are unable to do this.

When one studies age-identity changes systematically, some social conditions can be discovered that support ego identity, thereby forestalling the identity diffusion expressed in King Lear's terrifying query "Who am I?"

An individual's age conception is, of course, related to his actual age. But the variations in age identification between persons in the same age group, and the similarities between those whose actual age differs, indicate that chronological age is only a limiting condition and does not explain the changes in age identity that occur during an individual's life.

The answers to the Elmira study's question "How do you think of yourself as far as age goes—middle-aged, elderly, old, or what?" confirm that chronological age in itself does not reveal one's age identity. Although all respondents were sixty or beyond, only 38 percent thought of themselves as elderly or old; 60 percent considered themselves still middle-aged.[2]

But the likelihood that people consider themselves old rather than middle-aged steadily increases with chronological age. In Elmira, for example, among those under sixty-five, only 18 percent defined themselves as old; between

sixty-five and seventy, 37 percent did; but among those
seventy and beyond, this proportion rose to 59 percent.
Old age is, after all, something more than a state of mind,
since the aging process is marked by objective physical and
behavioral changes. Although these changes usually occur
gradually and therefore do not immediately intrude upon
the individual's consciousness, one might expect that they
will become increasingly apparent to him and his associates
as the years pass and thus finally bring about his identification with old people. Indeed, when Elmira respondents were
asked "How much have you changed in the past ten or
fifteen years—would you say hardly at all, somewhat, or a
good deal?" less than a fifth of those under seventy, compared with a third of those over seventy, felt that they had
changed "a good deal."

However, further analysis revealed that not all older
people, but only those who had shifted their age identification, were likely to perceive these changes in themselves. It
seems that neither the knowledge of their years nor even
their white hair and wrinkles induce older people to perceive
that they have changed.

As Proust writes:

It does us no good to know that the years go by, that youth gives
way to old age, that the most stable thrones and fortunes crumble,
that fame is ephemeral—our way of forming a conception—and,
so to speak, taking a photograph of this moving universe, hur-
ried along by time, seeks on the contrary to make it stand still.[3]

And so, to borrow Proust's metaphor, it is the conception of himself as old, not the weight of his years as such,
that forces the older person to give up the photograph and
reluctantly substitute the mirror.   **101**

TABLE 8
Percentages of Persons
Who Perceive "A Good Deal"
of Change in Themselves—
by Age Identification and Age

		Age Identification	
Age	Middle-Aged	Old	Total
Under 70	15 (206)	42 (31)	18 * (273)
70 and over	22 (73)	40 (88)	33 * (175)

* Difference is significant at the 0.01 level.

A similar phenomenon was observed with the older person's beliefs about the image others have of him. The older the person, the more frequently does he answer affirmatively when asked, "Do you think that the people you see and care most about think of you as an old man (woman)?" Only about one-eighth of those under seventy, but a third of those seventy and over, feel that their close associates consider them old. But regardless of their actual age, people come to believe that others consider them old only if they consider themselves old.[4]

In sum, the shifts in age identity from middle to old age promote various mental states that distinguish old people. All people age chronologically, but many maintain a *stable* identity and resist the social pressures to relinquish their middle-aged identity. By doing so, they preserve a sense of sameness in themselves and confidence in the continuity of how they are perceived by the people they know and care about.

It might be argued that it is unrealistic for people who are categorized as old to maintain a middle-aged self-image

TABLE 9

Percentages of Persons
Saying That Significant Others
Consider Them Old—
by Age Identification and Age

		Age Identification			
Age	Middle-Aged		Old		Total
Under 70	7 (206)		45 (31)		13 * (276)
70 and over	14 (73)		50 (88)		32 * (187)

* Difference is significant at the 0.01 level.

—the implication being that they *ought* to "adjust" their self-concept to social reality. But why should people ignore their subjective experience—granted an idiosyncratic one—and accept consignment to a social category based on the crudest, most generalizable criteria, which ignore the subtle marks of individuality that distinguish one person from another within every social category?

In this context, an observation made by the writer E. B. White around the time he turned seventy is refreshing and to the point:

"How should one adjust to age?" In principle, one shouldn't adjust. In fact one does. (Or I do.) When my head starts knocking because of my attempt to write, I quit writing instead of carrying on as I used to do when I was young. These are adjustments. But I gaze into the faces of our senior citizens in our Southern cities and they wear a sad look that disturbs me. I am sorry for all those who have agreed to grow old. I haven't agreed yet. Old age is a special problem for me because I've never been able to shed the mental image I have of myself—a lad of about nineteen.[5] **103** ɛ

White's comments suggest that the "irrationality" of the older person's refusal to consider himself old is beside the point; his need to preserve the sense of sameness within himself between the lad of nineteen that he was long ago and the man of seventy that he has become—this is the issue. It is a struggle to preserve, in Erikson's terms, his ego integrity.

Although retired, White continues to practice his craft. And though this is now difficult, he struggles to remain creative. He goes on to say that

> A writer certainly has a special problem with aging. The generative process is slowed down, yet the pain and frustration of not writing is as acute as ever. I feel frustrated and in pain a good deal of the time now; but I try to bear in mind the advice of Hubert Humphrey's father. "Never get sick, Hubert; there isn't time."

White is among the fortunate few who can continue to work—to practice a craft, not merely a hobby—after retirement from the occupational structure. Most people, however, have neither the skill nor the self-discipline to create independently a product that commands an audience or a price. Increasingly, the conditions of modern production call not for craftsmen, but for the learning of specialized tasks, performed by many different people, each with limited skills. When retirement takes place, therefore, they have no work that can be carried on outside the factory or the business in which they were formerly employed.

The loss of the occupational role, the mainstay of one's identity—not age or physical changes—leads people to change their age identity and accept old age.

When people of similar age are compared, those who are retired perceive themselves as old much more often than do their employed age-peers. In the Elmira study, only a small proportion of the employed in their sixties thought of themselves as old (18 percent); but retirants of the same age felt old nearly as often as employed people of seventy years and beyond (37 percent and 41 percent, respectively). Only retirants seventy and beyond perceived themselves as old in most cases (67 percent).

Interestingly, widowhood, in contrast to retirement, does not produce significant age-identity changes in older people. In the Elmira study, widowed people at all levels were slightly more inclined to perceive themselves as old than those who were still married, but the differences were far smaller than between the employed and the retired. There are several reasons why retirement, but not widowhood, has a pronounced effect on the older person's self-conception.

Retirement, first of all, endangers the self-esteem of the older person, as the following remark of a retirant illustrates:

> When did I start to feel old? Why, when I stopped working. I was always real proud that I'd come to Chicago and got a job and supported myself. Then when I couldn't work anymore, why, I wasn't good for anything.[6]

Retirement is a *social* pattern that implies an invidious judgment about old people's lack of fitness to perform a culturally significant and coveted role. By social definition, therefore, retirement signifies old age. Moreover, as the remark above implies, having a job—the principal aspect of an adult male's social identity—is bound up with his sex identity. When strangers meet, the first question directed **105** to men (but not, as a rule, to women) is "What do you do?" or even "What are you?"

In contrast to retirement, a marital partner's death is not confined to older people (although it is more common later in life), since it is *natural* event without socially invidious implications because it is beyond human judgment and control.[7]

Furthermore, because retirement disrupts the many informal relations developed on the job, whereas widowhood disrupts only a *single* relationship, I suggest that exit from a peer group has more pronounced effects on the individual's self-concept than does the loss of an intimate relationship.[8] This helps to explain the different effects of retirement and widowhood on age identity. The proposition can be tested by determining if membership in a friendship clique is more significant for maintaining a stable age identity than are relations with individual friends.

Respondents in the Elmira study were asked three questions about their social participation: "How many really close friends do you have here in town that you occasionally talk over confidential matters with?" "Now think of the friend that you know best here in town—how often do you get to see that friend?" "Would you say you go around with a certain bunch of close friends who visit back and forth in each other's homes?"

Neither the number of friendships nor the frequency of contact with the closest friend significantly affects age identity.[9] But older people who belong to a *friendship clique* consider themselves old less often than those who do not participate in such a group. Only 29 percent of the members, in contrast to 41 percent of the non-members, regard **106** themselves as old. However, this relationship may be spurious, since as people grow older they tend to participate less in friendship groups, and thus are more likely to think of themselves as old.

Indeed, when age is controlled, the relationship between clique membership and age identity disappears among those who are under seventy. Most people under seventy still define themselves as middle-aged whether or not they belong to a friendship group. But among people who are seventy and over, clique membership makes a considerable difference for age identity. Only half of those who participate in a friendship group, but nearly two-thirds of the others, consider themselves old.

That participation in a friendship clique makes no difference for age identification in the younger group only *appears* to refute the hypothesis that group memberships are more effective than single relationships in forestalling identity change. Actually, this hypothesis helps to explain why participation in a friendship clique is less important in the younger than in the older age group. People under seventy are likely to have alternative group memberships. For example, since most men of this age are still employed, they participate in work groups and other occupational groups. Younger women, as well, participate more in clubs and organizations than those who are older. Thus it makes little difference whether they also participate in a friendship group. But after seventy, when participation in these other social groups is the exception rather than the rule, the person's position in a friendship group becomes more important for sustaining a sense of sameness.

Similarly, how an individual perceives his image   **107** among his close associates is influenced by his participation in a social peer group, but not by the number of friends he has. Regardless of their age, those who belong to such a group feel less often than others that they are considered old. Indeed, among people seventy and over in the Elmira study, two-thirds of the clique members, compared with less than half of the others, believed that their associates did not consider them old.[10]

These indications that participation in a social group forestalls the psychological changes that mark old age more effectively than participation in a number of dyadic relationships can be explained by the characteristics of social groups. Studies of various small groups [11] show that recurrent interaction between individuals usually fixes each member's role. The images and expectations that arise among the group members tend to persist and to influence their subsequent behavior toward one another. The stability of the *network* of relationships within a group of friends or co-workers prevents mutual awareness of the gradual alterations taking place among the participants, particularly if these changes do not interfere with a person's ability to share in the group's activities. Consequently, the recurrent gatherings of the same people lend a sense of continuity to each participant's identity. For example, some people who have grown old together continue to refer to themselves as "the boys" or "the girls."

Participation in a friendship *group* does, indeed, serve to postpone shifts in age identity, and this supports the hypothesis that loss of the work *group* is one of the reasons why retirement influences an older person's self-concept more than widowhood does.

TABLE 10
Percentages of Persons
Identified as Old by Membership
in a Friendship Group and Marital Status

Marital			**Friendship Group**			
Status	Member		Non-member		Total	
Married	29	(85)	35 *	(133)	33	(218)
Widowed	34	(53)	51 *	(121)	46	(173)
Difference	5		16			

* This difference, as well as that between proportions among totals, is significant at the 0.05 level.

TABLE 11
Percentages Identified as Old
by Membership in a Friendship Group
and Employment Status

Employment			**Friendship Group**			
Status	Member		Non-member		Total	
Employed	21	(66)	25 *	(104)	24	(170)
Retired	42	(24)	62 *	(69)	57	(93)
Difference	21		37			

* This difference, as well as that between proportions among totals, is significant at the 0.01 level.

Both widowed and retired people who have a circle of friends continue to think of themselves as middle-aged more often than those without such a group—further evidence of the significance of friendship groups for sustaining the sameness of older people's self-concept.

Even though a marital partner's death does not, as I mentioned earlier, affect an older person's self-concept to a   **109** significant degree, nevertheless, widowed people more often continue to perceive themselves as middle-aged if they have a circle of friends than if they do not. Similarly, retirants with a friendship group more often sustain a middle-aged self-concept than those who are without this identity support.

The friendship clique, however, is less successful in counteracting the effects of retirement on age identity. Even among older people who have a circle of friends, twice as many of the retired as of the employed consider themselves old, but hardly any more of the widowed than of the married do so.

It is evident, then, that membership loss in a peer group after retirement only partly explains why age identity is more affected by retirement than by widowhood, since even retirants with a group of friends more frequently perceive themselves as old than do people who are still employed.

Retirement is a form of social exclusion directed at people when they reach the arbitrarily fixed age of sixty-five, and thus defines the onset of old age—just as age twenty-one has traditionally marked the beginning of adulthood. A man normally retires not because he feels old but because he is compelled to retire, regardless of how he feels. According to social definition, he *is* old. Subject to this kind of pressure, a person finds it difficult to sustain his middle-aged identity even if he has a circle of friends to serve as an "identity anchor." A change in a person's subjective age identity operates as a self-fulfilling prophecy. Because he sees himself as old, he is more apt to believe that others consider him old, and more apt to believe that he has changed a great deal. A self-concept of being old hurts one's self-esteem and morale. This in turn further underlines the disparity between his present and former self, and reinforces his perception of himself as old.[12]

Howard S. Becker and Anselm Strauss have observed that "stabilities in the organization of behavior and of self-regard are inextricably dependent upon stabilities of social structures." [13] This generalization is confirmed by the significance of friendship *networks* for sustaining a sense of enduring sameness of identity following major role exits. The generalization also helps us to understand why personal identity problems have become a major concern of people in contemporary society. Identity confusion and fragmentation of self are common sources of malaise in advanced industrial nations. The feeling, voiced by a character in Saroyan's play *The Time of Your Life,* that "there's no foundation all down the line" articulates a pervasive mood shared not only by intellectuals but by all segments of industrial society.

To a significant degree, this lack of a sense of continuity and coherence within ourselves arises from the fragmented character of people's social roles and the ephemeralness of the social networks in which they carry on their lives. We participate in many social relationships and social groups, each with a different set of people who are unknown to one another. In each group, the individual is confronted by different demands and different expectations. Within his family, he is expected to engage in warm and intimate interaction. With neighbors, he is expected to be friendly but not intrusive. With his co-workers, he is both competitive and cooperative, depending on the nature of his work, but is always expected to be outgoing and friendly.   111

More important in our context are the discontinuities over time in people's social networks. The geographical, residential, and social changes that an urban resident experiences make lifetime relationships difficult to sustain. The family and friendships that one had in childhood and youth often disintegrate after members disperse to go to work or to college, to marry, and to establish families elsewhere in the city, the suburbs, or other communities. People acquire new friends in the neighborhoods they settle in, on their jobs, or in other formal organizations. But usually friends in these different situations are not acquainted with one another. Friendships take on the same impermanent, fragmented, and differentiated character as the social roles that people play.

This lack of continuity in the social networks to which people belong from the beginning of adulthood and thereafter makes it more difficult to preserve a sense of inner sameness and continuity, particularly as the person grows older in a rapidly changing world. The younger generation begins to take over the jobs, the positions in organizations, and the houses in neighborhoods formerly occupied by members of one's own generation. Their ideas, their mode of living, their behavior are different and alien; and as people become older, they increasingly feel themselves to be, in Margaret Mead's graphic term, "immigrants in time."

As long as a person is married and continues to perform his customary occupational role, he has a continuity of experience and social response that fortify his identity and reassure him that he is what he thinks he is in spite of the changes continually occurring around him. No wonder modern men and women depend so heavily on their marriages, and place so many diverse demands upon this single relationship. Spouses must be friends and lovers, helpmates, and companions to one another. There is empirical evidence that people who have a social network of friends are less dependent on their spouse for socio-emotional support and companionship than are people who, though they have friends, are not part of a friendship clique.[14]

The roles played by a person in the past, especially by a man, cease to have any social reality unless he belongs to an enduring social network of people who have shared the same past. To have even one stable group in which others share with the older person the knowledge of who and what he was before he grew old acts to preserve sameness of identity.[15]

The size of urban communities, the high degree of residential and intercommunity mobility, and, therefore, the dispersal of old people greatly diminish opportunities to sustain membership in the enduring friendship networks common in traditional societies but rare in modern city life. Take, for example, the following description of the *cuaird* in rural Ireland:

. . . The old men's gathering imparts a deeper reality to what appears to be merely a companionable pastime of the old men. The evening *cuaird* of the old men takes on an institutional flavor. It is a clique, of course, a tightly knit group of males of similar interests and similar status, giving rise to nicknames within itself which . . . express the member's position in the internal arrangement of the group. It has a definite meeting place and meeting time. It excludes those of dissimilar traits; in this instance, the young men. But it is a clique which operates within a traditional setting: "That is the way it has always been and is the way it always will be." [16]   **113**

This description makes one realize that essentially the same kind of social phenomenon existed in countless communities in pre-industrial eras. One can better appreciate why Shakespeare chose to make Lear's "company of knights" the climactic issue in the struggle between the old king and his daughters. For, like the *cuaird* and the friendship clique, that "company" of contemporaries was the last remaining bulwark of his former identity. Within that social network of old friends, Lear continued to *be* the same man that he had been before his retirement from office. Among them he remained *King* Lear, not the "idle old man" that Goneril perceived, nor "my lady's father" that her steward perceived. Lear's struggle with his daughters to retain his companions was a struggle to preserve the continuity of his own identity.

That struggle for the opportunity to sustain an identity, which Erikson defines as ". . . a persistent sameness within oneself and a persistent sharing of some kind of essential character with others," has become a basic existential issue that confronts the individual in old age. To continue "to be," instead of being consigned to the status of a "has-been," is the problem that policy-makers, social scientists, and organized groups of senior citizens have yet to address.

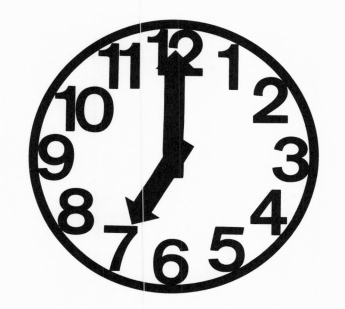

INFLUENCE
OF INTIMATES
ON IDENTITY
CHANGE

An individual's social identity can be thought of as being composed of three distinct elements: his conception of himself, his conception of how others view him, and, finally, the actual conceptions that others have of him. The first two were discussed in the previous chapter. Now we turn to the third aspect of identity—namely, the actual conceptions of older people held by their social intimates—to explore to what extent one's age identity corresponds with the conceptions of significant others.

To study identity changes from the "objective" perspective of others, as distinct from the subjective perspective of the aged, obviously requires not merely a sample of older people but also a sample of their associates. Because of the time and expense involved, such studies are rarely undertaken in survey research. The Kips Bay study of older people is unique in that each respondent, at the time he was interviewed, was asked for the name and address of his closest friend or relative, and these associates of approximately half of the sample (275 individuals) were subsequently interviewed.[1]

Three distinct but related issues based on these joint data will be examined in this chapter. The first is concerned with an older person's social characteristics that lead an intimate to view him as old or middle-aged. It parallels the analysis in the previous chapter of the way in which role exits precipitate changes in the self-image of older people. The second identifies some of the social conditions that pressure an older person to relinquish his middle-aged identity once an intimate comes to view him as old, as against those conditions that enable another old person to sustain a sense of "self-sameness," to borrow Erikson's phrase, and thereby preserve the self-integrity that is so necessary and yet so difficult to sustain in old age. Finally, the chapter distinguishes those conditions that influence the self-attitudes of older people from those attitudes toward social norms that prescribe different types of behaviors for the old and the non-old.

SOCIAL CHARACTERISTICS OF OLDER PEOPLE AND ASSOCIATES' CONCEPTIONS

Respondents in Kips Bay, as in Elmira, were asked, "How do you think of yourself as far as age goes—middle-aged, elderly, old, or what?" Associates were asked the same question about the respondents: "How do you think of (respondent) as far as age goes—do you think of him (her) as middle-aged, elderly, old, or what?" An intimate's conception of an older person varies somewhat with the type of relationship that they have. Thus a person's spouse is somewhat less likely to consider him old (53 percent) than would his children (59 percent) or a friend (63 percent). Although these differences are small and not statistically significant, they suggest that those associates who have known the older person longest are the least inclined to change their conception of him as he ages.

The respondent's actual age plays a more important part in determining whether or not his associates consider him old. But at each age level, people who still perform either of the major institutional roles are less often judged old by their associates than those who no longer do so. Widowed people in their sixties are more often considered old (48 percent) by their associates than the married in the same age group (38 percent), and these differences persist among people over seventy, as Table 12 shows. Their associates' conceptions vary even more with the employment   **117**

TABLE 12
Percentages of Respondents
Considered "Old" by Associates—
by Age and Marital Status

Marital		Age	
Status	Under 70	70 or Over	
Married	38 (69)	74 (35)	
Widowed	48 (52)	81 (59)	
Difference	10	7	

TABLE 13
Percentages of Respondents
Considered "Old" by Associates—
by Age and Employment Status

Employment		Age	
Status	Under 70	70 or Over	
Employed	32 (63)	61 (18)	
Retired	46 (39)	79 (53)	
Difference	14	18	

status of older people (Table 13). Among people in their sixties, only a third of the employed, but close to half of the retired, are considered old by their close associates, and this difference becomes somewhat larger among people over seventy. Retirement not only affects the older person's self-image more than widowhood does (as was shown in the previous chapter), but once he passes seventy it also is more likely than widowhood to affect his close associates' conceptions of him. Indeed, associates' conceptions greatly influence the changes in self-image among retirants.

TABLE 14

Percentages of Respondents
Whose Associates Consider Them "Old"—
by Age and Socio-economic Status

Socio-economic Status	Under 70		Age 70 or Over	
Higher	25	(16)	64	(11)
Middle	41	(87)	71	(45)
Lower	51	(35)	84	(55)

An individual is socially defined as old much earlier in some social classes than in others. In Kips Bay, only 25 percent in the higher class, in contrast to more than half in the lower class, are considered by their significant others to be old while still in their sixties. Although the chances of being considered old by an intimate increase markedly in all classes for those past seventy, the differences between classes still persist in the older group. However, as Table 14 shows, they are somewhat smaller here than in the younger one.[2]

CONDITIONS THAT AFFECT THE INFLUENCE OF ASSOCIATES ON AGE IDENTITY

In general, much agreement is found between the older person's age identity and his closest associate's conception of him. The chances of agreement are nearly twice as great as the chances of disagreement between them (see Table 15). When disagreement does exist, it is frequently because the older person still views himself as middle-aged while his intimate conceives of him as old, and not the reverse—an indication that we are readier to consign others to old age than to place ourselves in that category.

These relationships persist, although in a modified form, even when age is controlled. Thus a person in his sixties considers himself old more often if his associates regard him as old (40 percent) than if the associates consider him middle-aged (24 percent), and the differences are similar (75 percent and 55 percent, respectively) among people over seventy.

TABLE 15

Age Identification of Respondents by Associates' Conception

Self-Identifi-cation	Associates' Conception	
	Middle-Aged	Old
Middle-aged	57	34
Old	26	53
No answer	17	13
	100	100
	(106)	(144)

The conceptions of others with whom the older individual interacts are, as we might expect, important determinants of his own age identity.[3] Although people may be reluctant to relinquish their identification with the middle-aged and to admit that they are old, they also want to avoid their associates' ridicule if they should deny that they are old when their closest intimates disagree. As Leon Festinger, Stanley Schachter, and Kurt Back state, "an opinion or attitude which is not reinforced by others of the same opinion will become unstable generally." [4] This observation also is true for the individual's self-attitudes.

The relationship between self-image and conception of **120**

TABLE 16
Percentages of Persons
Who Define Themselves
as Old—by Employment Status
and Associate's Conception

Associate Sees as	Respondent's Employment Status			
	Employed		Retired	
Old	36	(28)	62	(53)
Middle-aged	24	(37)	32	(28)
Difference	12		30	

significant others is, perhaps, less surprising than the fact that this relationship is not more pronounced than it actually is. Indeed, even the relationship found tends to disappear under certain conditions. Older people who are still employed, for example, do not usually consider themselves old, and their closest intimates' conception exerts relatively little influence on their self-image.[5] Retirants, on the other hand, are influenced a good deal more by a single close associate. They are nearly twice as likely to consider themselves old if the associate does so than if he does not, as Table 16 shows.

A finding in experimental social psychology reported by Festinger and his colleagues helps to explain the greater readiness of retirants to conform to an intimate's conception: ". . . Where there is a high degree of dependence upon physical reality for the subjective validity of one's beliefs or opinions, the dependence upon other people for the confidence one has in these opinions or beliefs is very low . . . where the dependence upon physical reality is low, the dependence on social reality is correspondingly high." [6]   **121**

Although gainful employment does not constitute "physical" reality, it does constitute an objective social reality that validates the belief that a person is not yet old. In this situation, therefore, what his associates think of him makes little difference to an individual's self-image. Losing this objective validation of his claim to middle-aged status —employment—constrains the individual to adjust his self-image to the conception his close associates have of him, since this now becomes the significant social reality that validates his self-image.

There is still another, and perhaps more important, reason why retirants are influenced to a greater extent by the conceptions of a single associate than people who are still employed. Loss of the work role, as we have seen, often disrupts the older individual's social relationships. At the very least, it removes him from people with whom he had associated at work; and the consequences are often far-reaching, since the loss of interpersonal relationships narrows a person's scope of social referents. His social milieu becomes more constricted, and as a result the influence of his closest intimate increases.

How can we confirm this interpretation that retirement, because it not only entails the loss of a significant validation of adult identity but also has isolating effects, increases an older man's vulnerability to the influence of his close associate? This can be tested by ascertaining whether the relationship varies with extent of friendship participation. For if the interpretation is correct, it follows that a close associate's opinion should have less impact on the self-image of those persons who have several friends than on those who have only a few. Table 17 shows that this is the case.

Among people who have few friends, most agree with **122**

TABLE 17

Percentages of Persons
Who Identify Themselves
as Old—by Friendship Participation
and Associate's Conception

Associate Sees as	Friendship Participation of Respondent			
	Low		High	
Old	73	(82)	37	(43)
Middle-aged	29	(48)	35	(40)
Difference	44		2	

their intimate associates about their own age status. Nearly three-quarters of the people who are judged as old by their associates share that view, and 71 percent of those *not* considered old by their associates share that view. But among people who have many friends, virtually no relationship exists between self-appraisal and the conception of their closest associates. Two-thirds of these individuals consider themselves middle-aged, and the opinions of their closest associates seem to have no impact on their age identification.

Not only does the friendship participation of an older person affect his agreement with the opinion of his closest associate, but so does his kinship participation. His associate's conception influences his self-image if he has no regular contact with relatives (40 percent), but this influence is relatively slight if he sees two or more relatives regularly (11 percent).[7] These findings support the conclusion that when an older person has several social referents, his age identity is less influenced by a single significant associate than is that of the individual who is relatively isolated and less likely to have alternative social appraisals of his age status.

A hypothetical example of two older people—one who has only two close associates and another who has six—may help to clarify this conclusion. The problem is to determine to what extent their associates' appraisals influence the self-appraisals of these people. Evidently, if only one associate of each of these individuals is interviewed, we "sample" half of the "influentials" in the first case, but only one-sixth of those in the second one. One associate's opinions represent a larger proportion of all social influences experienced by the individual who has few associates than by the one who has many.[8] My findings, therefore, must not be misread to indicate that sociable people are less subject to social influences than are relatively isolated individuals. Whether this is the case could be determined only on the basis of information from all the associates of aged people. Two implications, however, can be derived from the data presented. First, they challenge the assumption that an adult's closest associate invariably exerts a decisive influence over his thinking and acting. (The decision to interview the closest associate of each respondent was based on this assumption.) The significance of a *number* of social relationships for sustaining a sense of self-sameness apparently outweighs that exerted by a person's most intimate relationship.[9] Second, the data indicate that the impact of a single intimate's opinion on an individual depends on the extent of the latter's social participation. This impact is great after significant role exits, but only if social contacts are limited.

Parallel results have been obtained in sociological studies of other realms of behavior. Seymour Martin Lipset, Martin Trow, and James S. Coleman, for example, report **124** that in small printing shops the union shop chairman's level of activity is related to the political participation of union members. The authors note that "no such relationship would be expected, nor is it found, in the *large* shops, where the level of activity of the chairman is no indicator of the political environment to which the large shop men are exposed." [10] Similarly, in a study of voting behavior, Bernard Berelson, Paul F. Lazarsfeld, and William McPhee found that people who talk politics most often are least likely to find themselves in agreement with their closest friends in political discussions. The authors observe that "the political complexion of friends does not affect everyone equally. Strangely enough, the friendship pattern is more influential in the case of those voters who talk politics less." [11] One would imagine that people with diverse social roles and extensive social relations have more opportunity to engage in political discussions, and there is consequently a greater likelihood that their political opinions are influenced not only by their three closest friends but by other associates with alternative points of view as well.

COMPARISON OF ASSOCIATE'S INFLUENCE ON NORMATIVE ORIENTATION AND AGE IDENTIFICATION

The likelihood that an older person will share his closest associate's conception of what constitutes proper conduct in old age depends also, but to a lesser degree, on the extent of his social participation.

A series of statements of a normative character was submitted both to respondents in Kips Bay and to their associates to determine how each would define the role of an old person. By comparing their answers, it is possible to as-

certain the degree of correspondence between the older individual's normative orientation and his associate's
expectations. A score based on a scale of four of these items
distinguishes those older people who accept differential rules
of conduct for old age (indicated by a score of three or
more) from those who reject them (indicated by a score of
two or less). The same scale, based on the responses of associates, serves as an indicator of their role expectations—
that is, whether or not they expect older people to conduct
themselves in a different manner from younger people. The
four items on which these scales are based are these:

	Respondents *	Associates
"It's undignified for older people to be interested in the opposite sex."		
Agree	27%	31%
"You can't expect older people to accept new ways of doing things."		
Agree	42%	54%
"Older people ought to go around with people of their own age rather than with younger people."		
Agree	55%	56%
"Older people should dress more conservatively than younger people."		
Agree	73%	69%
Number of cases	500	257

* Coefficient of reproducibility 0.91.

The closest intimate's influence on the normative   **126**

TABLE 18

Percentages of Persons
Who Accept Differential Norms—
by Friendship Participation
and Associate's Expectations

Associate Expects Differential Behavior	Friendship Participation			
	Low		High	
Yes	43	(77)	33	(30)
No	27	(82)	28	(68)
Difference	16		5	

orientation of an older person, as on his age identity, depends on the extent of the latter's friendship ties. Whether the elderly individual who has several friends believes that older people ought to conform to different rules of conduct from those governing the behavior of younger adults bears little relation to the role expectations of his closest associate (see Table 18). In contrast, the acceptance of such differential norms by relatively isolated individuals is more often affected by the role expectations of one intimate companion. In 43 percent of the cases in which the latter expects differential behavior, but only in 27 percent of those in which he does not, isolated old people accept differential behavioral norms. This suggests that the individual who has several friends, and who therefore can obtain social support for his beliefs from other quarters, feels less constrained to conform to his closest associate's expectations than does the person with limited social contacts, who is not as likely to be exposed to alternative points of view and therefore must accept his intimate's viewpoint.

Although a single associate's impact on normative orientation, as well as that on self-appraisal, varies with the extent of the older person's participation, his normative orientation is less affected by his close associate than is self-appraisal. Thus 57 percent of the respondents whose closest associate considers them old, and only 34 percent of those whose closest associate does not consider them old, define themselves as old, a difference of 27 percent, as Table 15 shows. This difference rises to 44 percent among relatively isolated respondents (Table 17). In contrast, 40 percent of the respondents whose closest associate expects older people to behave differently from others and 27 percent of those whose closest associate does not hold this expectation accept distinct behavioral norms for older people. This difference of only 13 percent rises to merely 16 percent among the relatively isolated respondents (Table 18).[12] Using percentage difference again as a rough measure of an associate's influence, it can be seen that influence is considerably greater on self-attitudes, such as age identification, than on more general normative issues, such as the rules of conduct appropriate in old age.

To sum up: the age identity of older people and their acceptance of different norms of conduct in old age are influenced by their intimate's views. But the *extent* of the intimate's influence is far more pronounced among relatively older people who have few friends than among those who have more plentiful social resources. The latter person's self-image is virtually unaffected by a single associate's conception, even when the two have very close ties of friendship or kinship. Similarly, whether or not an elderly individual believes that different conduct norms should apply to the old bears little relationship to his closest associate's opinions. In short, as people grow older, their self-judgments and their more general opinions and beliefs have greater autonomy if they can resist the isolating effects of role exit and can conserve old social resources or find new ones. Extensive social ties enhance an individual's personal freedom, while a lack of them binds him and makes him more dependent on the meager resources available to him. A person having no other role relationships becomes less involved in a network of social obligations and thus loses alternative resources of social response and support.

But close associates do not equally influence all beliefs of the individual. While intimates exert much influence over the older person's self-attitude, the former appear to have relatively little impact on older people's normative orientations, even among the relatively isolated.

George Herbert Mead's analysis of the self might clarify these findings:

> If the . . . individual is to develop a self in the fullest sense, it is not sufficient for him merely to take the attitude of . . . other individuals toward himself . . . ; he must also, in the same way that he takes the attitudes of other(s) . . . toward himself and toward one another, take their attitudes toward the various phases or aspects of the common social activity, or set of social undertakings in which, as members of an organized society or social group, they are all engaged; and he must then, by generalizing these individual attitudes of . . . society or social group . . . act toward different social projects. . . . It is in the form of the generalized other that the social process influences the behavior of individuals involved in it and . . . that the community exercises control over the conduct of its

129

individual members. . . . In abstract thought the individual takes the attitude of the generalized other toward himself, without reference to its expression in any particular other individuals; and in concrete thought he takes that attitude in so far as it is expressed in the attitudes toward his behavior of those other(s) with whom he is involved in the given social situation. . . .[13]

The foundations of the self-attitudinal structure are formed in childhood through interaction with the first significant persons in the child's world. But some aspects of the structure are continuously being modified through interaction with others who become significant to people as they mature and enlarge their social roles; this is, of course, especially true for age identity. Significant persons, besides strongly influencing the individual in concrete situations, as Mead points out, also influence those self-conceptions that are culturally expected to change at an unspecified time, such as age identity. In the absence of any clear-cut cultural definition of when one ceases to be middle-aged, it is the concrete social reality—the conceptions of significant others —that signals the specific time when the change in age identification from middle-aged to old occurs. Just as parents play a crucial role in forming a child's self-conceptions because the child is relatively isolated from other social influences, so the older person's self-image becomes more vulnerable to his closest associate's influence, as he is isolated following role exit.

Although close associates do not much influence isolated people in their normative orientations, this does not mean that such beliefs are not socially structured. It may well be that normative beliefs are more stable than self-attitudes because they are "anchored" in social groups. In

TABLE 19

Percentages of Persons
Who Accept Norms for the Old—
by Class Position and Associate's Expectations

Associate Expects Differential Behavior	Higher		Lower		**Class Position** Difference
Yes	21	(19)	43	(86)	22
No	18	(57)	33	(93)	15
Difference	3		10		
Percentage who Accept norms	18	(76)	38	(179)	

other words, generalized beliefs about what constitutes appropriate age-role or sex-role behavior usually refer to and reflect the prevailing attitudes of larger collectivities, such as one's social stratum. Once such beliefs become internalized, they are not readily modified by a single associate, even one with whom the individual shares the closest ties of friendship or kinship.

The dependence of distinct norms of conduct on a person's class position confirms the group character of normative orientations, as Table 19 shows. Members of the higher classes are unlikely to accept different norms, whether their closest associate accepts them (21 percent) or not (18 percent); members of the lower classes are more inclined to accept them even if their associate does not share them (33 percent). Furthermore, in the highest classes, in which opinion is heavily *against* acceptance of differential behavioral norms for older people (82 percent), their inti-

TABLE 20

Percentages of Persons Who Define
Themselves as "Old"—by Class
Position and Associate's Conception

Associate's Conception	Higher		Lower		**Class Position** Difference
Old	54	(35)	63	(89)	9
Middle-aged	25	(28)	36	(59)	11
Difference	29		27		

mate's opinions exert virtually no effect (3 percent). In the lower classes, however, in which there is less agreement on these norms (38 percent accept them, and 62 percent reject them), their closest associate's expectations make somewhat more difference (10 percent) for the normative orientation of respondents.

In contrast, the age identity of older people varies far more with the appraisal of their intimates than with their class membership, as Table 20 shows. Although lower-class individuals past sixty are more inclined to consider themselves old than those in the higher class, class membership is much less significant a determinant of age identity than the specific conception of their close social intimates. Thus, even though in general people in higher social classes maintain their middle-aged identity longer than working-class people, if their closest associates view them as old, the chances that they themselves will share that view are more than doubled. Similarly, even though in the working class a person of sixty or beyond is likely to be considered old, if his closest intimate perceives him as middle-aged, the chances that he will agree are considerably enhanced.

ILLness
and
WORK
aLienation
in OLD aGe

When social scientists study the same problem, they often report contradictory results. But the findings on retirement in America have been generally consistent. Most studies report that by far the greatest number of older people retire voluntarily or for health reasons. I suggest, however, that these findings are not very reliable, because the term "voluntary" is ambiguous. Upon closer examination, it becomes evident that the reasons given for "voluntary" retirement are not consistent with other evidence concerning the needs and abilities of older people.

Most studies, for example, accept older men's claims that they *chose* to retire. Yet figures purporting to show an increase in voluntary retirants fail to take into account that compulsory retirement has increased throughout the economy and that fewer workers today are free to decide when to retire. (More and more of the traditionally self-employed are becoming employees—witness the trend toward larger law firms, group medical practice, and accounting firms.)

Moreover, even though it can be said that compulsory retirement is an impersonal, bureaucratic decision based on old age alone and not on ability or fitness for work, it nevertheless threatens the older person's ego. Old people—like blacks, Jews, women, and other minority groups who are victims of exclusionary policies—recognize that these discriminatory policies are impersonal, yet they *experience* them as personal rejections that undermine their self-esteem.

People will try hard, as Freud demonstrated, to protect themselves from the pain and threat of social rejection. These ego threats mobilize the individual's defense mechanisms, such as denial and rationalization. These defenses provide the individual with a socially acceptable reason for his behavior. I submit that many "voluntary" retirements actually represent the older person's denial or rejection.[1]

Furthermore, there is evidence that, as compulsory retirement spreads, older workers are increasingly pressured by younger co-workers and by higher-ups. Instead of arbitrary dismissal, various subtle techniques are used to alienate the individual until his dissatisfaction with his social relations on the job overwhelm whatever previous gratifications he gained from his work.

The strategies employed to gain "voluntary" resignation will, of course, vary according to the group's composition. Working-class males and younger people generally use more explicit pressure to hasten a group member's exit. Typical techniques may include overt mockery, joking at his expense, or excluding him from group rituals. Samuel Lubell strikingly describes the informal exclusionary tactics used by younger factory workers to oust older employees:

> From comments voiced by other workers it is evident that in many plants a form of systematic hazing has taken hold, with younger workers jeering at the older ones, "How old are you today, Grandpa?" Or, "Old man, when are you going to quit?"
>
> In Canton, a 40-year-old mill hand boasted, "We had to razz one man a full year before he quit. We kept calling him henpecked."
>
> And in South Chicago, a young mill hand described a birthday party that had been given one 67-year-old worker. "We painted up a big sign with 'Happy Birthday' on it . . . then on the other side we drew one of those old tire company ads showing a youngster holding a candle and saying 'time to re-tire.' We all thought it was funny. But the old man didn't see the joke."[2]

Lewis Carliner [3] has provided evidence that these forms of pressure are increasing, not only on men in their sixties but also on those in their late forties and fifties.

White-collar workers resort to more subtle tactics; these include the withholding of status or monetary compensation, delegation of relatively menial jobs "below the dignity" of the older employee who is called upon to perform them, a cool demeanor, or lack of response to friendly overtures, as exemplified by the phrase, "Don't call me, I'll call you." All these tactics attempt to undermine a person's motivation to maintain membership in the work group, and thereby force his resignation where employees have no power of expulsion or dismissal or are reluctant to exercise it. Yet it seems that even under these degrading pressures some men approaching retirement age admit to a fear of retirement.

Few men past fifty-five say that they are *not* going to retire,[4] which is hardly surprising in view of the widespread increase in compulsory retirement. Most men expect to retire at sixty-five or earlier, and by that age nearly three-quarters of them *are* retired.[5] It is clear, in short, that, except for the self-employed, older people can rarely choose their own time of retirement, and that most of them claim to favor the present system. Curiously, when men sixty-five and older are asked why they retired, nearly two-thirds claim it was their own decision, only slightly over a third admitting that it was their employers' decision. Health is the reason most frequently mentioned by "voluntary" retirants for deciding to stop working. After retirement, they have little desire to return to the labor market, most men (69 percent) again giving poor health as the main deterrent to post-retirement employment.[6]

136

On the face of it, such reports suggest that an inevitable process of physiological deterioration takes place as people age, making a productive role impossible for the elderly in our society. Yet reports on older people's *health* show a very low incidence of acute or disabling illness. No more than 8 percent of the elderly are confined to their homes.[7] Of the 4 percent who are in hospitals or nursing homes, it has been estimated that over half could be rehabilitated if there were non-institutional settings where they could live and receive the services they need.[8]

Against this low incidence of acute illness stands a high rate of chronic illness among people sixty-five and older: 81 percent suffer from one or more chronic conditions. But generally overlooked is the important fact that about two-thirds of the American population report at least one chronic illness while still in middle age. Although the incidence of chronic illness rises among older people,[9] only 15 percent are unable, according to their own reports, to carry on a major activity such as work, keeping house, or attending school.[10] In short, there is a discrepancy between the proportion of people who give health as their reason for retirement and the proportion of people who, according to health statistics, are, despite their chronic ailments, capable of continuing to work.

Other evidence also suggests that the poor health given as the reason for retirement in many cases is more spurious than real, and that accepting such a claim at face value leads one to overlook its psychological meaning.

James S. Tynhurst, Lee Salk, and Miriam Kennedy, in a study of 250 males who retired at various periods and ages, report no differences in death rates; retirants tended to fulfill the life expectancy of the same age group in the general population. Moreover, a comparison of their health ratings before and after retirement revealed either no change or an improvement in health.[11] Similarly, Wayne E. Thomson and Gordon F. Streib, who studied a panel of workers before retirement, found that the shifts in health among retirants, based on physicians' evaluations as well as on self-evaluations of health status, closely paralleled those of their still-employed age peers. Indeed, among retirants rated as "fair" or "poor" in health before retirement, there was a tendency toward better health in retirement. These findings, at the very least, suggest that retirants are not actually in poorer health than older people who continue to work.[12]

It is possible that many of the elderly claiming poor health as their reason for retirement have had chronic illnesses which were not incapacitating during their middle years but have become aggravated with the approach of retirement. Often this type of illness may unexpectedly show a strong reversal once the person stops working, because he is no longer disturbed by the pressure to retire and by conflicts over retirement.

Serious consideration should be given, therefore, to the proposition that "illness" has a psychological function for older people in modern societies. When older people enter the only stage of life for which our society provides no clearly defined institutional roles, sickness serves as a socially acceptable way of legitimizing that rolelessness. As Talcott Parsons astutely observes, sickness constitutes a safety valve—offsetting the ego threat that rolelessness represents for the old.

The enormous American effort to improve health is legitimized above all in terms of our achievement values and of the equaliz- **138** ing of opportunity for achievement. At the same time, however, since it is conditionally legitimized, sickness provides for the individual, perhaps, the most important single escape hatch from the pressure of obligations to achieve; pressures which, because of the upgrading process which has been stressed here, are becoming, for the average individual, more rather than less intense. Seen in this light, illness is far from being an exclusive and unmitigated evil; it is also an important "safety valve" for the society. . . . It seems almost obvious that illness is a *particularly* important form of deviant behavior for [the aged]. . . .

If it is the broad societal verdict upon older people that they are "useless," then the obvious way to legitimize their status is to *be* useless through the incapacitation of illness.[13]

Viewed as a social role, sickness provides the old-person-as-patient with special rights and privileges that the old person who is well does not have and cannot invoke. It is a *social* mechanism for commanding attention and sympathy from friends and relatives, particularly from children who will visit and phone a parent when he is sick more often than when he is in good health. Irving Rosow reports that during an illness older people receive more attention and more care from children and other kin.[14]

Voluntary retirement for health reasons, in short, is often a face-saving social fiction practiced by the old, but one in which the rest of society is glad to share, for then retirement can be justified on physical or altruistic grounds rather than on bureaucratic, non-humanitarian ones. Indeed, "resignation for reasons of health" is a bureaucratic euphemism widely employed to mask arbitrary dismissal of any employee, old or young.[15]

Psychologically, illness is a narcissistic response to social deprivation. Gregory Rochlin has described the process **139** of "turning inward," the heightened self-concern so often characteristic of persons in their later years:

> Narcissism is expressed in taking the self as an object in which to invest one's libido, as others were taken in earlier phases. Freud's essay "On Narcissism" illustrates the point being made here: "Libido and ego-interest share the same fate and have once more become indistinguishable from each other. The familiar egoism of the sick person covers them both. We find it so natural because we are certain that in the same situation we should behave in the same way." A parallel process takes place in aging. . . . We have observed that the aging man gives up his previous critical judgment of himself and overestimates his value, just as he avoids anything that would diminish the importance of his ego. . . . In old age, narcissism and aging are indispensable. He no longer projects forward, as his ideal, that which represented or substituted for the given-up narcissism of childhood. An unremitting need results therefore to press for satisfaction perpetually, by countervailing what may be valued and lost, by taking as the substitute himself, faute de mieux.[16]

The correlation often found between low subjective health ratings and low morale has generally been interpreted to mean that poor health undermines morale. But if we recognize the narcissistic elements of poor health and its functional value as a substitute for role relationships and activities that had previously sustained the individual's sense of ego integrity, it becomes clear that the relationship between health and morale is a reversible one: role exit, loneliness, and inactivity can and frequently do engender physical malaise.

Just as older people's marginal status in contemporary society may promote more ill health among them than it would if they had meaningful social roles,[17] so it may also foster deterioration of mental abilities when the social environment does not provide opportunities for their exercise.[18] There is empirical evidence that mental deterioration is not characteristic of all older people, but occurs primarily among low-skilled, less-educated people whose work does not require the exercise of higher mental faculties or the acquisition of new knowledge. A recent study of retirants of better-than-average education found an overall excellence of health and mental ability, with only minor differences in either respect, between that group and a group of men in their early twenties. In fact, the retirants, on the average, had higher intelligence ratings than the young men in the comparison group.[19] Other studies, as well, indicate that those who suffer a decline in mental ability as they grow old tend to be of low socio-economic and educational status, and it is also in this group that chronic health problems leading to disability are most prevalent. The fact that the health and educational attainment of each successive generation is superior to that of previous generations in American society must also be taken into account in intergenerational comparisons of intellectual ability. In recent years, several investigators have been skeptical about the findings of older cross-sectional studies that regularly reported decrements in intellectual ability with age. They argue that such findings may be spurious because younger generations start out at a higher level of ability and have a higher educational attainment than do older generations. Longitudinal studies based on the *same* generation yield different results.[20]

In short, illness and decline in old age—to some degree, although, of course, not altogether—have social roots; **141** and some of their manifestations are not at all natural or inevitable. That is not to deny the importance of programs like Medicare, which are aimed at providing health services to older people. Such programs are necessary and valuable. But they do not come to grips with the *social causes* of illness in old age. Until new, socially meaningful roles for older people are institutionalized, it can be anticipated that more, rather than fewer, people will find the sick role a preferable alternative to being altogether roleless as they grow older. Otherwise the costs to society in terms of time and money spent to meet these needs will surely increase.

But aside from its social implications, sickness is a "maladaptive adaptation" for the individual. Although health complaints at first evoke sympathy and social response, eventually they demoralize the older person and alienate the people close to him who are burdened with his demands.

Work alienation, like illness, has a positive function for an old person who must relinquish his job. Alienation from routine, repetitive, highly mechanized, fragmented work continues to be a pervasive and persistent problem in contemporary industrial societies. The significant improvements in wages and working conditions following unionization of blue-collar workers have not dissipated the employees' discontent with the boredom and the powerlessness of industrial work. Indeed, there is some recent evidence that the discontent of younger workers today is primarily due to the routinization of the work and their powerlessness in the industrial plant—and not so much to unsatisfactory wages and security, the principal issues around which workers organized in the 1930's and 1940's.[21]

142

Marx said that alienation from work heightens proletarian class-consciousness in the revolutionary struggle. Three factors in American society help to explain why work alienation has not produced a revolutionary proletariat. First, the "Protestant ethic" persists in secular form to give meaning to work; second, the social ties formed at work are important alternative sources of gratification that offset work alienation; and third, the institutionalization of retirement, coupled with social security and work pensions, represents an "escape hatch" to the discontented worker who can look forward to release from tedious work.

People's attitudes toward their jobs of course influence their attitudes toward retirement.[22] Studies have shown that work satisfaction increases with occupational status. Professionals, businessmen, and the self-employed, whose jobs entail responsibility and self-direction, have the greatest attachment to their work and the greatest reluctance to retire.[23] Work alienation is more widespread, as Marx predicted, among lower-skilled workers, particularly those in highly mechanized industries such as automobiles and steel.[24] At these occupational levels the prospect of retirement is often welcomed, as this remark shows: "God bless the day I can leave. . . . I sure do want to retire." But a significant proportion of blue-collar workers enjoy their work and dread retirement, as revealed in this comment: "I'd be miserable if I couldn't work." [25]

In the Kips Bay study, still-employed respondents were asked about their attitudes toward their jobs, and retirants were asked what their attitude toward their jobs had been while they were still employed. A curious difference was observed. The attitudes of middle-class retirants toward   **143** their work closely matched those of the employed. But in the working class, a significantly higher proportion of retirants (61 percent) than of the still employed (47 percent) reported high work satisfaction. Although blue-collar workers as a rule exhibit more work alienation than those in white-collar jobs, *in retirement* their less favorable economic and social situation leads them, in retrospect, to think more favorably of their jobs than they did when they were employed.

But how does work alienation affect the morale of employed older people? It might be expected that a job protects the morale of the old person who enjoys his work. Conversely, it might be thought that morale improves in old age for the retirant who had obtained little satisfaction from his work. But this is not so. Instead, in the Kips Bay sample, low morale was considerably more frequent among retirants who had been alienated from their work (62 percent) than among the alienated employed (44 percent).

Even when an older person dislikes his *work,* the *job* supports his morale because social relations on the job mitigate the strains of alienation. Indeed, older employees who dislike their work tend to place greater emphasis on their work relationships than do other employees. Half of the dissatisfied employees in the Kips Bay study mentioned "mixing with people" as an important aspect of their job, as compared with only 37 per cent of those who enjoyed their work.[26]

The social participation of less-satisfied older employees is also more extensive, 42 percent, as opposed to 27 percent for those who like their work. This is true for both blue-collar and white-collar workers. Social participation thus serves as an adaptive mechanism in old age not only for retired people but also for those employees who are alienated from their work.[27] This does not mean that people who like their work and do it well are necessarily social isolates. Indeed, studies have shown that such employees are often highly esteemed by their co-workers.[28] But their need to socialize is not as great as it is for those whose indifference toward their work compels them to find other sources of gratification.

As long as men who enjoy their work remain in the occupational structure, they are able to sustain high morale. But retirement deprives such older people more than those who were alienated from their work.

I do not mean to imply that retirement deprives *only* those who enjoy their work. On the contrary; since the alienated worker establishes more social relations on the job than do others, his retirement, by depriving him of opportunities for sustaining these friendships, isolates him. Therefore, low morale among the work alienated is more frequent (68 percent) after retirement. But low morale is least frequent among such people if they are able to sustain or develop an active social life after retirement (34 percent). In short, the lack of friendship opportunities following retirement constitutes the principal deprivation for the alienated worker. If, however, he can remain socially active, his morale is as high in retirement as when he was working.

But the retirant who enjoyed working faces other problems. Although retirement affects his social life less than it does the alienated worker's, because he did less socializing on the job,[29] the loss of the work role affects his morale far more.[30] Among retirants with extensive social relations, low morale was more frequent for those who had enjoyed their work than for those who had not.[31] In short, extensive social relations are not as effective an alternative for the job among retirants who had been dedicated to their work as among those who had been alienated from their work.

There is a pronounced cultural discontinuity in a society that, on the one hand, seeks to instill the Protestant ethic toward work and, on the other, institutionalizes compulsory retirement at an arbitrarily fixed age. This bureaucratization of exit from the occupational structure most heavily penalizes those who strongly internalize culturally prescribed attitudes toward work.[32]

While dedication to work contributes to the efficient performance of duties and to the individual's sense of well-being as long as he is allowed to work, such an orientation harms him in retirement.

These findings have some implications for social policy. Measures designed to extend the social opportunities of older people may very well meet the retirement needs of alienated workers, but will be less effective for older people with an attachment to their work. For them the loss of meaningful work constitutes a relatively greater deprivation than for other elderly people. And it is in this subgroup that the need for post-retirement roles of a useful and challenging nature is most pressing. The forms these roles could take will be discussed in chapter 10.

PATTERNS
OF RESPONSE
TO AGING

Do not go gentle into that good night,
Old age should burn and rave at close of day;
Rage, rage against the dying of the light.
—**DYLAN THOMAS**

The study of adjustment and morale in old age, a heavily researched area in the empirical literature, examines two main issues: the definition of adjustment and morale, and the attitudes of those with high and low morale.

Expressions of satisfaction with life are most commonly taken as evidence of adjustment. This is, to be sure, one criterion for judging adaptation in any context, including that of old age. But subjective reports of satisfaction or contentment are not a sufficient criterion of what constitutes an effective mode of response in old age, or, for that matter, in any other stage of life.

A better criterion than mere contentment is whether a certain pattern of behavior allows the individual possibilities for growth, for realizing his needs, and for utilizing his capabilities as fully as possible. The old person who struggles against the pressures to withdraw to the sidelines risks disappointments and frustrations that the person who retreats to the rocking chair avoids. But the person who struggles also enhances his chances of discovering new interests and new friends—in short, of growing and extending his being, and of living out his remaining years with zest instead of passively accepting his fate. To retreat from seeking new opportunities and new challenges in old age is a defensive strategy that does permit the individual to achieve tranquility, but the price he must pay for peace is stagnation and decline. For if our powers of intellect and of feeling are not exercised, they become weakened, just as our bodies become debilitated from lack of exercise. That is not to deny that "slowing down" accompanies the aging process, nor that certain adjustments have to be made to slowing down and to illness. Growing old has disadvantages for an individual to varying degrees in various activities. For example, E. B. White, cited earlier, continues to write even though writing is more difficult and more enervating at seventy than it was in his earlier years. Things *have* changed, and he says, "My deadline now is death." [1] But he expresses a sense of urgency and a continuing attachment to his craft that overcome the pain and frustration of the creative process. Indeed, this engagement with a valued activity and the determination to carry on despite the obstacles imposed by an aging organism typifies such self-actualizing aged persons as White, Igor Stravinsky, and Bertrand Russell.

At every stage in life, an individual requires confirmation of his worth. This confirmation can be obtained through what he does—his activities that have value—and through what he is—his personal qualities that command affection or respect from others. Indeed, there is an interplay between activities and social relationships. Satisfying activities, whether a vocation or an avocation, enable a person to sustain respect for himself and to command respect from others. Similarly, satisfaction in interaction with others encourages him to share their activities and thus maintain a sense of efficacy and purpose. In short, the ability to love and the ability to work, which Freud considered the two basic criteria of a healthy personality, continue to be as important in old age as in earlier stages of life.

Erikson's delineation of man's principal developmental tasks is an important theoretical contribution to an understanding of the identity problems facing contemporary man. While the foundations of an integrated personality are laid   **149** down in childhood, the struggle to achieve and sustain ego integrity extends over a person's entire lifetime.

> The lack or loss of the accrued ego integration is signified by despair and an often unconscious fear of death: the one and only life cycle is not accepted as the ultimate of life. Despair expresses the feeling that the time is short, too short, for the attempt to start another life and to try out an alternate road to integrity. Such a despair is often hidden behind a show of disgust, a misanthropy, or a chronic contemptuous displeasure with particular institutions and particular people—a disgust and a displeasure which (when allied with constructive ideas and a life of cooperation) only signify the individual's contempt of himself.[2]

Erikson sees identity diffusion as the opposite of ego integrity. David Riesman has further elaborated the types of resolution of the identity struggle in old age:

> If we observe the aging of individuals, in the period after middle life, it seems to me that we can distinguish *three ideal-typical outcomes*. Some individuals bear within themselves some psychological sources of self renewal; aging brings for them accretions of wisdom, with no loss of spontaneity and ability to enjoy life, and they are relatively independent of the culture's strictures and penalties imposed on the aged. Other individuals, possibly the majority, bear within them no such resources but are the beneficiaries of a cultural preservative (derived from work, power, position, etc.) which sustains them although only so long as the cultural conditions remain stable and protective. A third group, protected neither from within nor from without, simply decay. In terms more fully delineated elsewhere, we may have autonomous, adjusted, and anomic reactions to aging.[3]

The three "ideal-typical" outcomes that Riesman de- **150** lineates correspond closely to empirically derived patterns of response that I will discuss presently. A fourth type of response that he does not mention, but that can also be found in old age—a pattern that I call *retreatism*—is analogous to what Elaine Cumming and William D. Henry describe as "disengagement." [4] According to them, disengagement is "normal" during the aging process, preparing the individual to face the inevitability of death.

I do not know what Cumming and Henry mean by "normal." If they mean that disengagement is the typical response to aging, they are wrong. While it is found among some older people, it is the exception rather than the rule. If they mean that disengagement is inevitable, they are again wrong, since it is not the sole or even the characteristic response that has been observed in older people. And, finally, I must disagree if by "normal" they mean that disengagement is a healthy or desirable response to aging. For empirical evidence shows that *as a rule* just exactly the opposite is the case. Numerous studies [5] in a variety of communities and in institutions for old people report that activity, whether in the form of work or an avocation, and sociability, whether in the form of a single intimate relationship or more extensive social relationships of a less intimate character, are the most stable and consistent correlates of high morale in old age.[6]

The facts are—as I have repeatedly said—that old age in contemporary society signifies the loss of the two principal social roles that define adult identity, and that social roles that might serve as compensation for these major losses have not yet been institutionalized. Because these role exits take older people out of the mainstream of social life, old age constitutes a stigma; and like any other stigma, it is feared and dreaded. Many people, to be sure, "gracefully" accept being "farmed out to pasture" for the remaining fifteen or twenty years of their "one and only life cycle." They "accept" their fate in the existing social order. When asked, they purport to be "satisfied" with life. To take such reports at face value, however, is to ignore contrary evidence of widespread complaints of loneliness; the disproportionate and rising number of suicides among older men; and the disproportionate number of older people relegated to nursing homes, hospitals, and mental institutions. But, as a rule, older people rarely join together to protest the ignominy of their position. Should they feel resentment, outrage, or despair (as they surely must), they hide these feelings from others and often even from themselves, because their discontents might be construed as evidence of personal maladjustment. They are told, after all, that "disengagement" is normal and inevitable with aging. And how many people have the temerity or the autonomy to separate fact from "scientific" fiction?

The disengagement theory, as originally formulated by Cumming and Henry, has little, if any, scientific value. Indeed, the modifications and qualifications that they have since made in their theory indicate that they, too, have come to see its shortcomings. Unfortunately, when theories, even discredited ones, once enter the public domain they often have unintended but nevertheless harmful effects on human behavior and social policy. The disengagement theory deserves to be publicly attacked, because it can so easily be used as a rationale by the non-old, who constitute the "normals" in society, to avoid confronting and dealing with the issue of old people's marginality and rolelessness in American society. In this sense it bears a close kinship to the fiction, widely current in American society before the sixties, that blacks were happy people, so inherently different from white people that they enjoyed their subordinate position. It turned out, as we all now know, to have been a dangerous fiction, because it served to insulate whites from the deep-seated resentment and despair beneath the bland, public masks the blacks displayed to the white majority.[7]

Erving Goffman accurately describes the two-faced game that goes on between stigmatized minorities and normals:

> . . . The stigmatized person [is required] cheerfully and un-selfconsciously [to] accept himself as the same as normals, while at the same time he voluntarily withholds himself from those situations in which normals would find it difficult to give lip service to their similar acceptance of him . . . it means that the normals will not have to admit to themselves how limited their tactfulness and tolerance is; and it means that normals can remain relatively uncontaminated by intimate contact with the stigmatized, relatively unthreatened in their identity beliefs.
> It is just from these meanings, in fact, that the specifications of a good adjustment derive.[8]

From the standpoint of the non-old, good adjustment in old age is all too often equated with silent, acquiescent conformity, as a reader's query in the *Chicago Daily News* shows:

> Why doesn't Englishman Bertrand Russell settle down to the gentle life of an elder statesman instead of meddling in everyone's business?—A. R.   **153**

In response, the newspaper quoted Bertrand Russell:

> Time, they say, makes a man mellow. I do not believe it. Time makes a man afraid and fear makes him conciliatory, and being conciliatory he endeavors to appear to others what they will think mellow. And with fear comes the need of affection, of some warmth to keep away the chill of the cold universe. When I speak of fear . . . I am thinking of the fear that enters the soul through the experience of the major evils to which life is subject; the treachery of friends, the death of those whom we love, the discovery of the cruelty that lurks in average human nature.[9]

The appearance of "mellowness" in many older people is a tactic to win acceptance and support. To protest their marginality would only alienate others, and this the person without any socially useful role cannot do because he lacks the opportunities for finding alternative social resources to replace his remaining social ties.

Just as the young child will express hostility toward parents because he is dependent upon them and fears abandonment, so the old person will pretend obliviousness to younger people's indifference and neglect in order not to jeopardize his relations with them, for he understands that in the present scheme of things he needs them more than they need him.[10]

The comments below illustrate two patterns of response in old age each of which, in its own way, leads not to growth but to decay.

> I've rather got used to being alone. I live in the past, I guess. I have lots of memories of good times, and when I get to feeling lonesome I just try to remember those. . . . **154**

I have no family . . . I have no money, and all my close friends are dead. No one cares what happens to me. My fling is over, and I would just as soon die as not. My life is perfectly meaningless—I can expect nothing of it except more of the same and the prospect doesn't please me. There's nothing in this kind of life that is worthwhile.[11]

Both of these older people have lost a major role—the first is a widow and the second is a retirant; yet it is evident that their patterns of response differ considerably, not only in degree but also in kind. The first statement illustrates *retreatism,* and the second, *alienation.*

A retreatist frequently "daydreams of the past," enjoys "just sitting and thinking about things," and is "absent-minded.[12] He is the escapist par excellence. Absent-mindedness can be considered a diffuse form of forgetfulness. Freud described the psychological function of forgetfulness in this way: "In this tendency towards avoidance of pain from recollection or other mental processes, this flight of the mind from that which is unpleasant, we may perceive the ultimate purpose behind not merely the forgetting of names, but also many other errors, omissions and mistakes." [13] When most aspects of daily reality are unpleasant, as in the case of the isolated person, this psychological mechanism becomes more diffuse, and the forgetting of specific events turns into general absent-mindedness.

Just as absent-mindedness can be considered a mechanism to avoid whatever evokes unpleasant associations, so daydreaming, the other characteristic element of retreatism, evokes pleasurable experiences from the past when these are not forthcoming in the present. Freud made the well-   **155**

TABLE 21
Percentages of Persons Who Manifest
Alienation and Retreatism—
by Socio-economic Status

Response	Socio-economic Status		
	Higher	Middle	Low
Alienation	13 *	23 †	40
Retreatism	8	11	14
Total maladapted	21	34	54
Number of cases	90	237	105

* Significant at the 0.05 level.
† Significant at the 0.01 level.

known observation that the daydream is " a response to an
unsatisfied longing. . . . [The person] turns away from
reality and transfers all his interest . . . into the creation
of his wishes in the life of phantasy." [14]

Alienation is an extreme form of maladaptation, characterized by the feeling that "there is just no point in living,"
by feelings of regret over the past, by the idea that "things
just keep getting worse and worse," and by abandonment
of all future plans.[15]

People with this response do not just voice extreme
dissatisfaction with their present situation: even the past is
a cause for regret rather than a source of comfort. Moreover, their attitude toward the future belies the aphorism
that "where there is life, there is hope." For these people are
filled with hopelessness and despair to the point where life
itself no longer appears worth living. Such people repeatedly
express feelings of rejection by others: ". . . When you get
to be my age, you might as well be dead—nobody wants you **156**

around any more." Self-deprecation is also common: "You know what they ought to do with old men like me? Take us out and shoot us. We're no good for anything. What the hell am I alive for? I'm no good to myself, no good to anybody else." [16]

Low morale, as seen in chapter 2, is most frequent among relatively isolated people who have lost a major role. But responses to retirement and widowhood differ. Isolated retirants are more likely to be alienated (49 percent) than the isolated widowed (35 percent), whereas the latter are slightly more inclined to be retreatists (26 percent) than the retired (20 percent). Thus retirement not only affects morale more in old age than does widowhood but it also tends to precipitate a more severe type of maladaptation.

Since the occupational role is of primary importance for males in our culture, retirement produces particular strains for them. In both the Elmira and Kips Bay studies, retired men are more prone to become alienated than retired women. Retreatism, on the other hand, tends to occur more often among widowed women than among widowed men.

Furthermore, the socio-economic status [17] of older people strongly influences their chances of becoming alienated, while having only a slight effect on their chances of developing retreatism. Alienation is much less frequent in the high socio-economic group than in the low one,[18] but class differences in the incidence of retreatism, although in the same direction, are very small. Ethnic status, too, affects the incidence of alienation, but not that of retreatism. Foreign-born older people are more apt to manifest alienation than are native-born, quite independently of their socio-economic position.

157

That alienation is the typical response in the lower class suggests that this type of maladaptation, in contrast to retreatism, is more apt to occur among older people who, because they are poor, feel that they are "failures," since pecuniary success is so highly stressed in American society. Indeed, in answer to the question "How well . . . would you say . . . you've done in trying to get ahead in life?" alienated people far more often expressed a sense of failure than retreatists, who did not differ at all in this respect from well-adjusted respondents.

The discouragement and frustration that accompany failure to achieve culturally valued objectives is expressed in such statements as "I have to struggle for everything in life." [19] Twice as many alienated older persons agree with this statement (69 percent) as retreatists (33 percent). The retreatist is not only less inclined than the alienated individual to take this view but is also less likely to do so than the well-adapted older person (48 percent). This suggests that retreatism lessens feelings of frustration that might otherwise arise when difficulties are encountered, albeit at the cost of active concern with improving the difficult situation.

The alienated individual, but not the retreatist, generally attributes his difficulties to pure chance or "luck." In answer to the question "How much do you feel that the 'breaks' in life were against you?" nearly three-quarters of the alienated, but only two-fifths of the retreatists, in the Elmira study, expressed the belief that "most" or "some" of the "breaks" were against them. The lower-class old person, in particular, finds it difficult to reconcile his failure with a cultural ideology that emphasizes equality of opportunity. **158**

Since success is culturally assumed to be a reward for effort and merit, the onus for failure falls on the individual. But people do not readily accept this responsibility, since to do so would be too threatening to their self-esteem. Thus, as Robert K. Merton observes, "For the unsuccessful, and particularly for those among the unsuccessful who find little reward for their merit and their effort, the doctrine of luck serves the psychological function of enabling them to preserve their self-esteem in the face of failure." [20]

Thwarted aspirations, often the lot of alienated persons, embitter and leave an imprint on one's attitudes toward people. The alienated are less inclined than the retreatists (who do not differ in this respect from well-adapted people) to believe that "people can be trusted." Needless to say, a lack of trust in people interferes with the individual's ability to establish and maintain friendly interpersonal relations. Indeed, there is a direct relationship between expressions of mistrust and the extent of a person's social participation. Thus, the proportion who evidence mistrust is highest among those with the lowest participation scores, and lowest among those with the highest scores.

In the absence of panel data, it is impossible to decide whether this suspicious attitude produces isolation or results from it—most likely influence is reciprocal. The individual whose close associates support and reassure him as he confronts the problems of old age is probably less apt to develop a distrustful attitude toward people than the one who is without friends. When a person says that "no one cares about an old man," he indicates a sense of rejection and resentment. The implication follows that someone *ought* to care and that other people's indifference means that they are not worthy of trust. This orientation, even if it is a reaction to social isolation, is self-defeating, since most people avoid a distrustful and suspicious individual.

The retreatist does not, as a rule, share the alienated person's anomic outlook. Indeed, he is no more likely than the well-adjusted older person to express mistrust, or to regard himself as a failure, or to consider himself a victim of "bad breaks." This suggests that the psychological mechanism of withdrawal helps to forestall complete demoralization in the face of adverse conditions. While retreatists resemble well-adapted old people in their general outlook, their markedly lessened interest in virtually all forms of activity clearly distinguishes them from the latter.[21]

Evidence shows that retreatists are less motivated than other older people, including the alienated, to seek social companionship. Respondents were asked, "Would you say you are more like the people who need a lot of love and respect, or more like those who don't need so much?" Retreatists answered "a lot of love" less often than any other group (24 percent), in marked contrast to innovators (63 percent), the best adjusted group (whose response will be discussed below).

Retreatism is a mechanism of escape that promotes a measure of equanimity at the expense of weakening the individual's motivation to participate in social life. An elderly widow's comment illustrates this:

> Sometimes I think, "I just can't stand to be here by myself"; then I say to myself, "You are, so you might as well make the most of it." . . . I'm probably not as dependent on other people as I might be. I've rather got used to living alone. . . . I **160**

have lots of memories of good times, and when I get to feeling
lonesome, I just try to remember those. . . .[22]

She is aware that "other people" and her "memories of
good times" relieve loneliness. Through daydreaming she
has made an adjustment, such as it is, to a solitary existence.
But by choosing this alternative, she has become less motivated to seek social companionship, as indicated by her
statement, "I'm probably not as dependent on others as I
might be." It may be that without the escape mechanism of
daydreaming, her loneliness would have forced her to seek
companionship, enabling her to remain better adjusted; on
the other hand, it may also be that without this mechanism
she would have experienced the full destructive force of
loneliness and become alienated.[23]

The alienated person's mistrust and the retreatist's escapism could be called dysfunctional alternatives. Although
the retreatist does not particularly distrust people, his unwillingness to acknowledge his need for others serves the
same dysfunction as distrust and makes isolation in old age
as likely for him as for the alienated person.

Both responses—retreatism and alienation—constitute
maladaptations, because they reinforce the conditions that
give rise to these responses in the first place. (Similarly, the
"culture" of poverty contains elements both of retreatism
and of alienation. It is, to be sure, an adaptation that permits the poor to survive in the face of brutish conditions, but
it also inhibits exactly those behaviors that would make it
possible for the individual to escape his lower-class destiny.[24]) Maladaptations can be likened to narcotics. They
reduce pain but undermine the individual's will to take mea-   **161**

sures that would enable him to escape from, or to alter, the conditions that oppress him. In the face of the same kind of stress, some individuals attempt to change the *conditions* that cause them to suffer, while others become permanently "trapped" as they develop defense mechanisms to accept these conditions.

Retreatism and alienation are similar to Freud's neurotic defense mechanisms [25] in emotional disorder and to Hans Selye's "diseases of adaptation" in organic disease.[26] These conceptions have in common the recognition that some physical and psychological defenses are pathological insofar as they do not result in better adaptation of the organism, and ultimately prove injurious to the organism.

David Bakan, discussing the convergence between Freud and Selye, elucidates the similarities in their formulations:

> . . . Selye's observations and conclusions come remarkably close to those associated with the idea of the "death instinct," "the hypothesis that all living substance is bound to die from internal causes," which Freud explicated in *Beyond the Pleasure Principle*. Selye has succeeded in showing in great detail how mechanisms in the organism bring about its own disease and death. . . . [The] death instinct . . . is manifested precisely in "defenses" which do not defend, which injure, and which nonetheless *appear* to defend from injury.[27]

PATTERNS OF ADAPTATION

In marked contrast to both retreatism and alienation are the patterns of response illustrated by the following comments:

. . . After she lost her husband she made a terrific effort to get   **162** independent interests and was successful. She accentuated her old interests—church work, old ladies home work . . . she made up her mind to be useful fifteen or twenty years longer.

You just have to adjust to growing older, to having things change around you. Lots of times you don't like the new things but there isn't anything you can do about them. You just have to accept them.

These comments illustrate some of the differences between *innovation* and *conformity,* two different modes of *adaptation* in old age. Although these types of older people, unlike the alienated and the retreatists, score high on morale tests,[28] innovation is a more effective form of adaptation than conformity, particularly in respect to the older person's integration in the social and political community.

The innovator is exemplified by the "spry octogenarian," although he is rarely quite that old. He takes old age in his stride because he develops new interests and establishes new friendships. He remains integrated even though some of his former social relationships may have been disrupted.

The innovator is defined as an individual who "enjoys life more now than at fifty," "goes out of his way to make friends," rarely feels that his "life today is not very useful," and has made new friends in recent years.[29]

Conformity is a residual category that includes the 203 respondents (43 percent) in Elmira who received low scores on all three response scales—innovation, alienation, and retreat. Such remarks as "you have to take things as they are" and "you just have to adjust to growing older" characterize the conformist's tendency to adapt *to* conditions. In contrast, the innovator makes a determined effort

163

to adjust *the* conditions—he (or she) "goes out of his way" to make friends, makes a "terrific effort to get independent interests," "makes up her mind to be useful." The older person who simply "takes things as they are" may very well enjoy life and continue to see "old" friends as long as conditions permit, but he is not as likely to enter new social relationships and develop new interests as the person who makes a deliberate effort to do so. The difference between innovators and conformists in this respect is found in their answers to the question "Thinking back to when you were fifty [which of these activities] gave you more satisfaction then or now?" Included were friendships, recreation outside the home, religion or church work, and solitary hobbies at home.

In contrast to maladapted older people, conformists do not, as a rule, lose interest in an active life, but they are significantly less inclined than innovators to become more interested in activities. In short, the conformist is satisfied with the way things are—no small achievement in old age —but he does not take an active role in adjusting conditions to his new needs as the innovator does. Riesman's delineation of the "adjusted" older person also describes the conformist:

> . . . For the adjusted group it matters decisively what institutions they hitch or are hitched onto. . . . Their one-and-only life cycle gets fatally mixed up with the larger institutional cycles.[30]

Institutional roles and extensive social participation, as seen in chapter 4, serve as functional alternatives for adaptation in old age. That is, most of the employed and the **164** married, whatever their extent of participation, score high on all morale measures, and so do most of those who participate extensively, whether retired or employed, widowed or married. Now we can see that an institutional role or extensive social relations are indeed *alternative* mechanisms of adaptation with respect to innovation. In other words, among the employed elderly, the incidence of conformity is about the same among those with low participation scores as among those with high scores, and this is also true for the married.[31] Similarly, among older people with high social participation, the conformist pattern was about as frequent for retirants as for the employed, and for the widowed as for the married.[32] But employment status and participation have a cumulative effect on the older person's chances of becoming an innovator. For example, more than a third of the socially active employed are innovators, but only a fifth of the isolated employed, a quarter of the socially active retirants, and a mere sixteenth of the isolated retirants. Marital status and participation also have a cumulative effect on the incidence of innovation, although it is somewhat less pronounced.

Innovation occurs more among men (23 percent) than among women (16 percent), but this difference completely disappears when employment status is controlled: The proportion of innovators among employed men and women is identical (28 percent). Hence contact opportunities on the job, not sex status as such, explain the higher rate of innovation among men.

The incidence of conformity varies with socio-economic position, but that of innovation does not. Sixty percent of those in the higher class display conformity, as com- **165** pared with 47 percent in the middle class and 29 percent in the lower class. Thus the typical response in the middle and higher class is conformity, but in the lower class it is alienation.[33] Although older people on higher socio-economic levels generally have more extensive social relations than those in lower-class positions, this does not completely account for the differential incidence of conformity, since conformity occurs less even among socially active lower-class people than among relatively isolated persons in middle- or higher-class positions.

Although conformity is less frequent among those in the lower class, the extent of their social relations has a stronger effect on their chances of remaining conformists, rather than becoming maladapted, than it does on those in the middle or higher class.[34] In the higher classes, the incidence of conformity varies hardly at all with social participation. But those in the lower class with more extensive social relationships are more likely to exhibit conformity than the more isolated. In other words, social relationships assume greater importance for minimal adjustment where structural conditions create the greatest strain toward maladaptation. This is implied in the comment of an elderly widow on relief, who says:

> My biggest problem is having no money and being lonely. It's so lonely to live alone. I don't mind about the money so much, but being lonely is hard. I would like to have more friends . . . someone you know better and longer . . . who has a home where you can go visit.

It becomes easier to bear economic privation and the ignominy of "being on relief" if one at least has friends.[35]

Forming new friendships in old age, one of the characteristics that distinguishes innovators from conformists, would seem to depend on three conditions: first, the individual's opportunities to meet new acquaintances; second, his motivation to enter into a friendship with them; and third, the willingness of others to reciprocate the older person's friendly overtures.

Older people in the Kips Bay study were asked, "How did you happen to meet . . . the closest new friend you have made in recent years?" The three most frequent answers were "we were neighbors" (25 percent), "through another friend or relative (22 percent), and "through work" (18 percent). Two of these opportunities for meeting new people are more readily available to innovators than to others, since most of them have a number of friends (78 percent are high participants) who might introduce them to new acquaintances, and many also have a job (58 percent) in which they might meet new people. Conformists are not quite as fortunate, but a considerable proportion of them also have extensive social relations (61 percent) and are still employed (43 percent). Yet is it not merely his opportunities for meeting new people but particularly his orientation toward them that differentiates the innovator from the conformist.

Obviously, not all social contacts develop into friendships. Two acquaintances are likely to become friends only if one of them initiates friendly overtures. Many people are more than willing to accept an invitation from a new acquaintance if it is forthcoming, but are reluctant to make such overtures themselves. Thus friendships often fail to develop between acquaintances simply because each waits for   **167** the other to take the first step. But the innovator, taking greater advantage of his opportunities, does not hesitate to proffer an invitation when meeting someone he likes.

Initiative in new social situations entails the risk that one's friendly overtures may not be reciprocated. Therefore it is only the secure individual who can afford to expose himself to the risk of having his bid for friendship rejected.

The concept of interpersonal integration refers to the degree of acceptance and respect that an individual enjoys among a group of close associates. Ideally, integration would have to be determined by ascertaining the attitudes of all close associates of each respondent toward him and using these data to construct socio-metric indices. Since such information is not available in survey research, we must be content with examining the significance of the respondents' feelings of integration, which is an important factor in its own right, but which must not be assumed to be a direct expression of the actual extent of their interpersonal integration.[36] Indicative of the subjective experience of integration are, for example, answers to the question "Do you think you are easier to get along with than other people, or maybe a little bit harder to get along with?" While the majority of innovators and conformists expressed the belief that they were "easier to get along with" (in contrast, for example, to alienated people), a significantly greater proportion of innovators (79 percent) than of conformists (65 percent) gave this reply. Similarly, when asked "How often do members of your family or friends ask your advice about things?" a significantly greater proportion of innovators (49 percent) than of conformists (35 percent) indicated that their close associates consulted them "often." Although these data   168 do not furnish reliable evidence of actual differences in integration, they do indicate that innovators are more inclined to *feel* integrated—that is, to feel that others accept and respect them.

There are at least two reasons why the person who feels securely integrated can afford to take the initiative in new social situations more easily than others. First, the belief that his associates think highly of him gives him confidence that new acquaintances will also respond favorably to his friendly overtures. Second, the possibility that others will not reciprocate his bid for friendship is less threatening, because his well-integrated position permits him to maintain his self-esteem even in the face of occasional failure.[37]

The most marked difference between innovators and conformists occurs in their answers to the question "Would you say that you are more like the people who need a lot of love and respect or more like those who don't need so much?" It is worth noting that only among the innovators did a majority give the answer "a lot of love" (63 percent) —an indication that as a rule only this type of older person is sufficiently secure in his interpersonal relations to admit freely to himself and to a stranger (the interviewer) that he is emotionally dependent on others. Conformists, in contrast, differ little from maladapted old people. They admit that they need "a lot of love" (35 percent) no more often than do alienated individuals (36 percent), and not much more often than the retreatists, who, it will be recalled, constitute opposites in this respect (24 percent).

This difference between conformists and innovators suggests how innovation becomes self-reinforcing. Since the innovator feels more securely integrated, he is able to admit   **169** to himself the need for social companionship; and this awareness, in turn, reinforces his motivation to seek new friends. On the other hand, the person who protects himself against the threat of isolation by denying his need of others thereby reduces his incentive to cultivate friendships. This tendency is most characteristic of the retreatist who suppresses his need for love by evoking pleasant memories of the past, but it also characterizes the large majority of conformists.

Older people's responses have implications not only for their effectiveness in interpersonal relationships but also for their political effectiveness. We have seen that the chances of personal adjustment are worse for older people in lower class positions than for those in higher ones; worse for retirants than for the employed; and worse for isolated persons than for active social participants. Thus poverty, idleness, and isolation would seem to be the main problem areas in which social action is needed to alleviate the alienating effects of old age. The chances for such action may well depend, in part, on older people's willingness to take an active political role in the community and to organize and use their voting power to bring their needs to the attention of political circles.

Two indicators of "public" participation, as distinguished from participation in primary relationships, are voting in elections and membership in formal organizations. Table 22 shows the relationship between the responses of older people and their participation in these activities.

It is clear that the innovator is most likely to remain an active member of the community in his old age. Compared **170**

TABLE 22

Types Re- sponding	Percentages of Persons Who Voted in National Election (1948)	Percentages Who Belong to One or More Organi- zations	Number of Cases
Innovators	84	81	(81)
Conformists	77	55	(203)
Retreatists	63	52	(46)
Alienated	57	35	(102)

with others in his age group, he seems to be in the best position to influence the community to take action in behalf of older people.[38]

Conformists are less inclined to take an active part in community affairs; indeed, they are no more likely than retreatists to belong to organizations, even though their personal relationships (61 percent have high participation scores) far exceed those of retreatists (35 percent). The alienated individual is least inclined to participate in the political process, even in presidential elections; and it is only among the alienated that the majority do not belong to any organization.

From the standpoint of political action, therefore, the innovator and the alienated person represent opposites. To be sure, the alienated individual, but not the innovator, is usually in the lower class—which is a deterrent to organizational participation. But even when class position is controlled, these differences between innovators and alienated

Types Re-	**Socio-economic Status**					
sponding	Low		Middle		High	
Innovators	100	(15)	74	(46)	85	(20)
Alienated	20 †	(36)	45 †	(53)	38 *	(13)

* Difference significant at the 0.05 level.
† Difference significant at the 0.01 level.

respondents persist; at each level a significantly higher proportion of the innovators than of the alienated belong to one
or more organizations (Table 23).

The differences in voting behavior between innovators
and the alienated also remain when class position is controlled, as Table 24 shows. Although the proportion of older
people who voted in a presidential election increases directly
with class position, at *each* class level the proportion of
voters is higher among the innovators than among the
alienated.

These findings suggest that the outlook of alienated
older people—their sense of defeat, their belief that chance
determines the outcome of human affairs, and their mistrust
of others—discourages political participation by undermin-
ing the belief that common gains can be achieved by joining
with others in a similar position and with like interests. Their
hopelessness, in turn, reinforces their powerlessness.

In contrast to actual participation in social action, in
which the two groups stand at opposite extremes, the
alienated and the innovators hardly differ from one another

TABLE 24
Percentages of Innovators
and Alienated Who Voted
in the 1948 Presidential Election—
by Socio-economic Status

Types Re-sponding	Socio-economic Status					
	Low		Middle		High	
Innovators	73	(15)	83	(46)	95	(20)
Alienated	50	(36)	51 *	(53)	85	(13)

* Difference significant at the 0.01 level.

in respect to their belief that such action *ought* to be taken. The question was asked, "How much need would you say there is for a program to improve the position of older people in this country?" Alienated people say that there is "a very great need" for political action nearly as often as do innovators and considerably more often than do conformists and retreatists, as Table 25 shows.

Although the alienated individual appears to be as concerned with social action as is the innovator, he is far less likely to join others in bringing it about. That those who suffer most from the disadvantageous position of older people in this society are least inclined to take an active role in the community and thereby to help improve their position indicates most pointedly, perhaps, the social and political dysfunctions of alienation. It is a futile form of protest, because it reduces the individual's motivation to protest with others. By default, if not by intent, the alienated person helps to perpetuate the conditions that spell unhappiness and atrophy for him and for others in old age.[39]

Harold Wilensky has delineated the political dangers

TABLE 25

Percentage of Each Type
Who See "a Very Great Need"
for Social Action

Types Responding	Percent Who Say "a Very Great Need"	Number of Cases
Innovators	55	(81)
Conformists	34	(203)
Retreatists	41	(46)
Alienated-retreatists	37	(38)
Alienated	50	(64)

that may arise from the marginality, the apathy, and the alienation that exist to a significant degree among older people in American society:

> . . . In the absence of effective mediating ties, of meaningful participation in voluntary associations the young and old become vulnerable to political extremism, more susceptible to personality appeals in politics, more ready for the demagogues who exploit fanatical faiths of nation and race. . . . The aged must be seen as a peculiarly potent pool of extremism; apathy and activism, may in the end, be blood brothers.[40]

new
ROLes
FOR
LaTeR LiFe

It is when the human heart faces its destiny and
notwithstanding sings—sings of itself, its life, its
death—that poetry is possible.
—ARCHIBALD MAC LEISH

That the life cycle of the human organism, like any organism, begins with birth and is ended by death is a universal fact of nature. But the length of life of individuals and of a generation is a variable conditioned by the values, resources, and knowledge of their society. And the stages in the human life cycle—their duration, meaning, and content—are determined not merely by biological processes but also by social values and social institutions.

A steadily lengthening life expectancy is one of several phenomena that have created new social problems for postindustrial societies. Until recently, life was short, people faced and feared the prospect of death while still performing significant social roles. But as more and more people survive beyond the time of their children's leaving the household, as more and more men live beyond the age of retirement and more and more women are confronted with a decade or more of widowhood, the fear of early death has been replaced by the fear of aging and its connotation of a living death.

This paradox, that the lengthening of the life span is accompanied by an increasing fear of becoming old, is traceable to the absence of significant roles for people in later life. The life cycle, as traditionally perceived, consists of four stages: childhood, youth, adulthood, and old age. The first two stages are considered preparation for adulthood. Life's purpose and meaning, we have been led to believe, are to be found principally in the enactment of three adult roles—marriage, parenthood, and, for males, an occupation. These are not, of course, the only worthwhile social roles. Adults may also have leisure pursuits—friends, avocations, politics, voluntary associations, sport, and play. But such

176

activities are optional and lack the obligatory character and the authority of institutional roles. People judge themselves, and are judged by others, to be "successful" if they achieve a happy marriage, have children who "turn out well," and have jobs that command high remuneration and respect.

The enactment of these three core adult roles has been viewed as the apex of the life cycle, mainly because they constitute the roles, to borrow the metaphor of the theater, most fully defined and elaborated by our cultural scripts. These are the roles people are taught to aspire to and to prepare for. Institutional mechanisms and public opinion influence individuals, as they approach adulthood, to commit themselves to these roles, and, once committed, to discharge "to term" the role responsibilities they have undertaken. The commitment to one's marital partner, according to the marital vows, is "until death do us part"; the parental commitment is also for a lifetime; and commitment to one occupation for all of one's working life has become the norm, at least in the professions and business.

Since people think of a specific set of roles as the culmination of their personal existence, they fear old age because it means adandoning these roles and having no prospect of any other culturally significant roles for the remainder of their lives—which, with an extended life expectancy, can be a long time. Ordinary men and women have relied on cultural scripts throughout their earlier lives, and when these no longer exist, they often lack the resources and the experience to improvise new ones. Instead, many older people just cling to life as they wait to be relieved of a lonely and useless existence.

The problem is not confined to the absence of institutionalized roles for the aged but extends to the traditional conceptions of youth and middle age that still prevail in most of the world. The conception of the life cycle in Western society is a cultural construct. This is not to say it is not real. All beliefs widely shared by any collectivity are real, because, to paraphrase W. I. Thomas, beliefs have real consequences when acted upon. But ideas and beliefs are not immutable; they change with historical circumstances, although more slowly, as seen in society's conception of the nature and content of adulthood. Our ways of thinking about youth, middle age, and old age have not yet caught up with the significant demographic changes and effects of mechanization that have occurred in the twentieth century. Consequently, long before old age many people experience existential strains that they do not understand, for which they are unprepared, and with which they are unable to cope effectively.

Previously, a generation lasted fifty years or less. People occasionally lived longer, but they were the exception rather than the rule. When we say that an individual's life expectancy has steadily increased since the turn of the century, we also mean that his generation's life span has been extended. Most adults now in their forties can expect to live another twenty-five years. In advanced industrial societies, the combined trends of earlier marriage, smaller families, and earlier departure of children from the home are now freeing men and women from the financial and social obligations of parenthood relatively earlier than before. But the culturally prescribed scripts remain the same as they have always been. There are no new *obligatory* social roles in middle age to spur the individual to purposeful activity once **178**

NEW ROLES FOR LATER LIFE

actual parenthood ends, even though people in their forties
can expect to live another twenty or twenty-five years. At
this point in their lives, some people become enervated and
less active; others become restive or depressed, beset by such
questions as "Is that all there is?" or "What now?"

Because a woman is involved in homemaking and
child-rearing roles, she often experiences these strains
earlier than her husband. Increasingly, women respond to
the "empty nest syndrome" by returning to the labor force
in middle age, usually to clerical and sales jobs that do not
require much training or skill. But many women, particularly in the educated, affluent middle class, desire more
challenging work. This may require more education than
they have had, or the renewal of skills that have become
obsolete because of rapid changes taking place in all professions.

More venturesome women, despite the absence of culturally prescribed scripts, have therefore begun to seek
further formal education in middle age. Reports in women's
sections of newspapers and in women's magazines frequently
detail the initial doubts and fears of those who return to
school:

> Four years ago, Mrs. Margaret Duffy thought she was "too
> old" to go to college. But today this Rogers Park mother of ten
> and grandmother of three has taken more than half the courses
> she needs to earn a college degree. . . . She admits it's not
> easy for a woman in her mid-forties to make the move. "I was
> afraid at first—this stirred around in my mind for quite a while.
> . . . I wondered if I could really do it. You think: I'll be a cow-
> ard, I'll fail and the kids will laugh. Then I got mad at myself for
> signing myself off before I tried." . . .   **179**

When asked if she felt "out of place" in classes with eighteen and twenty year olds, she said:
"Age just seems to disappear in the classroom. I had to
study a little longer, but it wasn't bad." [1]

Women like that are the "innovators" of an emergent social
pattern that will spread and become part of the cultural
script for the next generation of women. Today's feminist
movement is not simply an attempt to gain equality with
men or to emulate them. It is also a response to the demographic changes that I have repeatedly enumerated. The
prospect of living an additional twenty-five years after the
completion of child rearing; the knowledge that women are
outliving men and that the gap is increasing; the earlier age
of marriage and smaller families—all this has made women
realize that simply being a wife and then a widow for a long
time is an anachronism in contemporary society. To them,
indeed to both sexes, society is equipped to offer better
health, better socialization, and better education; but society is wasting these opportunities. And most of all—to
borrow Erikson's phrase—a person's one-and-only life cycle
is being abused. Women not only can have marriage and
babies *and also an occupation or career,* but they *should*
have all three roles, just as men do. It is precisely because
society gives them the option of not working or seriously
pursuing some avocation that too many women are victims
of the "empty nest syndrome" and the so-called menopausal
syndrome in middle age. The work role is not merely a responsibility; it is also an additional resource that helps to
alleviate the strains of a woman's exit from the maternal
role. Probably in future generations, it will not be the working wives who will have to be defensive—as they still are to-   **180**

day—but the wives who lack the energy, will, and self-respect to forge themselves an independent existence through learning and work.

Under the present pattern, white women, as a rule, leave the labor force during the childbearing and child-rearing years, although the numbers who continue in the labor force through this period are increasing.[2] But the widespread establishment of day-care facilities at places of work and at institutions of higher learning would allow more women uninterrupted employment and education during their entire adult life. Such communal facilities could also create new roles for older people. (I will reserve this point for later discussion.)

The need for a different perspective on the man's life cycle and social roles has not yet been fully recognized. But I believe it, too, will come, because no significant change can take place in the social roles of one sex without consequences for the roles of the opposite sex. Furthermore, the prolongation of adulthood has affected the lives of men as much as those of women, but in less obvious ways.

Since the Second World War, the American economy has grown at an unprecedented rate. Job opportunities at the middle and higher occupational levels have greatly multiplied, and larger proportions of men are going to college and to graduate school. But they also have been marrying earlier, so parental help, the G.I. Bill, government scholarships and loans, and help from their wives have subsidized their higher education.

Technological innovations have created new occupational opportunities for young men. They enter jobs at higher pay and prestige than in former years and can ad-   **181** vance more rapidly. With greater affluence and easier credit, the luxuries young married people once worked and saved for over many years are attainable far sooner. To repay their debts on things needed to provide an affluent style of life, men must work harder, particularly when their wives do not work.

While their children are born and growing up, men are heavily involved in the rat race. The rearing and socialization of children, therefore, have increasingly come to be viewed as mainly the mother's responsibility. Recent studies of college youth show that not only girls but also boys, as a rule, feel closer to their mothers than to their fathers.[3]

By the time American men are in their forties, a great many of them are weary and bored with their jobs. They have either "made it" or scaled down their ambitions. They discover that in the years when they were frantic about "making a buck," repaying debts, and gaining recognition, they lost touch with their children, with their wives, and, worst of all, with themselves.

To a great extent, the alienation of men and women from one another in middle age stems from the pronounced division of labor between the sexes that begins when a married couple become parents. For it is at that point in their lives that contemporary women retire from outside work and wholly embrace the domestic pattern. What usually follows is what Philip Slater describes as "the domesticization and neutralization of the wife" as a stimulating human being and an erotic object. By serving as a full-time "domestic" in a mechanized household, she has freed her husband from household responsibility so that he, as sole supporter of the family, can give himself single-mindedly to his job.

But according to society's norms it is not enough for a man simply to do his job; he must be ambitious and strive to get ahead. "Putting the job first" is considered a laudable quality in our corporate society. Such exaggeration is what commands raises and promotions for a man. But it is enervating to be always aggressive and competitive, while being good-natured toward superiors, co-workers, and customers. Home is where men can collapse into an easy chair, remove their masks, stop thinking and scheming. They have spent themselves at work. At home they want to be looked after, nurtured, and then "let alone," to become the spectator of television drama, conversation, or sport. Since Daddy works so hard and his income makes possible the nice house, the cars, the toys, and the college education that all middle-class children must have, it would be ungrateful for a wife to complain of his dullness, his neglect of her and the children. Ungrateful, indeed! A good wife humors her tired husband and protects him from his children's boisterousness and their demands for communication. To quote Slater again, "Alienation from the body, from the emotional life, is largely a white male invention" [4] in contemporary industrial society.

Warnings of the dire effects of "momism" on male youth are voiced from time to time. Ironically, those who complain also defend the status quo. They are the ones who consider it "only natural" that "the job comes first" for men, and who view it as proper that men should invest their intellect, their emotions, and their energy primarily in their jobs, leaving to women the work of rearing and socializing children.

This marked division of labor between the sexes—the male assuming responsibility for the family unit's material needs, the female looking after its expressive needs—is, according to Talcott Parsons and Robert Freed Bales, the most efficient family form for an industrial, socially mobile society. Perhaps it is—in the same way that the assembly line is a highly efficient and economical way to turn out machines. Efficiency, however, does not justify a pattern that imposes unnecessarily heavy costs on those who adhere to it. What the division of labor does to women in later middle age and beyond has already been noted, but the costs are also borne by men and children.

When the children grow up and leave home, women miss the things they did for and with them. Men, in contrast, often regret the chances they missed to do things for and with their children. Most children, not only when they are little but also when they are growing up, enjoy being with their parents as they approach adolescence and begin to want to talk, to argue, to query. However, many find that their parents are too busy or too weary and preoccupied to listen, much less to enter into a dialogue with their progeny. College students often tell me that their middle-aged parents don't listen to them, and so in frustration they have stopped talking. The parents, pained by their children's estrangement and hostility, then complain that they can't "reach" their adolescents.

Boys say they feel estranged from their fathers more than from their mothers. Today's male youth, in large numbers and with much pain, reject their fathers as models. They reject their fathers' aspirations for them and they reject their advice because they view them—to use T. S. Eliot's words —as "hollow men." They seem, in middle age, smug, scared, unloving, and unfulfilled human beings, who themselves don't understand the malaise that besets them and drives them to assorted substitutes—alcohol, tranquilizers, television, and young women. By their forties, too many men in affluent America feel estranged from their children, bored with their wives, and alienated from their work.

The traditional conception of middle age must be revised. Middle age is represented as the high plateau of the life cycle—the prime of life. Yet, increasingly, men and women at this age feel "let down." They see no further challenges and they feel trapped. They are often bored with work and with their marriages. "The trick," Harvey Swados says, "is how to go on living even after you've found out what kind of world it really is." Middle-aged people invoke various "tricks" to assuage their malaise. They diet, adopt novelties in dress, change their hair style, and use cosmetics and surgery to preserve themselves. Such changes are of course only skin deep, and do not represent any significant form of inner change, of self-renewal.

Inner change requires some basic alteration in the activities and social relationships to which we adhere because they are part of the routine of daily existence, but which have ceased to present us with the challenge of new problems that call for new solutions. Riesman has observed that it is the "socially provided script" that causes an individual to give his roles less than his full self.[5] But a great many adults become *too well adjusted* to society's expectations and insufficiently attuned to their own nature and needs. Occupational success, once attained, all too often fails to provide the psychic rewards that a person feels are necessary for the attainment of his own integrity. The successful men and women who discover later in life the inner impoverishment that has resulted from their conformity to the cultural script have become clichés, both in real life and in the literature of contemporary society.

We all fear tragedy because of the pain and disruption of normal existence that they inflict upon us. Yet personal tragedies, although painful, often lead to the discovery and cultivation of inner resources, because they make our lives less stable. People are forced to improvise when life does not follow the cultural script and when events precipitate exits from customary roles. Improvisations necessitated by what first appear to be disasters or tragedies cause many people to discover inner resources they did not know they had. Crippling illness, the death of a spouse or child, the breakdown of a marriage, or dismissal from a job are misfortunes that we all know *may* occur but as a rule do not. The paradox is that unless middle-aged people are forced by a disruptive misfortune to abandon the familiar scripts that lend order and meaning to their life, they forget that they are not simply spouses and parents and breadwinners. They forget that they had a distinct identity before, and a destiny to fulfill after, their exit from marriage, or parenthood, or their jobs.

The proliferation of spectator activities—television, sports, entertainment—at the expense of avocations that entail new learning or service to others, outside the family and work orbits, is an ominous sign of the psychic impoverishment that often follows a literal adherence to demands of institutional roles. Such total devotion to formal roles and such a lack of informal activities are poor preparation for the later years of life.

It seems that the people who are most often bored and 186

weary of middle age and, above all, fearful of old age are those who have most faithfully and exclusively invested themselves in the institutional roles provided by the cultural script—the women who have been fully occupied with homemaking, child rearing, and being "good" and "devoted" wives; the men who have assiduously pursued the goal of occupational success. One looks at successful men in their forties and wonders why they were in such a *hurry* to "make it." Once they have reached the peak of material success and recognition, there is little else for them to do. Curiously, one frequently observes that the less successful men fare best in their later years. Those who either were less ambitious to begin with or who discovered early that they would not make it sought and found gratification outside their jobs, such as doing things with their wives, children, and friends, and pursuing a satisfying avocation. In the vernacular of materialistic societies, the losers in the marketplace are the winners in the second half of life, and the winners end up as losers. They clearly exemplify what William Simon terms "the anomie of affluence."

Middle-aged people should not be satisfied with the way things are. As psychiatrist Robert N. Butler writes, "One of the greatest dangers in life is being frozen into rigid roles that limit one's self-development and self-expression. We need to enhance the reality and the sense of personal growth throughout the course of life until its very end." [6] Nor should the later years be merely a time for the pursuit of happiness, if happiness signifies a desperate search for diversion or a frantic effort to recapture youth by imitating the young.

Middle age constitutes a point of arrival, but it should **187** also be defined as one of departure, as a time of reassessment and of change. Since change means giving up familiar ways of behaving and discovering new and untried courses, some anxiety and pain are inevitable. The same is true for adolescence, because it, too, is a period of transition. But there is an important difference between the two periods. The adolescent is under a cultural obligation to emancipate himself from childhood and from his parents, and to prepare himself for work and marriage. Social mechanisms explicitly or implicitly move him in these directions.

Moreover, the adolescent's problem is that he is no longer the child he was nor the adult he will become. Lacking a firm identity, he is nevertheless called upon to make decisions and commitments for a lifetime without having much experience. He will be warned that he will "ruin his life" if he follows his own inclinations rather than the expectations of his parents and his teachers. If he does what he is told, he feels he has betrayed himself and abdicated to others his right to live his own life and make his own mistakes. His "own" inclinations are often little more than reflections of what his peers term important, unless he is that rare person who, even in youth, is self-directed.

By middle age, on the other hand, the individual is experienced. He has lived with the consequences of the choices and commitments he made in his youth, and can judge *for himself* whether he is satisfied with the way he has lived his life. Between adolescence and middle age, people change. What they thought was important at twenty-five no longer seems worthwhile at forty-five. Conversely, needs and goals that seemed unimportant in youth, and were neglected over the years, reassert themselves and demand satisfaction.

188

A common query in middle age is, "If you had your life to live over again, what would you do?" The past, of course, cannot be relived. But people *can* change the present and alter their future, even in middle age. To be sure, the culture does not *prescribe* further roles, and therefore most people believe that they must continue to follow their conventional patterns because "it is too late to change."

"Too late" means several things. For one, that a person lacks the will and fortitude to depart from the usual pattern because he fears the consequences of breaking the mold —the disruption of routine, the discomfort and disarray that accompany significant role changes. These people are the lethargic ones. "Too late" also means that a person is afraid of the consequences of defying convention and is unwilling to incur the disapproval of those he values. The social pressure of friends and kin today is usually on the side of upholding the original role commitments made during one's youth. There is also fear of failure, fear of making a fool of himself, fear of rejection by others. These people are the fearful ones. A third meaning of "too late" is that a person's emotional bond to his occupation or his spouse continues to be sufficiently strong so that the need to be faithful to others outweighs the pains and strains of one's present role. These people are the faithful ones.

"Too late" can also mean a lack of visible and available options. It is easier to abandon a line of work if one is interested and skilled in an avocation than if one has none. Similarly, many people, although unhappy in their marriages, do not leave their spouses because they do not have any desirable alternatives. Lacking other visible and readily accessible options, people, as a rule, cling to unfulfilling

189

jobs or marriages rather than risk uncertainty. Losing the security of an institutional role can cause a person as much anxiety as he felt in adolescence.

We view adolescence as the only transitional phase in the life cycle, bridging childhood and adulthood. The young person must prepare himself—through formal mechanisms, such as schools, and informal social mechanisms, such as relationships with boys and girls—for the adult roles that he knows lie ahead. A major source of anxiety during this period is the need to make the critical choices and lifelong commitments that adults insist upon.

Still, adolescence is socially recognized as a period of instability and change. Middle age is not. The middle-aged person who forsakes significant roles is regarded as a social deviant. Butler eloquently sums up the social constraints on change and growth in our culture:

> To obviate the necessity of pseudo-lives, infra-lives, and "lives of quiet desperation," there must be greater freedom over and against identity—the freedom to rebel against the freeze. Today, to leave or switch careers in midlife, as trains switch tracks, or to cop out of the career ladder is regarded as "sick." The definition of "sickness" is critical to the evolution of social and personal "solutions." As it is in some contemporary circumstances, the more "sick" things one does the "healthier" one is —to leave careers and marriages, especially, is defined as maladaptive.
> Recognition of the human capacity for error is essential. This requires humility. But we seem to be moving in the opposite direction.
> With the threat of so many social and technological changes, instead of an unfreezing of roles, tasks, and identities, there

has been a greater intensification in many respects and in many
quarters.
At the same time, however, there are experimenters, individuals who are playing with change and are likely to represent the life styles of the future. Similarly, there are new organizational forms, and also anarchic, scattered forms.
It is surprising how punitive society can be toward those
who evolve new life styles.[7]

People expect to live another twenty years or more beyond middle age. Thus when a young person contemplates
a lifetime commitment to one spouse or one career he quite
properly hesitates and often defers or even refuses to make
commitments when a lifetime signifies not twenty years but
fifty years at age twenty.

The conventional conception of the life cycle is out-
moded because it is still predicated on the life span that
existed seventy years ago and does not correspond to today's realities. But sooner or later, new definitions will be
established and the conception of middle age as a period
of change, not unlike adolescence, will spread and become
institutionalized. The question is, What forms can these
changes in middle and later life take?

One harbinger of change in any institutional system, as
Butler suggests, are the "dropouts," or the "innovators"
who possess the financial and psychological resources to
depart from the security of the conventional life. One type
of middle-aged risk-taker is the man or woman who changes
careers.

In *The New York Times,* for example, an article ap-
peared called "Life Begins Anew with a Second Career."
Here are some interesting excerpts:

191

The two-career life, like the two-car garage, is beginning to become a part of the American scene, said Frank Cass, vice president in charge of research for Deutsch & Shea, specialists in manpower and personnel. . . .

Professor Allan H. Stuart of the School of Continuing Education at New York University cited the technological developments in such areas as computer programming and systems analysis as factors promoting change. "It's amazing to see the parade of men between thirty-five and fifty who come in wanting to change jobs. . . . Some of them feel obsolescent and want to be updated. Others have become financially stable, their kids are out of college and they're looking for a more exciting, more stimulating job for their later years."

Dr. Victor Fuchs of the National Bureau of Economic Research . . . observed . . . that in a prosperous, full-employment economy, career change is more feasible and less of a risk than it used to be.

The article cites cases and reports the reasons why people decided to change careers. For example:

To kick over the traces, get out of the "rat race" and try something they have aways wanted to do.

A forty-two-year-old successful salesman who was elected a trustee of the library in the suburb in which he lived got interested in library work, took a year to return to school, and became a librarian at a large university, said, "What really matters is that I'm now doing something for a living that I would be willing to do for nothing." [8]

The article also cites the example of a retired fire captain in a New York suburb who "always had an interest in history," entered Columbia's New Careers Program, and is now a full-time student working for his Ph.D. in preparation for becoming a history teacher.

Another case described is of a retired policeman who "had no desire to vegetate in a rocker," and found a position as a clerk-coordinator with a railroad.

Several interesting and suggestive themes can be gleaned from such accounts of how middle-aged or elderly innovators came to realize that improvisation was possible. First, it is apparent that they had developed interests outside their jobs through reading, through attending classes, and through voluntary work in organizations. In short, even before they changed careers, they had not adhered to the cultural script exclusively but had engaged in various optional roles that exposed them to new problems, ideas, and perspectives that served as sources of self-renewal. Faced with a lagging interest in, or outright boredom with, their jobs, they apparently did not seek to escape in drink, drugs, television, sexual liaisons, travel, or other kinds of "fun," but used some part of their leisure to acquire new knowledge, skills, and experiences.

There is a distinction between using leisure to escape oneself and one's problems, and using leisure to expand one's self-awareness and understanding. New knowledge and skills generate new interests and help a person to discover hidden resources within himself that can aid in his self-*recovery* and self-*discovery*. These processes are, I believe, necessary preliminaries to the establishment of integrity, which Erikson sees as the culminating nuclear conflict of any individual. Too often during a lifetime of "getting and spending, we lay waste our powers" of reflection and understanding. Life's satisfactory resolution should include a bet- **193** ter understanding of the forces that have made us what we are. Education and study should not be mere instruments for vocational preparation, although this view is the one institutionally promoted in materialistic societies. In traditional Judaism, in contrast, study serves quite a different function. It assigns to the individual the obligation to study the holy texts every day of his life, recognizing this as a necessary accompaniment to the business of living, one that serves the need for self-renewal and self-refreshment better than any form of play.

The emergence and proliferation of encounter groups not only among the young but also among the middle-aged are an expression, I believe, of a need to gain a clearer understanding of one's authentic self, as distinct from the expectations and demands imposed by institutional roles. People do not understand the forces that put them into these roles, but once they adopt them, they become so involved in their family life and in their work that they fail to distinguish the whole of themselves from the parts that they play. They look to encounter groups to free themselves from these social pressures and social constraints, being dimly aware that self-understanding is a necessary step toward the achievement of inner freedom.

They are right, but they are wrong if they believe that a better understanding of *themselves* is sufficient to achieve liberation. We are all products of a particular social order and historical era. Without knowledge of other social ideologies, other social orders, and other historical eras, we believe that what is, must be. Such fatalism imposes the worst kind of bondage on the individual. Society's poor and uneducated masses are the most fatalistic and the most

19

powerless because they have the least knowledge and under-standing of the social order into which they were born and in which they live out their lives. Lacking any awareness of other perspectives and other alternatives, they see no possi-bilities for change. Without a knowledge of alternatives, they cannot even hope for betterment. Creativity of every kind, including liberation, requires imagination, and imagi-nation requires knowledge not only of ourselves but of the historical and social conditions that form and constrain us. Self-understanding and self-liberation go hand in hand with a knowledge and understanding of nature, of society, and of history.

The anti-intellectualism of today's youth rests on a mis-understanding of the uses of knowledge. They are right to reject the conception of knowledge for *itself*. But knowledge can also be for *oneself*. By this I do *not* mean that education can help a person get a more remunerative or prestigious job. I mean that self-understanding requires an appreciation of the social and historical conditions that mold and con-strict us. Only then can we begin to separate what is the *authentic self* and what is merely a response to social and historical constraints imposed upon us. Out of this arduous process can come not only self-liberation but also an im-petus and direction for changing our society so that others—not merely in our own time but in our children's time and beyond—will be freer than we.

The idea that education is only for the young, and nec-essary only in order to obtain a good job, is one source of the boredom and the malaise of the middle-aged and the old. It helps to explain why so many people come to be dominated by the cultural scripts and lose the capacity for **195** improvisation they had in their youth. With learning and reflection, along with the experience of living, can come greater autonomy, greater self-understanding, and greater compassion for others. Otherwise we become automatons that follow society's scripts; when the lines and the stage directions cease, we are left dispersed across the stage, repeating over and over again the same lines mastered long ago. Each of us is locked in his own loneliness and confusion; but still we cling to that stage, reiterating the same lines, playing the same parts. If *that* is living, then what is death?

Middle age should not be a period for slowing down, or for mere repetition of what we have done for so long. There is little time. Indeed, what marks the onset of middle age, what provokes the pain and the panic, is that shattering moment when we finally believe in our own mortality. It does no good to be told, when we are young, that all men are mortal. To youth, all hopes are possibilities. How can they believe in their own death?

But in middle age we know that though we still have time, it is not unlimited. Certain obligations, such as the rearing and financial support of children, are either discharged or soon will be. Women return to work. We have accumulated material goods, and therefore are freer in middle age than in early adulthood to pursue new interests and to develop new skills of our own choice and for our own pleasure.

The unhappy fact is, however, that most people lack the initiative and discipline to find new interests and acquire the skills necessary to implement them. People reared in homes and taught in schools that stress obedience and pun- **196** ish autonomy do not suddenly blossom into autonomous beings once they are free. They merely become immobilized or distraught. Such people, however, can become active with new cultural scripts that specify role obligations beyond the family and work.

Howard S. Becker has made an important observation especially relevant here:

> A structural explanation of personal change has important implications for attempts to deliberately mold human behavior. In particular, it suggests that we need not try to develop deep and lasting interests, be they values or personality traits, in order to produce the behavior we want. It is enough to create situations which will coerce people into behaving as we want them to and then to create the conditions under which other rewards will become linked to continue this behavior.[9]

Attitudes toward education—that it is only for the young and intended primarily for getting a good job—need radical revision, supported by structural innovations, if our aim is to improve the quality of life.

The "generation gap" that erupted in the sixties is partly the result of a knowledge gap. I do not mean merely that a higher proportion of young people attend college today, but also that the *content* of a college education today is very different from that of twenty-five or forty years ago. The average middle-aged and older person is only dimly aware of the important changes that have taken place in every domain of knowledge. No wonder so many people past forty—again to borrow Margaret Mead's graphic phrase—are like "immigrants in time." The gap in knowledge and perspectives between actual immigrants of the early part of this century and *their* children was no greater than the gap that exists between the young and their parents or grandparents.

Middle-aged and older people who have returned to college or to graduate school are not, I notice, alien to or alienated from the young. They disagree, of course, on many issues. But the young disagree with one another, too. The differences in basic assumptions and in communication between the generations outside the university are less apparent on campuses.

Indeed, the increasing presence of middle-aged *and* older people in institutions of higher learning is evidence of a trend that needs to be supported and implemented in various ways: through the mass media, through labor unions and voluntary associations, through community and governmental subsidies to build and staff community colleges, and through subsidies to existing educational institutions for additional space and staff. Incentives, such as periodic sabbaticals in earlier and later middle age, should be instituted in business, in industry, and in government. More than persuasion and exhortation are necessary to establish and disseminate a new social pattern. Opportunities and incentives need to be introduced on a large scale to motivate the ordinary person to rouse himself from his lethargy.

The institutionalization of continuing education would be one way to stimulate new interests and open new perspectives to people in middle and later life. This would lead people to make changes in their lives and thereby promote the process of self-renewal—a process that is easy to recommend but difficult to implement. The concept of continuing education, once established, would also serve as an institutional link in which the individual could still perform useful **198** social roles after retirement and widowhood, bridging the discontinuity of existence after significant role exit.

Furthermore, to the extent that it becomes an accepted practice for people in middle age and beyond to continue their education in some concrete social collectivity, their coming together would create new opportunities for the formation of friendships between people with similar interests and similar experiences—which I have shown is an especially pressing need following the role exits of old age—and would reduce the gulf that now exists between the middle-aged and the old. The creation of new roles in the public sector is another way older people could continue to be useful, integral members of society. This would help their self-respect and that of others.

"For all things there is a season. . . ." A season for service to others should be considered during those stages of life when a person is no longer earning a living. The exigencies of life in contemporary societies are such that in adulthood we direct our energies mainly to our families and to our jobs. We serve those we know and love, but in doing so we neglect our powers of sympathy and compassion for the multitude of other human beings who need help but who remain anonymous.

One is struck by the sympathy and outpourings of help elicited among people in all walks of life when a newspaper prints a human-interest story about the tragic plight of an individual or family—a family burned out of its dwelling; a need for a specific medical treatment or facility for a child whose family is unable to pay for it; an abandoned or neglected child; an old person without friends or resources; or a father with a large family in desperate need of a job.   **199**

The size and impersonality of the group made up of the poor, the sick, and the handicapped, and their segregation from healthy and affluent citizens, have made it impossible for those who need help and those who need *to* help to come together and communicate with each other. It is one thing to read statistics about the poor, the sick, and the lonely in a community and quite another thing to learn about or encounter a specific, identifiable individual who needs a form of help that many people can and wish to give.

Like so much else in advanced industrial societies, altruism has become bureaucratic. We help the unfortunate largely through taxes and through private philanthropy administered by professionals and officials. The stigmatized and the unsuccessful are herded together in institutions or in distinct areas that the "normal" majority is aware of but rarely, if ever, personally experiences. From time to time, the mass media discover the myriad islands of wretchedness that exist in our midst. But for the most part, the poor, the sick, the abandoned are abstractions, not concrete individuals who not only need material help but the personal care and concern of another human being.

Both the receiver and the giver are humanized in the altruistic transaction. When communities were smaller and technology was simpler, there was a tradition of mutual aid among people of modest means, and noblesse oblige among the aristocracy. There was, to be sure, a great deal of inequality and injustice as well, and I certainly am not suggesting a return to the past. I am merely saying that altruistic activity is a very important element in creating and sustaining a sense of community. Industrialization, urbanization, and bureaucratization undermine the opportunity **200** and the motivation of society's members to enact the role of citizen in a direct and meaningful way. When this is missing from the collective life of a people, it impoverishes an individual's life, weakens the bonds between society's members, and thereby ultimately undermines the collectivity as a whole.

Many years ago, Simmel made an observation about America that unfortunately continues to be true today:

. . . An English proverb says: "the business of everybody is the business of nobody." The peculiar fact that actions become negative once a plurality engages in them, is also shown in the motive in terms of which an attempt has been made at explaining the forbearance and indolence, in regard to public evils, of the (otherwise so energetic) North Americans. Public opinion there, the explanation runs, is supposed to bring about everything. Hence the fatalism which, "making each individual feel his insignificance, disposes him to leave to the multitude the task of setting right what is everyone's business just as much as his own." [10]

Since Simmel made this astute observation we have moved away from a policy of laissez-faire and toward the welfare state. Altruism has been organized and bureaucratized. The individual citizen's responsibility is merely to pay taxes for the establishment and maintenance of various programs run by professionals and officials. Yet there is a vast difference between altruistic activity that involves merely the obligatory and regular payment of money and that which involves individual service to others or to a specific neighborhood or community. To be sure, people can still volunteer their services in various private or quasi-private social service enterprises. But the number who feel obligated to en-   **201** gage in community or public service are a tiny fraction of the population, far smaller than those who marry, raise children, or are gainfully employed. We continue to believe that the public good is best served by pursuing our own private goals and interests. Merely paying taxes that pay the salaries of public officials does not, however, produce a sense of community. The fact that most people give no public service of any kind, and except in the case of military service, are not obliged to do so, explains the lack of public concern and social responsibility in American society.

Machines and bureaucratic organizations have freed us from the tasks that once filled and enriched people's lives. Ordinary citizens today, particularly youth and older people, have more leisure than ever before. Increasingly, people in later life sense that their lives lost meaning when their child-rearing responsibilities ended. The same dissatisfaction is found among many young people, particularly those from more affluent homes. Because they themselves have had all forms of care and comfort and because they know these advantages do not rest on their own merit or achievement but merely on the accident of birth, they feel guilty and unworthy. Many of them go to college because that is what their parents want them to do. But it is not what they want, because going to college means postponing the opportunity to perform socially productive work—that is, work that furthers the public good and not merely their own self-interest.

Affluent societies waste not only their material resources but also youth's energy and idealism. Instead of providing social mechanisms to make use of such precious resources, adults exhort youth to be "realistic"; that is to say, self-interested, ambitious, and self-seeking. Many par- **202** ents fear and oppose their children's altruistic inclinations because altruism is not part of a materialistic society's cultural script. Pecuniary and status ambitions are the driving forces in the adult world, not altruism. This is the reason for America's inability to use all its resources to eradicate poverty and its attendant problems.

This same society ignores older people—their accumulated experience, their skills, and, most of all, their desire to perform useful roles that would sustain their self-respect and earn them the respect of others. The young and the old are excluded from society's productive or generative systems. They are "free" of responsibility for anyone but themselves, and this demoralizes them. Simmel writes of the reason for this:

> Man does not only want to be free, but wants to use his freedom for some purpose. . . . To a great extent, freedom consists in a process of liberation; it rises above a bond, contrasts with a bond; it finds its meaning, consciousness, and value only as a reaction to it. But it no less consists of a power relation to others, in the possibility of making oneself count within a given social relationship, in the obligation of submission of others, in which alone it finds its value and application. The significance of freedom as something limited to the subject himself thus appears as the watershed between its two social functions as it were; and they are based on the simple fact that the individual is tied by others and ties others. . . .[11]

Both the young and the old occupy a marginal position in the family and occupational structure. Neither group feels itself a part of any common enterprise. Youth views the university as an "ivory tower," not an integral part of collective life. I do not share this view of the university. But if young people, during their years at school, have no productive work that benefits any collectivity, their freedom becomes oppressive. Hurrying them into higher education, marriage, work, and parenthood when they can expect to live to age seventy and beyond is close to insanity. Certainly it is irrational to push people into the occupational structure at an early age so that we can retire earlier—and just as irrational to encourage early marriage if we are concerned about overpopulation.

The young need an opportunity to perform useful, socially relevant roles so as to establish a sense of efficacy; older people need productive roles for the same reason. The answer to both groups' needs, it seems to me, lies in the creation of new obligatory social roles in the public sector. Massive problems confront American society. Despite its enormous wealth, despite modest attempts to deal with our national problems in the areas of poverty, health care, and education, the ills of our society persist and proliferate. Much significant, essential work lies waiting while there are millions of young and old people eager to be useful. These human resources, now wasted, can and must be mobilized and organized to perform the work.

We have institutionalized the national service of young men to wage war. We are equally capable, if we have the will and imagination, to institutionalize obligatory civic service, not once but at several points in the lives of *all* citizens. For example, a period of civilian service following high school would involve youth in the task of reconstructing society. Instead of merely acting as critics, they can and should be mobilized to participate in the solution of national and communal problems. Youths from advantaged

204

homes should be given the opportunity to learn and perform manual tasks. Those from disadvantaged homes should be given compensatory education to overcome the handicaps they face in the labor market. And *the personnel for training the young can be drawn from the ranks of retired people.* Young people's energy and enthusiasm can be brought together with older people's experience and knowledge. The care and socialization of children in agriculture, the crafts, and the professions would involve the elderly population's skills that now go unused. The elderly could also work in a network of day nurseries and health clinics in cooperation with the young.

The institution of obligatory service would mean a vast amount of planning and organization. But no other society has better resources and skills to undertake and successfully carry through such a vast undertaking.

It is time to revise our concept of what constitute the obligations of citizenship. Our laissez-faire approach to the solution of national problems undercuts our avowed concern for creating in Americans a sense of national purpose. The more affluent we become as a nation, the more we mechanize and automate our systems of production and consumption; the more leisure we create, the more fragmented and demoralized our society will become. Erazim Kohak explains why this is so in his analysis of youth in post-industrial society:

> A basic problem for any society beyond subsistence level is one of providing compensatory mechanisms for technological alienation. . . . In the age of scarcity, liberals assumed that once the goods of daily life became available with minimum effort, human life would be freed from drudgery, and human

energy would flow into "creative" tasks. They did not anticipate the secondary effect: that human life will be deprived of the token tasks through which man builds a sense of self-confident identity, relates effort and effect, and gains the habits of work demanded by creative effort; in short, that man, no longer forced to manipulate his world, will lose his ability to conceptualize it.

In the postindustrial age, a quasi-magical relation of push-button and instant product replaces effort as the basic experienced link between man and his world. It not only expresses but also reinforces human alienation in the machine world.[12]

Because America is the most advanced industrial society in the world, we are often a model for less developed nations. Those that follow our example, it is already clear, will also inherit our problems. As they increase the quantity of goods and leisure, they will suffer the same impoverishment of national spirit and purpose now visible in America.

Only one underdeveloped nation with massive problems of overpopulation has deliberately avoided using the American pattern as a model. That nation, of course, is China. I believe that we could benefit if we studied how it has gone about mobilizing its vast population to construct a modern nation. Particularly interesting is China's willingness to subordinate material goals to ideological principles. When the political leadership discerned among the more privileged sections of Chinese society a diminution of fervor toward the revolution in favor of increasing their private interests and advantages, the "cultural revolution," reputedly conceived and led by Mao, was launched to rekindle a collective revolutionary spirit, a rededication to the original goals of the revolution. To most Americans, dedicated as we are to materialism, it seemed irrational for the Chinese to interrupt their drive toward economic progress for ideological reasons. Nevertheless, though many of its methods are alien to us, the Chinese experience is instructive, if we believe James Reston's reports from China.

> . . . Everywhere the scenes are intensely human and alive—but everywhere.
> This sense of youthful activity is not only physical but mental. In the twenty-one years since the Communist takeover, the people had not had time to settle into any stable routine, and even when they seemed to be doing so in 1966, the leadership convulsed them into new and dramatic patterns of life with the Cultural Revolution. This has now passed through its violent phase when the young were encouraged to challenge the leaders of the bureaucracy and even some of the leaders of the Communist party, but it is far from over yet.
> Accordingly, China is still in a highly active state of transformation where all workers, peasants, teachers, students and even technicians and other professionals are challenged daily to self-criticism and self-improvement in the performance of their tasks. Thus there is no time even for older men and women to settle down and relax. One is constantly reminded here of what American life must have been like on the frontier a century ago. The emphasis is on self-reliance and hard work, innovation and the spirit of cooperation in building something better and larger than anything they have known before.[13]

America needs this kind of community spirit. Toward its creation we must actively direct our thought, material resources, and organizational skills. We must recognize that the pursuit of personal happiness is not a satisfactory ideology for a society to live by, for happiness is strangely elu-

207

sive when it is pursued solely for private ends and by private means. But a sense of community and of collective purpose cannot be created without enhancing the role of citizen far beyond what it is today. Everyone should enjoy productive, socially useful work. Constructing labels like "senior citizen" as a euphemism for old people will no longer do. "Senior citizen" is not an effective social role but one that excludes older people from much of society. Were older people given an opportunity to enact the role of citizen, in its fullest sense, by performing active service in and for the community, that label could have a substance and meaning that it does not now have. When that happens, growing old will no longer be the grim and fearsome prospect it is today; it will become that stage in life when men and women, no longer spending and acquiring, can look forward to attaining humanity and self-integrity, not through the pursuit of pleasure and diversion but mainly through altruistic activity.

ROLe exIT:

A THEORETICAL ESSAY

Role exit occurs whenever any stable pattern of interaction and shared activities between two or more persons ceases. "Loss," "separation," "departure," and "ending" are terms that signify exit from a social role. They engender feelings of deprivation, sadness, depression, and uncertainty similar in character, if not in intensity or duration, to those precipitated by a loved person's death. For the sense of bereavement is caused not merely by the death itself but also by the termination of any enduring pattern of activity between one person and a significant other.[1]

PROCESS AND MEANING

Role exit comes about in one of four ways. One way is through an act of nature, outside the domain of human volition, a role partner's death being the prototype. The roleless status of widowhood or of orphanhood designates such an exit from institutional roles.[2] Another way is through voluntary action, when a person decides to leave a relationship or a group. Desertion of others is the prototype of this mode of role exit. Its reciprocal form, involuntary exit, is the third way: to be left by a role partner is to be abandoned. The fourth way is expulsion by a group or larger collectivity, which is equivalent to banishment or excommunication.

There are important differences in the meaning of these four events. An exit precipitated by death from natural causes or some other disaster does *not* have invidious implications because it is not the motivated act of a human agent. The response to death is grief, undiluted by either shame or guilt.[3]

Role exits precipitated by a motivated act always have　**210** an invidious meaning. A person who voluntarily leaves his role partner feels guilty because he has violated the norms of faithfulness and loyalty that he internalized in childhood: to desert others is to betray trust and inflict pain upon them.[4] Guilt feelings are most intense in exits from diffuse, enduring relationships, such as marriage and filial relationships. But they are also present, in a modified degree, when a person leaves one job for another, moves out of a neighborhood, or emigrates to another community or country; he is abandoning those people with whom he had established relationships in these social contexts.[5]

People who voluntarily relinquish a social role do so, as a rule, not merely because they are alienated from a role partner or role set but also because they have the hope or promise of greater satisfactions or benefits from some other role. These expected rewards make them willing to bear the guilt that is the cost of an actual (or even a contemplated) desertion of a significant person or collectivity.

Role exits that come about through abandonment by a partner or a collectivity have the most invidious implications of all. In such cases one individual is rejected by another, and to be thus abandoned is to feel unloved, betrayed, and demeaned. Shame, not guilt, is the by-product of desertion by another person or banishment by a group. Such feelings constitute basic threats to self-esteem. For, to a very large degree, self-evaluations are social products forged out of other people's responses in various social role contexts. Although a person's primary underlying self-concept is formed during childhood within the context of his own family, it is continually modified in other social contexts in which he plays roles in relation to different individuals. Personal identity is not merely the sum of roles played but also the self-image formed while performing them. Identity evolves, to some degree, with each role change; self-integrity is jeopardized at every role exit and at every role entrance. At these points, the sense of enduring self-sameness, to use Erikson's term, is disturbed, signaled by the depression that accompanies role exits and the anxiety that accompanies role entrances. When a person gives up a role, he loses a part of himself and is uncertain and has self-doubts about his identity, depending on the significance the role had for him and also on what precipitated his exit from that role.

Voluntary relinquishment of a role, for several reasons, usually produces less disturbance in the self. First, the choice of continuing the role or relinquishing it is up to the person who leaves, not his role partner. Although the period of decision before role exit may cause some strain, a process of anticipatory socialization occurs, which prepares the individual for assuming the new role and relinquishing the old one. Most important, however, is that the decision to relinquish a role is generally not made until the individual has some other role option, or is considering one, and this can be a restitution for the role he is giving up. Voluntary role exit, in short, implies that the process of reintegration of the self began before the exit and that restitution for the relinquished role is at hand, so to speak, in the form of the new role the person is entering.

Involuntary exits, whether precipitated by a natural, sudden event or by the desertion of another, offer no comparable forms of anticipatory detachment to facilitate exit and to allay the diffusion of identity engendered by role exit. The person's feelings of desolation and impoverishment are

212

more prolonged; he experiences uncertainty and self-doubt. The old pattern of his existence has been disrupted and he has no immediate plans or prospects around which to re-form his self-concept.

The individual who has been deserted by a significant role partner or banished by a collectivity is, in addition to the strains already mentioned, burdened by the pain induced by social rejection—that is, the loss of another's love, concern, compassion, or esteem. He is not merely diminished by exit from a role but also demeaned in the process. At issue is not only the diffusion of identity induced by role changes but also the additional strain of feeling rejected and demeaned. Self-love and self-respect in *every* stage of life are contingent on responses of those role partners and those role sets that are most significant to the individual. Generally speaking, an adult and his society believe that institutional roles—marriage, parenthood, occupation—are the ones most important. Therefore marital, filial, and occupational relationships become the anchoring points of adult identity, particularly if the individual lacks other role resources that can extend the range of his influence and of the social influences that form and sustain his identity.

Understanding how the two major role exits of old age come about helps to explain the difference in their meaning and effect. An unanticipated finding of my study, corroborated by others, is that retirement has more detrimental effects than widowhood on the associational life, morale, and self-concept of older people, particularly men.

Widowhood, because it is not the result of a motivated human act, does not have an invidious meaning for the surviving marital partner. Although it constitutes a personal

213

tragedy and evokes more intense suffering, grief, and desolation in the short run than does retirement, the pain is lessened by the passage of time and the solicitude of kin and friends.

Retirement—particularly compulsory, abrupt, total retirement at an arbitrarily fixed age—is a relatively new *social* practice that increasingly victimizes large numbers of elderly people. It is not considered a tragedy because society accords it legitimacy. Were a retirant to display the grief and pain caused by ending his occupational life, or even admit them to himself, his response would be viewed as excessive and inappropriate, whereas the expression of grief is expected and allowed when a spouse dies. No rituals of bereavement and mourning mark this momentous status passage, except perhaps for the farewell party with speeches and a gift from the company. Yet this social occasion is comparable to a funeral because it too has a boundary-maintenance function. The funeral is a social ritual that immediately precedes the burial; it is the last social act directed toward the individual, except for the actual interment of the body; it is the final separation of the dead from the living.

Symbolically, the retirant's farewell party has the same function, marking his separation from his work group, his firm, and the world of the gainfully employed. The important differences, of course, are that the ritual of separation and banishment concerns a conscious human being and that the exit results from a *motivated* act of fellowmen. It reflects the social judgment and policy of a collectivity that men or women beyond a certain age are not fit to work or that their services are no longer necessary. The impersonal **214** character of the decision does not vitiate its invidious meaning. If anything, it does the opposite, for it rules out consideration of a person's past contributions, present ability, or willingness to work. It is social rejection not unlike the job discrimination practiced against other minority groups—blacks, Puerto Ricans, women. But retirement at an arbitrary age has official and public sanction, whereas exclusionary practices toward other minorities are covert and unofficial. Retirement does not merely exclude the older person from the world of work; it is a form of banishment of one individual by a collectivity. The retirant has been a member of the same occupational collectivity from which he is expelled in old age, just as the excommunicant has been a member of the church, or the dishonorably discharged soldier a member of the army. The difference is that the excommunicant and the ex-soldier are banished because they violated an important norm of the collectivity, not because they happened to reach a certain age.

Aging is an inevitable and natural phenomenon that all living things experience, as they do death. Since retirement is imposed arbitrarily and not because of any transgression by the individual, the collectivity makes some restitution to the person for his banishment. Social security and private pension systems represent the principal forms of official restitution thus far institutionalized.[6] Separation pay, the farewell party, and the retirement gift are other forms of restitution, but these are mainly symbolic rituals, of meager material help to the banished person. They do not in any significant way compensate for the social cost of losing his valued activities and relationships.

As an ego defense, many people deny the threat, pain,

and shame evoked by social rejection. Thus a person abandoned by a spouse or lover frequently believes the relationship ended at his instigation, not that of the role partner. Or a person facing the threat of dismissal from a position will be allowed the face-saving device of resigning for "reasons of health" or for "personal reasons." In much the same way, many older retirants claim health as the reason for their retirement. Researchers take this claim at face value and classify them under the category of "voluntary" retirees. But this simply contradicts the fact that most firms have a policy of *compulsory* retirement at a certain age, beyond which a worker cannot remain employed. The only option open to employees is to retire early, usually at a smaller pension, or to remain on the job until they are dismissed by their employer, making them eligible for a full pension. In other words, older employees can avoid the threat of banishment by quitting their jobs—but at the cost of a smaller pension. That many people nevertheless retire early is merely an indication of how pervasive is the need to save face and avoid the pain of rejection.

Illness and physical incapacity are the only culturally legitimate grounds on which adult males are freed from the obligation to work. Men governed by the Protestant work ethic often find it difficult or impossible to reconcile themselves to the idleness retirement imposes on them in old age. They frequently express feelings of uselessness and worthlessness. But if troublesome physical symptoms develop, their idleness can be legitimated on natural grounds and they can escape the guilt and feelings of worthlessness that normally accompany normative violations.

Indeed, two longitudinal studies of retirants, based on **216** physicians' ratings as well as subjective ones, show that it is not unusual for older workers before retirement to develop physical and psychological symptoms that subside or disappear after retirement. Evidence of this kind strongly suggests that the prospect of, and the conflicts associated with, retirement can cause illness, rather than that illness leads to retirement, as has been commonly supposed. It is as though the psyche produces confirmatory evidence in the form of somatic symptoms to support the claim of older men that they *chose* to retire for health reasons.

Psychoanalytic and psychosomatic medical literature recognizes the narcissism of the sick and the old as a common form of defense against the ego threat caused by personal losses.[7] Illness enables the individual to retreat from role strains and conflicts, providing a rationale for him to focus his solicitude and concern upon himself.

Illness also constitutes a social role for people who have been deprived of a value role or who believe this prospect to be imminent.[8] Children, kin, and friends feel constrained to visit and perform services for an older person who is ill, which they would do less frequently were he well. At the hospital, his contacts with physicians and other medical personnel represent another source of help and attention not available to the healthy older person. The sick role, in short, provides an individual with a defense against the shame engendered by desertion and banishment, and a form of restitution for the roles he is forced to relinquish.

But only for a short time. When the illness becomes prolonged, the elderly patient's children and relatives seek relief from the burden of caring for him by sending him to a hospital or nursing home—from which he never returns because there is no other place for him to go. A *temporary* illness, in short, has social and psychological uses for the older person. When it is prolonged, however, it serves to legitimate the permanent banishment of the aged to total-care institutions.[9]

ROLE EXIT AND IDENTITY

Traditionally, the boundary between middle and old age has been ambiguous and variable. In American society, the enactment of the Social Security Act in 1935, which set sixty-five as the age when a person becomes eligible for a pension, established a formal definition of the lower limit of old age. It also established a norm that governs retirement from the occupational structure. The existence of this norm exerts pressure on older people, particularly retirants, to relinquish their middle-aged identity. Nevertheless, most people in their sixties maintain a middle-aged self-concept, an indication that people resist the influence of formal norms that threaten their integrity. Older people try to believe they are middle-aged as long as they can, not only because of a need to sustain their sense of sameness but also because old age is devalued in a changing, youth-oriented society.

The nature of the *psychological* mechanisms that people mobilize to defend and sustain their identity is the province of psychology. But identification of the *social* mechanisms that defend and sustain identity is the province of sociology.

An indication that chronological age is merely a limiting condition, and not the major determinant of age identity, is that people in their sixties and beyond who still perform institutional roles continue to think of themselves as middle-aged and that their close associates agree with this view. These roles, therefore, constitute an anchor of middle-aged identity that enables older people to resist the influence of the official norm.

Exit from either the occupational role or the role of marital partner, through retirement or widowhood, undermines older people's resistance to the official norm and makes them more vulnerable to its pressure to relinquish their middle-aged identity. But retirement, more than widowhood, makes this identity change difficult to resist, because it removes them from a *set* of social relationships, whereas widowhood involves the loss of a single, albeit highly significant, relationship.

That social networks, as distinct from discrete relationships, are important for identity becomes evident when the self-concepts of older people who have experienced role exit but participate in a friendship network are compared with those who do not. People maintain their middle-aged identity more frequently if they belong to a friendship clique. Age identity, however, does not vary, as morale does, with the *number* of friends reported by older people. It is the difference in the *nature* of influence exerted by social groups, as opposed to that exercised in discrete relationships, that explains these findings and also helps explain why individuals imbedded in a social network are in a better position to resist official norms that threaten their integrity.

A certain immutability of identity is conferred by an enduring group on its members. In stable social networks of friends, kin, or co-workers, the recurrent interaction among **219** them gradually becomes patterned. As shared images and expectations arise, these tend to persist and to influence subsequent interaction in the group. Moreover, because such groups generally survive the exit of any single member, they carry an authority not present in a relationship between two individuals, which ends with one partner's exit.

For these reasons, groups are better anchors of identity than discrete friendships, serve more effectively to sustain each member's sense of sameness, and make him more resistant to the influence of official norms that threaten his integrity. Thus, in old age, widowed and retired people who participate in a friendly clique more often retain their middle-aged identity than others of their own age who have experienced similar role exits but lack this bulwark of group support. An indication that the *network* of social relations is the significant variable is that age identity does not vary with the number of friendships retirants and widows have, as does morale, but only with clique membership.[10]

The number of friendships older people have does, however, operate to sustain the middle-aged identity of older people after role exit *under certain conditions*.

Retirement, as I mentioned earlier, socially signifies the onset of old age and, as a rule, has the same meaning to the older person's closest associate. Moreover, the proportion of older people who share their closest associates' conceptions of them as old is very much higher among retirants than among the still-employed.

Holding a job constitutes "objective" validation to older people and others for their claim to middle-aged status. As long as an older man performs this role, it makes little difference whether even his closest intimate thinks of **220** him as old. But retirement destroys this source of validation, and the older person's concept of his age identity then becomes more vulnerable to his closest associate's influence. The proportion of people in agreement with their associates is far higher among the retired than among the employed. This holds true, however, only for retirants who are relatively isolated from other social influences.

Retirants with more extensive friendships or kinship relations are subject to a wider range of social influences. They are therefore better able to sustain their middle-aged self-concept, even after their closest intimates come to think of them as old. Thus the opportunities for social contacts with a number of people that a job affords would appear to be an important variable in preserving an individual's autonomy in relation to his closest intimate.

Although this generalization is derived from a study of older people and their closest associates, it can easily be extended to other contexts as well. For example, it would explain why many housewives are influenced more by their husbands than their husbands are by them. But in families in which both man and wife hold jobs, an equalitarian power structure is more common. Similarly, a mother exercises a great influence over a very young child, but her influence wanes as he extends the range of his social relationships to include others in the family, and then peers, teachers, and the like. Adolescents who have extensive social contacts outside their family are less apt to be influenced by their parents than those who are relatively solitary.

Whenever people exit from a significant social role and the sameness of their identity is threatened, they become more vulnerable to their closest associates' influence.   **221**

Not merely their self-attitudes but other attitudes as well tend to become more like those of their intimates. They will seek restitution for their relinquished role by deepening their involvement in one or more of the roles that they perform permanently—or until they replace the old role, or add a new one. Thus an intimate's influence will be tempered by the other roles still in a person's repertory that operate as competing sources of influence and satisfaction. A related proposition is that the smaller a person's repertory of roles, the more subject he or she will be to the influence of a single close intimate and the less likely to exit voluntarily from that relationship.

The nature and number of social roles in a person's repertory, therefore, condition the degree of autonomy he can exercise in any given social relationship. The same variables probably also account to some degree for the differences in people's commitment to a specific role.[11]

SIGNIFICANCE OF ROLE SEQUENCES

The foregoing discussion has dealt mainly with role exit in the context of old age. Role exit, however, is also a *recurring order of events* in earlier stages of life, because there are very few statuses that people normally retain over an entire lifetime, and these few are all of an ascribed character. Although an individual maintains for a lifetime the same gender identity, race, ethnicity, and membership in a kinship group, most social roles in modern, complex societies have a more limited duration, and many of them also have a sequential character. As a rule, tenure in a particular role lasts for a varying but limited period of time, and then it is relinquished for the next in a sequence of roles that constitute a particular institutional nexus. Such role sequences are usually closely tied to stages of the life cycle, which in turn are ordered by chronological age, although the boundaries of each stage vary with the normal length of the life span. In those societies and historical epochs in which the typical life span of the individual is short, the duration of each stage of life is shorter than in contemporary, industrial societies, in which life expectancy has been considerably extended and each stage of life correspondingly prolonged. Thus in ancient times a man of forty was already old; today, life expectancy being around seventy, he is defined as middle-aged. The nature and number of the roles that the individual is expected to enact are therefore contingent more directly on his stage of life than on his chronological age.

From infancy through adulthood, the repertory of roles that a person is called upon to enact is progressively enlarged, particularly in more complex societies. As the number of group memberships expands—from the family, to peers, to the school, to a varying number of interest groups —the network of rights and obligations in which a person is involved becomes enlarged. At the same time, his expanding repertory of roles affords him the possibility of autonomy from specific others and the opportunity of influencing others. A very young child who occupies a status only within a single collectivity—the family—is wholly dependent on that particular role set, because he lacks alternatives resources of social influence and social support. Autonomy is possible only in those contexts in which the individual is in a position to make choices among alternative courses of action and alternative sources of influence. **223**

During the time the child extends his repertory of roles, his family continues as the principal role set that operates to bridge the discontinuities introduced into his life by the role entrances and exits that the cultural scripts prescribe. For example, starting school is a major role change that children—and sometimes their mothers—both anticipate and fear. It takes the child time to learn and to accustom himself to the behavior and attitudes expected of him in this new, unfamiliar social structure. Passing from one grade into another may be the child's first immediate encounter with role sequence. In this situation there are strains. Leaving a teacher to whom the child has become attached, leaving classmates, and even leaving the familiarity of a classroom induce some regret and sadness. At the same time, there is the pride that comes with promotion to a higher grade, and the anticipation of new challenges and new experiences alleviates the strains of separation from the old role. Throughout the child's role changes, his continuing membership in the family provides (at least in healthy families) an anchor of identity and a mechanism that help him to cope with the strains engendered by successive entrances and exits in school and in peer groups.

Adolescence is a difficult period because it is a time when a person is expected to loosen his bonds to his parents in preparation for leaving them and establishing his own family. This means that the young person must disengage himself from the very role set that sustained his underlying sense of sameness during the entrances and exits of childhood—and at a time when he is making decisions that will profoundly affect his future life.

The relinquishing of familiar, highly significant ties

temporarily disrupts the integrity of the self. In the middle class, adolescence, along with its identity diffusion, lasts longer than in the working class, because there is a longer period between the onset of the distancing process and the time the young person marries and takes a job—status changes that mark the passage of youth into adulthood. The adolescent in both classes, to counteract the feeling of instability and uncertainty that follow exit from his childhood role, binds himself to another role set, generally of his own sex peers or to a young person of the opposite sex. In these new bonds, the youth seeks restitution, so to speak, for losing the strong family bonds to which his identity had formerly been anchored.

Parents also undergo many of the strains associated with adolescent role exit. They, too, are in the process of relinquishing a long-enduring role marked by a high degree of activity and interaction. Parents carry a heavy burden of responsibility when their offspring are young, but they also enjoy the many rights they have over them. All too many contemporary parents, however, are more eager to relinquish the responsibilities toward their children than the rights they exercise over them—that is, they want to have their cake and eat it too.[12]

Some degree of strain always follows the end of any enduring social role, whatever satisfactions or dissatisfactions are entailed in its performance. The sense of sameness is disrupted, and the individual feels diminished and depressed for a time. Role exit, in short, produces alterations in self-concept and in mood, or what sociologists call morale. An injury to the body causes physical pain; an injury to the self induces psychic pain. Indeed, these two forms of injury constitute the principal sources of human suffering. Terms such as "lowered self-concept," "low morale," and "role strain" all refer to experiential components of what in ordinary language is meant by suffering.

It is more difficult to relinquish a satisfying relationship than one beset with strain and conflict. Nevertheless, even unhappily married people experience a sense of bereavement upon the dissolution of their marriage that is not significantly different in *kind* from the bereavement experienced by the surviving partner at the death of a spouse. Similarly, whether or not people have enjoyed their work or going to school, they miss for a time the activities and social relationships these entailed. The sense of loss, the depression of spirit, and the need for restitution are endemic to the experience of role exit. Whatever form it takes, it leaves a void, so to speak, in the self.

Gregory Rochlin has observed:

The self, when demeaned, produces conflicts and responses similar to those that may be observed in object loss. In fact, where there is a loss, self-esteem is affected. Loss and hence damage to self-esteem remain bound throughout life from early childhood onward. Therefore, in the dissolution of a meaningful relationship, a satisfying image of the self tends in part to be given up and the experience of loss becomes intensified. It is no less true, however, that loss is always followed by attempts at restitution. . . . Freud . . . stated that we never relinquish anything willingly, and in any case only when we can find a substitute for it. Depression comes to an end when a substitute for our disappointment and our lowered self-esteem is found. Restitution for impairment or a disability must be made in order that the ensuing process of lowered self-esteem and depression may terminate.[13]   **226**

Just as the basic socializing experience of infancy and early childhood can be thought of as prototypical of the process of initiation and adaptation generally entailed in role entrances, so the response to the death of a beloved or familiar person is the prototype of responses usually engendered by role exits.

The meaning and consequences of role exit are most amenable to observation and study either when a considerable time elapses between exit from a role and entry into another, as in the case of nonscheduled, fortuitous exits, such as divorce or unemployment in adulthood, or when exit from one role is not followed by a culturally prescribed entrance into another social role, as in the case of widowhood or retirement in old age.

Before old age, the *sequential ordering* of institutionalized social roles operates to obscure the recurring phenomenon of role exit. For with each culturally significant role that the maturing individual is called upon to surrender, he has a promise, so to speak, of a replacement for it—one that is usually represented as having more value, more honor, and more privileges. In addition to such inducements, a variety of social practices and mechanisms help prepare the individual to abandon old, familiar roles for new, more complex ones, at least until old age. Certain generalized orientations, first of all, are taught early: one must strive for and anticipate the rewards promised by later, more demanding roles in order to overcome the inclination to cling to the security afforded by the known, familiar aspects of living.

In American society, for example, children are taught to be ambitious and to seek success, first at home, then at school, and subsequently at work. A person is considered a failure, and invites a variety of negative sanctions, if he does not follow the progression of exits and entrances according to the prescribed timetable. The fear of failure thus overcomes the attachments the child may have formed for his teacher or classmates. He would sooner tolerate the strains of separation than risk being labeled a failure. In adulthood, a man is expected to attach greater value to the requirements of his job than to his relationship with kin, friends, his old community, and even his wife and children. A man who is not willing to relinquish such ties for a position elsewhere that promises higher status, greater remuneration, or more power is labeled ambitionless and a poor promotion risk. Similarly, children are taught early that getting married and having a family of one's own represents the highest form of happiness. Not to marry and not to bear children represent failure.

Various mechanisms are invoked or encouraged to inhibit or weaken the strong bonds of attachment that develop between parents and children, particularly in a small, isolated, nuclear family. To promote emotional "independence" in their children, parents encourage early involvement with peers and early dating, and send adolescents away to college. The cultivation of independence in children is believed to lay the foundation of an adaptable personality—that is, one that readily relinquishes old roles in the interest of acquiring new ones, undeterred by the strains engendered in doing so.

Moreover, such generalized orientations motivate the person to proceed according to the culturally prescribed timetables. Not to go the full route in any of these institutional sequences is tantamount to failure. "Dropping out" and "falling behind" have invidious connotations in American society. The meaning of both can be better understood when they are thought of in relation to the concept of role exit within the context of systems of age grading that is found in every society.

The importance of age as a sociological variable is that in all societies age grading is the basis for assigning and withholding institutional statuses. To be at the same stage in life as one's age-peers, therefore, means that one is likely to have numerous experiences in common with them—not merely similar social roles, but also being at the age when entrances and exits to and from these roles are expected to take place. Premature or delayed changes in status put an individual "out of phase" with most others in his age category. This, in turn, reduces his opportunities for association with his own age peers and reduces the pool of shared experiences between them. To be "out of phase," in short, places an individual in a deviant position vis-à-vis others in his own age group. Therefore it is likely to have some invidious effects on the person's associational life and self-concept.

"Dropout" is applied to those who prematurely exit from an institutionalized role instead of maintaining the length of tenure prescribed by that system. Although the term is used in connection with young people who fail to complete successfully the twelve years of schooling required for graduation from high school, it also applies to the youth who, going against the American middle-class pattern, chooses not to go to college directly after high school. Middle-class adults have the notion that, besides four years of college and an undergraduate degree as the minimum acceptable amount of formal education for their children, it is also necessary to maintain *continuous* tenure in the educational system, from kindergarten through college graduation. In recent years, resistance to this pattern has developed among a significant proportion of middle-class youth, who have opted for exploring other alternatives for a time —taking menial jobs, traveling, experimenting with communal forms of living, and so forth. The first reaction of parents and college officials to this departure from the subcultural middle-class script and timetable—that it was "sick" —has become tempered by time and subsequent developments. It has become clear, for example, that many young people were not so much "dropping out" as "taking time out" from a regulated, plush existence to explore other paths, discover different challenges, test their competence. Most of them do, in fact, return to school and to the cultural scripts, often with more self-direction and motivation than they would have had had they simply followed the expected pattern. Colleges and universities have begun to recognize this and to allow students more flexibility in the pursuit of a college degree, permitting them to participate in other activities and interests. In short, what we may be witnessing is a change or modification of an existing social pattern. What began as a premature role exit, carrying with it invidious connotations, may become an alternative pattern as acceptable as the traditional one. Possibly it may even become the preferred pattern, with a variety of institutionalized mechanisms to implement it in future generations.

Divorce is another instance of premature role exit, the rising incidence of which may augur significant changes in the traditional script regulating the institution of the family. **230**

Divorce represents a violation of the marriage vows to remain joined together "until death do us part." Death, being beyond human control, is, strictly speaking, the only legitimate way out of a marriage. Widowhood, therefore, whatever the age of the marital partners, does not have the invidious significance that divorce does, although both are alike in that they signify exit from a marital relationship. Widowhood is construed as a tragic outcome, but it does not, like divorce, carry with it the onus of failure.

Furthermore, widowhood in later life becomes a normal phenomenon because in contemporary societies most women seventy and beyond have experienced this form of role exit. Since the supply of men in later age groups declines considerably more than that of women, correspondingly fewer opportunities exist for older women to remarry. Widowhood in later life, therefore, represents a terminal role exit, a permanent detachment of the woman from participation in institutionalized forms of family life. Divorce, in contrast, is still an abnormal phenomenon in any age group, although in certain subgroups the divorce rate is so high that people at least once divorced probably constitute the majority group. Nevertheless, even in such contexts, divorce is experienced and viewed as failure, because it constitutes a premature role exit and a violation of the norm of permanency in marriage.

The concept of role exit is useful not merely because it directs our attention to the similarities between various forms of exit from the same social role—for example, widowhood and divorce—but also because it allows us to discover similarities in the effects of exits from different roles —for example, widowhood and retirement—when they oc- **231** cur prematurely as compared with when they occur "on time."

In my research on old age, I discovered that widowhood has a detrimental effect on the friendship associations of people in their sixties if most of their friends are still married, but it does not have the same effect on people in their seventies and beyond, when the majority of women and a larger minority of men are widowed.

This finding led me to the generalization that the effect of a major role exit on an older person's associational life depends on its *prevalence* among his age, sex, and social-class peers, because these three variables govern the selection and maintenance of friendships in all stages of life. My analysis of the effects of retirement, the other major form of role exit in old age, provided confirmation for the generalization.

From these findings, based on a study of older people, it is possible to formulate an even broader generalization: Role exit does not uniformly affect a person's social life; only role exits that occur "out of phase" with his age-sex-class peers will have isolating effects, whereas those that occur at the "normal" time will not. But it would be extremely difficult to derive this order of generalization from a study of the general adult population. For widowhood, divorce, unemployment, "dropping out" of school—each signifying exit from a social role in a core institutional system—are phenomena that involve only a minority. Because each of these role exits places the individual in a different status from most of his age-sex-class peers, each can be expected to have detrimental effects on his social life, to the extent that the latter has been contingent on the performance of

232

that particular role. But if within his own sub-set—that is, his circle of friends and acquaintances—a particular form of role exit *is* prevalent, then it will be the social life of the person who maintains tenure in that role that will suffer. Thus it could be predicted that the rarer a role exit is in a given subgroup, the more likely it is that the individual who experiences it will find himself more isolated socially, at least for a time, than he has formerly been.

The converse is true in those social contexts in which a particular form of role exit is culturally prescribed and/or prevalent. There the social life of persons who do not experience role exit at the customary time will be adversely affected, at least for a while, to the extent that their social life is confined primarily to age and sex peers. The school-child who is left behind when his age group is promoted will be forced to seek friendships with the younger children in his grade. Post-college youths who stay single at a time when their peers are marrying immediately after graduation are likely to be left out of the young couples' social activities and will have to seek new social settings in which to meet other unmarried young people.[14]

OTHER FORMS OF ROLE RESTITUTION

Role sequences represent only one form of restitution for culturally prescribed role exits. A second common form of restitution consists of repetition of the relinquished role. Remarriage, reemployment, job transfers, conversion to another faith, changing from one political party to another, immigration to a new country—all constitute role repetitions. The rights and responsibilities are similar to those of the former role, although no two role partners or role

233

sets are identical. Thus a widow or divorcee, already accustomed to living as a married person, is usually eager to remarry—the easiest and most direct form of restitution for the loss of familiar habits and pleasures. Role repetitions do not require, as a rule, the same amount of personal change as do new and different social roles; and if the relinquished role was satisfying, a person is inclined to seek a replica of a former role partner or role set. If it was not satisfying, he will seek a role partner or role set with different qualities. Yet the inclination to repeat a role, rather than find a new and different role, is very common, particularly with institutional roles. Because they *are* obligatory, such roles come to be considered the most important achievements in life. For example, a divorced person may find many of the same satisfactions, or possibly even more happiness, in an enduring love affair. Nevertheless, such a relationship, whatever meaning and authenticity it offers the lovers, does not have the cultural legitimacy of marriage. Lovers are pressured either to legitimate their relationship by transforming it into a marriage or, if that is impossible, to relinquish that relationship in favor of one in which marriage is possible. For even when marriage does not promise much gratification, it confers a coveted status on the individual because it carries with it the public rights and privileges, whatever the private reality may be, that a love affair does not. Moreover, to marry is to conform not merely to cultural expectations but also to most other people. Not to marry, in contrast, places the person in a deviant position and exposes him or her to the difficulties society creates for those who are different.

The same pressures operate upon men to perform some kind of occupational role. Even wealthy men with ample independent resources feel constrained to perform gainful work, which distinguishes a vocation—considered obligatory and carried out by most men—from an avocation, which is merely optional. Occupation is the core role for American males. More than any other, it determines and defines their adult social identity. That is one reason why retirement, even though institutionalized, has more pronounced effects on the identity and morale of older men than it does on older women, for whom the occupational role is not obligatory but merely optional. Marriage and motherhood are the main roles that define the social identity and associational life of adult women.

A third analytically distinct mode of restitution connected with role exit is for the person to reallocate involvement in remaining roles in his repertory, thereby restoring the sense of integrity or of wholeness to the self that was disrupted by relinquishment of the former role. For example, following widowhood or divorce, people often begin to invest more time and effort in their jobs. Greater involvement and investment of time in each other has been reported on the part of aging married people after their children leave home and after retirement. Among divorcees, more intense involvement with their children is a common compensatory response. Adolescents loosening their bonds to parents attach themselves more strongly to a set of friends, or to someone of the opposite sex. Older people spend more time with friends or relatives who have experienced similar exits after widowhood and retirement under certain conditions. New immigrants gravitate toward communities, neighborhoods, and organizations composed of fellow immigrants from the same country. In short, people often immerse themselves in other roles in their repertory as a means of alleviating the strains and deprivations engendered by exit from a significant role.

The number of roles in a person's repertory assumes new importance in this context, for these indicate the social resources that he has at hand to deploy when a significant role must be relinquished. Although people, as a rule, invest mainly in institutional roles—marriage, parenthood, work—those who do so exclusively are more vulnerable to demoralization and ego diffusion after role exit than are people who have engaged in non-obligatory social roles as well. The operation of this principle can be most systematically studied in old age, for only then does exit from the two core social roles tend to become typical. But the principle also operates in other stages of life and helps to account for differences in people's responses to the vicissitudes of social living.

In old age, for example, many studies, including my own, show that a person suffers a cumulative decline in morale, depending on the number of major role exits he has experienced. The proportion of the elderly who exhibit low morale is highest among those who are widowed *and* retired, and lowest among those still married *and* employed. The proportion with high morale among those who have experienced one form of role exit is intermediate. In other words, old people who retain one major institutional role can utilize it to counteract the strains of having lost the other role by investing themselves more heavily in the activities and relationships that the remaining obligatory role still affords them. For the person who loses both roles, this type of restitution is, of course, not available.

Those alienated from a significant role also seek restitution. Thus it is not unusual that when men experience dissatisfactions or tensions at work they look for alleviation of these strains in their home life. Indeed, an important responsibility of women is to nurture and help not only their children but also their husbands. Conversely, a common male response to marital dissatisfaction is a heavier investment in the occupational role; they work harder and longer and take more business trips. Since employment traditionally is not an obligatory role for women, this form of restitution for marital strain is less often available to them. They are more inclined, therefore, to seek alternative satisfactions in their children or in friendships with members of their own sex.

Most people experience a progressive impoverishment in their role resources as they grow older. Children leave home, old friends die or move away, a married couple's patterns of sociability are disrupted by the death of a spouse, and social contacts on the job are disrupted by retirement. At this point in life, therefore, optional social roles—particularly avocations and friendships—assume great significance in sustaining life satisfaction and self-integrity. My research shows, for example, that the number of friends people have makes little difference in the morale and self-concepts of older people so long as they are married or employed, but among the retired and widowed, the extent of social participation becomes critical for the maintenance of morale. Other studies show that avocations, or "non-interpersonal activities," sustain morale in later life in much the same way as do interpersonal activities.[15]

The morale and the self-concept of older working-class   **237** people are more vulnerable than those of middle-class people. Working-class people have fewer role resources during their adulthood. As a rule, they follow the cultural scripts more closely and exclusively than do the middle-class, and are therefore even more susceptible to the vicissitudes of old age. They have less formal education, and often a more constricted outlook on life. They read less, and have fewer skills and little interest in an avocation. They belong to fewer organizations and engage less in all forms of political activity than do middle-class people. They have fewer friendships, and those they have tend to be centered in the neighborhood and on the job. Since they stay in school for only the legally prescribed number of years, their options on the job market are restricted. This generally insulates them from an awareness and interest in the other role options available in complex, urban societies—options that better-educated, more cosmopolitan, and more affluent members of society are more likely to discover and utilize. Working-class people, in short, have a smaller, less varied repertory of optional social roles, and as a result must lead a more restricted existence than the middle class.

The proposition being advanced here is that the greater the number of optional role resources with which the individual enters old age, the better he or she will withstand the demoralizing effects of exit from the obligatory roles ordinarily given priority in adulthood. Each role in the adult's repertory represents a reserve of social resources, to be drawn upon in times of need—like savings in times of economic hardship. The same principle probably also operates before old age whenever a crisis necessitates the abrogation of a culturally significant social role. (But the crises

that are exceptional during adulthood become routine in
old age, to paraphrase Everett Hughes's astute comment
about physicians.)

It is important to enter old age with optional roles because opportunities to gain new ones are far more restricted
then than in earlier stages of life. Friendships, participation
in voluntary associations, and even avocational interests are,
to a great degree, contingent on the performance of an institutional role. This often becomes apparent only following
role exit. Job-connected friendships, for example, are disrupted when an individual retires. The opportunities for
contact between the retirant and his former associates, as
well as the common run of experiences on the basis of
which such friendships flourish, decline. Similarly, a
spouse's death disrupts friendships with other couples. The
surviving partner, as a lone individual, becomes less useful
in social occasions dominated by married couples, in which,
for example, divisions in conversation occur along sex
lines, or dinner tables and card tables are set up for couples.

The same processes that disrupt role-contingent friendships in old age also restrict opportunities to form new
friendships. People generally do not form friendships hap-
hazardly, but mainly in the particular role contexts in which
they have opportunities for recurrent contact with others of
like age and social status—at school, at work, in the neighborhood, and in voluntary associations. Large differences in
age operate as a barrier to the formation of friendships, because people's roles, and therefore their needs and interests,
differ from one stage to another. As they grow older they
discover that younger people predominate in most formal
organizations and voluntary associations, often filling offices   **239**

vacated by the death or retirement of older members. The same process occurs in neighborhoods. The aging population tends to leave a neighborhood of single-family residences and to move to smaller, less expensive quarters. Those older people who remain in any of these contexts become an ever-declining minority. They feel out of place and isolated, so they withdraw. But every departure or withdrawal diminishes their chances to meet people socially and to form new friendships.

This process becomes reversed only in those social contexts in which one's age group is clustered. Opportunities for new friendships and other optional roles are promoted by concentrations of older people in particular communities, apartments, and housing projects.[16] This goes against the ideological grain of Americans, who like to pretend that creed, color, age, and sex have nothing to do with the social opportunity structure, despite strong empirical evidence to the contrary.

So long as older people are excluded from participation in society's major social institutions—jobs, schools, the family—those who live in areas with a high density of older people will have social opportunities that would not be available if they were dispersed throughout the community. Should new roles for the aging become institutionalized, alternative mechanisms would arise to create new social opportunities. Then place of residence, as such, would become less important as a force to counteract the isolating effects of exit from the core social roles.

The three forms of restitution outlined above can be invoked not merely after role exit occurs but also before and in anticipation of it. A period of courtship before marriage eases the young couple's exit from their family homes and paves the way for their assumption of the marital role. The senior research paper required of honors students for graduation from college prepares them for the more rigorous requirements of graduate school. An employee aspiring to promotion often takes on duties similar or identical to those of the new role before exiting from his old position. Marriage partners planning a divorce may facilitate the transition in several ways. One or both may enter an extramarital sexual relationship. The wife may return to school or take a job before exiting from marriage. Or each of the partners may begin to see more of old friends or renew old solitary pastimes so that they may better fortify themselves against the strain of leaving or being left by the other marital partner. Learning the language and customs of another country often signals a person's intent to emigrate from his native land. Upwardly mobile people who aspire toward a higher social stratum will first strive to acquire the attitudes and values characteristic of that stratum.

The concept of "anticipatory socialization," as formulated by Robert Merton and Alice Rossi, is pertinent to role exit, since it refers to those changes in attitudes or behavior that precede entrance into new groups or collectivities. Implicit in the concept is that the same attitudes and behavior that orient individuals to new roles also facilitate exits from old ones. Although in concrete terms the two processes are often indistinguishable, it is important to make an analytical distinction between them. For role changes involve not merely the "pull" of a new role but also the "push" from an old one. In the process of role change, some external pres- **241** sure to relinquish a role, or an inner alienation from it, constitutes the initiatory phase. The process may be aborted at this stage or may continue if the individual becomes aware of a better alternative. His knowledge and selection of an alternative to the present role begins the process of anticipatory socialization that furthers his readiness to relinquish the old role in favor of a new one. But actual role exit from the one requires opportunities for access to the other. In short, the promise of, and opportunities for, restitution must exist before a person voluntarily relinquishes a role, no matter how unsatisfactory it may be.

Arnold van Gennep, the German anthropologist, long ago identified three elements universally found in rites of passage—those ceremonies that accompany culturally significant turning points in the life cycle. Symbolically represented in these rites are the phases of separation from an earlier status, transition from one status to another, and incorporation into a new status.

Entrances into new roles are characteristically accompanied by initiation rites. The individual must make vows, as in the marriage ceremony, or fill out documents. Or he may be required to pass tests of skill or endurance as conditions of entry into new statuses and/or new collectivities, such as educational institutions, professions, work organizations, the armed services, or voluntary associations. Following his certification, there is generally some customary form of initiation, or socialization, into the rights and duties of the new role: the honeymoon following marriage; the novitiate in religious orders; the rookie period in professional sports; the apprenticeship in crafts and skilled trades; the orientation period in educational institutions and business firms;

242

basic training in the army; and so forth. All these socialization experiences are an attenuated reenactment of the pervasive, more extended process of socialization that takes place in everyone's infancy and early childhood. Indeed, socialization is a key concept in sociology, serving as the analytical link between the diverse forms of entry into new relationships and new collectivities that individuals experience during their lives. Socialization theory deals with the processes that help people to acquire the knowledge, attitudes, and skills necessary to meet the expectations of role partners and role sets.

Though this theory is still in a rudimentary stage of development, it at least constitutes a generic concept useful for making analytic comparisons between substantively distinct types of role entrances. But the same cannot be said for the process of separation from social roles, although it too constitutes a generic process in social life.

Criticism of sociological jargon is not entirely unwarranted. It is important, however, to distinguish jargon from concepts. Concepts are primary and indispensable tools of every generalization discipline, for they select and order those aspects of reality to be observed and explained by a discipline. They serve to identify some analytically similar property shared by phenomena that in reality are distinct and different from each other. Until a concept exists to identify such similarities, no relationship will be perceived between them.

The term "role loss," commonly used in the literature on old age to refer to retirement and widowhood, tends to emphasize the involuntary character of these two experiences. One does not think of such events as graduation, promotion, or marriage as involving role losses, because such status changes have positive connotations, implying not merely a person's departure from a status in one collectivity but also entry into another status.

"Role exit" is a more neutral and more comprehensive term. Although I had no problem conceiving of widowhood and retirement as comparable events, I missed the similarities between those status changes of old age and the multitude of other such changes that occur in earlier stages of life—until I formulated the concept of role exit. After that, it was impossible *not* to see that role exit is a generic process in social life.

The concept, in turn, produced a series of theoretical propositions. Role exit has three kinds of specifiable and verifiable effects on individuals: it produces changes in an individual's associational life, his self-concept, and his mood. The duration and intensity of these effects are conditioned by the nature and extent of other role resources at his disposal and by the prevalence of a given role exit among his peers. These two variables govern opportunities for, and access to, restitution through which reintegration of the self is achieved. The form of restitution, in turn, determines whether the enduring effects of role exit will be in the direction of growth or of impoverishment and atrophy of the individual as a social being.

I believe that it is time to begin working toward a fusion of the systematic and the humanistic perspectives in sociology. Efforts to bridge the gap between these two "cultures" would, I believe, promote the growth of each tradition and enhance the importance of sociology as a science relevant to the human condition. A great deal of

244

human suffering has social causes, as Durkheim so well understood. His work directed sociologists to the analysis of social structures from the standpoint both of the constraints they impose and the opportunities they create for lending meaning and purpose to human life. Between his macroscopic theory and Freud's microscopic theory stretches the domain of role theory, which is now in a state of arrested development. Beyond entrances, socialization, and performance of social roles lies role exit.

After role exit, what? That is an important existential issue for the human being. It is also one that can be dealt with systematically by sociologists, provided a theory exists that specifies the order of variables entailed in the process. The purpose of this essay has been to outline such a theory. It goes without saying that I hope it will stimulate further research designed to test its validity.

notes

CHAPTER I

1 Elaine Cumming and William E. Henry, *Growing Old: The Process of Disengagement* (New York: Basic Books, 1961).

2 Erich Fromm, *Escape from Freedom* (New York: Farrar and Rinehart, 1941).

3 See Matilda White Riley and Anne Foner, *Aging and Society,* vol. I, *An Inventory of Research Findings* (New York: Russell Sage Foundation, 1968), pp. 15–37. Also see United States Bureau of the Census, *Historical Statistics of the United States, 1960,* p. 8; *Current Population Reports, 1964,* P-25, no. 279, p. 5; and *Current Population Reports, 1966,* P-25, no. 359, p. 14.

4 Louis Dublin, Alfred Lotka, and Mortimer Spiegelman, *Length of Life* (New York: Ronald Press, 1949), p. 42; and Mortimer Spiegelman, *Significant Mortality and Morbidity Trends in the United States Since 1900* (Bryn Mawr, Pa.: American College of Underwriters, 1964), p. 2.

5 National Center for Health Statistics, *Vital and Health Statistics, 1964,* series 3, no. 1, pp. 8–9.

6 Conrad and Irene Tauber, *The Changing Population of the United States* (New York: Wiley, 1958), pp. 31–32; and U.S. Bureau of the Census, *Current Population Reports, 1966,* P-25, no. 286, p. 10.

7 Riley and Foner, 1968, pp. 18–19; and U.S. Bureau of the Census, *Current Population Reports, 1964,* P-25, no. 286, p. 10.

8 Paul C. Glick, David M. Heer, John C. Beresford, "Family Composition: Trends and Prospects," paper presented at the annual meeting of the American Association for the Advancement of Science, Chicago, Illinois, December, 1959, p. 12; U.S. Bureau of the Census, *1960 Census of the Population,* vol. I, pp. 424–25.

9 The process described above, long established in American society, is also taking place in new nations in an earlier stage of industrialization. For example, Marris reports that in Lagos, Nigeria, the change to smaller housing units and higher rents, from old quarters that had accommodated many members of the extended family or unrelated individuals, had a detrimental effect on formal and informal family cohesion. It also disturbed the network of social relations and mutual

obligations that existed when spatial proximity made frequent social contacts the common pattern. These social relationships had also constituted an important source of social control, and constrained even upwardly mobile individuals to carry out obligations toward members of the extended family—in the form of financial help, finding employment, and advice—thus linking non-mobiles to the larger social system, with its new opportunities and requirements. See Peter Marris, *Family and Social Change in an African City* (London: Routledge and Kegan Paul, 1961).

10 See Marvin Sussman, "The Help Patterns in the Middle Class Family," *American Sociological Review,* XVIII (1953), 22–28.

11 For a poignant delineation of the social distance that can arise between "successful" children and modestly situated older parents, see Honoré Balzac's *Old Goriot.*

12 *Statistical Abstract of the United States, 1964,* Table 309. Farm ownership, which traditionally constituted the major source of self-employment in the American economy, has, with the progressive urbanization of the population and the mechanization of agriculture, declined most sharply.

13 It is interesting to note the finding of a recent cross-national study of old age that seven out of every ten men *over* sixty-five who are still working expect to keep working until they die. In short, the large majority of men who can exercise the option choose not to retire, but this option, as I have already indicated, is not generally available. The proportion of sixty-five-year-old men still in the labor force is relatively low in all three countries studied (32 percent in the United States, 28 percent in Great Britain, and 38 percent in Denmark). See Ethel Shanas, Peter Townsend, Dorothy Wedderburn, Henning Friis, Paul Milhøj, and Jan Stenouwer, *Old People in Three Industrial Societies* (New York: Atherton Press, 1968).

14 One of the demands won by the UAW in its 1970 negotiations with automobile manufacturers is the right to retirement with some pension after thirty years' service. Such a plan could mean that a man who started work at eighteen might retire at forty-eight after thirty years' continuous service in one company.

15 "Findings of the 1963 Survey of the Aged," *Social Security Bulletin,* XXVII, 3–10.

16 Lewis Carliner, "Labor: The Anti-Youth Establishment," *New Generation,* II (Spring, 1969), 27–31.

17 Samuel Lubell, "Young Workers Harass Oldsters: 'Get Out, Retire?'," *Chicago Daily News,* May 1, 1959. The economy was in a recession when this survey was made. When jobs are plentiful, such pressures on older workers probably diminish, but it is doubtful that they vanish altogether.

18 The aged were first recognized as a special category in the U.S. Social Security Act (SSA), passed in 1935 to replace the then depression-induced direct relief programs with a program of federal financial aid to the states. The act spelled out a work program for the able-bodied unemployed and established financial relief for three distinct categories of needy people—the aged, the blind, and the dependent children, and established old age, survivors, and disability insurance (OASDI).

19 The extension of social security coverage to farmers in 1954 has promoted the pattern of retirement at age sixty-five, or even earlier, among farmers as well. "Before the extension of Social Security to farmers no formal rule even suggested a time for retirement." University of Iowa, Institute of Gerontology, *Supplement to the Bulletin,* XIII, January, 1966.

20 Talcott Parsons, "Age and Sex in the Social Structure of the United States," in *Essays in Sociological Theory, Pure and Applied* (Glencoe, Ill.: Free Press, 1949), pp. 230–31.

21 The remarriage rate for widowers sixty-five and over is 15.5 percent, while that for widows is only 2.1. See "Marriage Rates by Previous Marital Status, Age, and Marriage Registration Area," *Vital Statistics Rates in the United States: 1940–1960* (Washington, D.C.: U.S. Department of Health, Education and Welfare, 1960), p. 103.

22 "Employment After Retirement," Research Report no. 21 (Washington, D.C.: United States Department of Health, Education and Welfare, 1968).

23 See "Marital Status by Age and Sex for the United States Civilian Population," *U.S. Current Population Reports,* P-20, no. 105, March, 1962.

24 Erdman Palmore, "Retirement Patterns Among Aged Men: Findings of the 1963 Survey of the Aged," *Social Security Bulletin,* XXVII, 3–15. A much higher proportion of retirement among women can be expected in future generations. A comparison of the proportions of employed women between the ages of forty-five and sixty-four over several decades shows that in 1900 only 14 percent were employed, but by 1968 this proportion had risen to 48 percent. See *Handbook of Women Workers,* Bulletin 294 (Washington, D.C.: United States Department of Labor, Women's Bureau, 1969).

25 Gregory Rochlin, M.D., *Griefs and Discontents: Sources of Change* (Boston: Little, Brown, 1965), p. 24.

26 Thus, among people sixty-five and older in 1960, only a tiny portion had never married (7.7 among men and 8.5 among women). See *United States Census of Population, 1960,* vol. I, part 1, pp. 424–25.

27 Peter Brown, *Augustine of Hippo* (Berkeley, Cal.: University of California Press, 1967), p. 408.

CHAPTER II

1 David Schneider, *American Kinship: A Cultural Account* (Englewood Cliffs, N.J.: Prentice-Hall, 1968).

2 One study, made in the 1940's, found that in many cases parents are entirely free of child-rearing responsibilities by the time they are fifty to fifty-five years of age. See Paul Glick, "The Family Cycle," *American Sociological Review,* XII (April, 1947), 164–74. A later study in the 1950's shows that most people have completed their child-rearing responsibilities in their later forties. Paul Glick, David M. Heer, and John C. Beresford, "Family Formation and Family Composition: Trends and Prospects," paper read at the annual meeting of the American Association for the Advancement of Science, Chicago, December, 1959, p. 12.

3 See *Continuing Education Programs for Women,* Pamphlet 10 (Washington, D.C.: U.S. Department of Labor, Wage and Standards Administration, 1967), p. 10; also *Handbook of Women Workers,* Bulletin 294 (Washington, D.C.: U.S. Department of Labor, Women's Bureau, 1969), p. 18.

4 See A. Lipman, "Role Conceptions and Morale of Couples in Retirement," *Journal of Gerontology,* XVI (1961), 267–71; and Robert O. Blood and Donald M. Wolfe, *Husbands and Wives: The Dynamics of Married Living* (Glencoe: Free Press, 1960). However, the dispersal of children, along with a couple's knowledge of extended life expectancy, may also have the opposite effect on marital relationships—as evidenced by the rising divorce rate among middle-aged couples. Some husbands and wives discover that they have become estranged from one another. For a variety of reasons they had remained unaware of this, or perhaps deliberately maintained a facade of contentment for the sake of the children. After the children leave home, however, their commitment to preserving their marriage wanes. A woman's return to the labor market may hasten the demise of such a marriage or, conversely, may enable her to better withstand the strains of an impending divorce. A man, on

the other hand, may seek a new love relationship to offset his fear of declining virility or to relieve boredom. The enduring biological capacity of men to father children allows them the option, in middle age and beyond, to marry younger women and start a second family.

5 Marvin B. Sussman, "The Help Pattern in the Middle Class Family," *American Sociological Review,* XVIII (February 1953), 24.

6 "Side Effects: An Interview with Stravinsky," *New York Review of Books,* March 14, 1968, p. 8.

7 See Zena Smith Blau, "Old Age: A Study of Change in Status," unpublished Ph.D. dissertation, Columbia University, 1957.

8 Both quotations are taken from interviews with older people in William Harlan, "Isolation and Conduct in Later Life," unpublished Ph.D. dissertation, University of Chicago, 1950.

9 This is not to say that many men in the affluent, consumer-oriented society of today do not have fantasies about being so rich that they could afford to become "playboys" and devote themselves to la dolce vita. Hugh Hefner has recognized the widespread nature of this fantasy, and has devised new ways to cater to it and to cultivate it in his various enterprises, such as *Playboy* magazine, Playboy clubs, and Playboy resorts. But his audience and his customers are not the very rich—who today usually choose to work in industry or politics, although they don't need the money.

10 Eugene A. Friedman and Robert J. Havighurst, eds., *The Meaning of Work and Retirement* (Chicago: University of Chicago Press, 1954), p. 30.

11 The Kips Bay study provided empirical confirmation of this generalization. It shows an incidence of low morale scores among retired men that is nearly three times higher than among employed men, while this difference between retired and employed women amounts to only 12 percent. A further indication that the work role is more significant for men is the finding that low morale is less frequent among employed men (26 percent) than among employed women (38 percent) but more frequent among retired men (60 percent) than among retired women (50 percent). See Z. S. Blau, 1957, p. 47.

12 W. Harlan, 1950, p. 40.

13 The continuity that characterizes the role of housewife contrasts sharply with the discontinuity that occupational retirement engenders in old age. There is no socially defined age ceiling on housework, and **252**

consequently housewives continue to perform their customary tasks as long as they are able to do so. This helps explain why the morale of housewives, although lower than that of employed older people, is higher than that of retirants. Z. S. Blau, 1957, p. 45.

14 W. Harlan, 1950, p. 233.

15 Z. S. Blau, 1957, p. 27.

16 E. Shanas, et al., *Old Age in Three Industrial Societies* (New York: Atherton Press, 1968).

17 W. Harlan, 1950, p. 195.

18 Friedman and Havighurst, 1954, p. 90.

19 W. Harlan, 1950, p. 195.

20 Ibid., p. 3.

21 Z. S. Blau, 1957, p. 35.

22 The division of the sexes that often takes place at social gatherings of married people is, of course, a reflection of the differences in sex roles. The pattern may also have the latent function of reducing opportunities for flirtations between married people. The disapproval that women, especially, express toward the occasional woman who deviates from the pattern and joins the conversation of the men suggests the normative nature of the pattern and the sanctions that are employed to maintain conformity with it.

23 Z. S. Blau, 1957, p. 39. For a discussion of the changes in the social life of women precipitated by widowhood, see also Helen Lopata, "Loneliness: Forms and Components," *Social Problems,* xvii (1969), 248–61, a more recent and intensive study of widows.

24 See Z. S. Blau, 1957; Irving R. Rosow, *Social Integration of the Aged* (New York: Free Press, 1967); Marjorie Fiske Lowenthal and Clayton Haven, "Interaction and Adaptation: Intimacy as a Critical Variable," *American Sociological Review,* xxxiii (February, 1968), 20–30.

25 Chronic physical problems become more frequent as the organism ages, but the proportion of people beyond age sixty with incapacitating physical problems is very small, and it is concentrated, of course, in the most aged groups. For an elaboration of this point, see, in particular, Robert Butler, "The Facade of Chronological Age: An Interpretative Summary," in Bernice L. Neugarten, ed., *Middle Age and Aging* (Chi-

cago: University of Chicago Press, 1968), pp. 235–44. Moreover, there is evidence that disability does not increase so rapidly with age among older people who work as in the general population; see Mortimer Spiegelman, "Significant Mortality and Morbidity Trends in the United States since 1900" (Bryn Mawr, Pa.: American College of Underwriters, 1964, 1966). Among older people of similar levels of health and socio-economic status, retirants consistently exhibit lower morale than those who continue to work; see Gordon Streib, "Morale of the Retired," *Social Problems,* III (1956), 270–76.

CHAPTER III

1 See, in particular, Gordon F. Streib, "Family Patterns in Retirement," *Journal of Social Issues,* XIV (1958), 46–60; and Henry D. Sheldon, *The Older Population of the United States* (New York: Wiley, 1958).

2 Lear presumably had been married, but not a single allusion to his marital life or to other events in his past occurs in the play. Although the death of a spouse is usually experienced as a tragedy by the surviving marital partner, it does not qualify as a fitting subject for the writer of tragedy, perhaps because it is an event that lies outside the province of human will and control, just as any other natural disaster does. Only when the agent of an act or event is the human being—singly or collectively—exercising choice or expressing his will does it fall within the domain of tragedy. Thus murder, assassination, suicide lend themselves to dramatic treatment in a way that natural death does not. By the same token, it is not the fact that he is old, nor the decline in his physical powers, that has precipitated the tragic chain of events that befall Lear. The heart of the tragedy is that *he* engineers his own tragic fate, by his decision to retire and to abdicate his independence.

3 A number of studies of interaction patterns between the *dependent* aged and their adult children suggest role reversal to be a common characteristic of these relationships. Further, they show that such role reversals often lead to or intensify conflict both for the aged and their children. See Evelyn M. Duvall, *In-Laws Pro and Con: An Original Study of Inter-Personal Relations* (New York: Association Press, 1954); Paul H. Glasser and Lois N. Glasser, "Role Reversal and Conflict Between Aged Parents and Their Children," *Marriage and Family Living,* XXIV, no. 1 (February, 1962), 46–51; Arthur E. Gravatt, "Family Relations in Middle and Old Age: A Review," *Journal of Gerontology,* VIII (1953), 197–201.

4 Georg Simmel, *The Sociology of Georg Simmel,* trans. Kurt H. Wolf (New York: Free Press, 1950), p. 392.

5 At the same time, there has been a growing emphasis on the rights of parents to have "lives of their own." Parents, then, progressively encourage their children to seek gratification of the affiliative needs in their own peer groups instead of in the family, with the predictable result that their ability to communicate with, and exercise influence over, their children often becomes seriously undermined by the time the latter reach adolescence.

6 G. Simmel, 1950, p. 394.

7 David Schneider, *American Kinship: A Cultural Account* (Englewood Cliffs, N.J.: Prentice-Hall, 1968), pp. 50–52.

8 Close to 75 percent of married people sixty-five and over in the United States share a household only with a spouse. See Paul C. Glick, *American Families* (New York: Wiley, 1957). A similar pattern is reported in other Western societies. See E. Shanas, et al., *Old Age in Three Industrial Societies* (New York: Atherton Press, 1968).

9 The proportion of people covered by Social Security and by private pension plans has been steadily rising over the past thirty-five years, and some attention has been given in recent years to the housing needs of the elderly. That is not to say that the problems of poverty among old people have been solved. But there is general acknowledgment that the problem exists and that its resolution mainly requires the extension and elaboration of programs already in existence, and the allocation of more economic resources to implement them.

10 According to Rosow (1960), financial assistance on the part of children to their parents does not, as one might expect, show any significant relationship to parents' place of residence. Thus even in cases where the older couple is to some extent financially dependent on their children, separate residences are often maintained. There is also evidence to suggest that as levels of living increase, adult offspring become increasingly less willing to support aged parents. See R. M. Dinkel, "Attitudes of Children Toward Supporting Aged Parents," *American Sociological Review*, ix (1944), 370–79; W. M. Smith, J. H. Britton, and J. O. Britton, *Relationships Within Three Generational Families*, Research Publication No. 155 (University Park: Pennsylvania State University, College of Home Economics, 1958).

11 A study of 500 persons aged sixty and over and their families concludes that "While parents and children are expected to maintain close psychological relationships through visiting, mutual aid and other ways, the independence of each of the conjugal family units is considered

sacrosanct." See Bernard Kutner, et al., *Five Hundred over Sixty* (New York: Russell Sage Foundation, 1966). A similar conclusion is reported in a study of a rural community; see J. H. Britton, W. G. Mather, and A. K. Lansing, "Expectations for Older Persons in a Rural Community: Living Arrangements and Family Relationships," *Journal of Gerontology,* xvi (1961), 156–62. Even among the widowed, separate residences are the preferred form of living arrangement. See E. Shanas, et al., 1968.

12 From "Guest Columnist," *Chicago Daily News,* November 21, 1968.

13 Correspondingly, we term the family of birth "my family" during the years of childhood and adolescence, and then transfer that same appellation to the family that we set up when we marry and bear children.

14 The relationships between daughters and their "mum" in East London described by Peter Townsend seem to have a more intimate character than those found in the middle class, possibly because these people usually reside in the same neighborhood and share the same working-class culture. It would be interesting to repeat Townsend's study on a sample of former Bethnal Green residents who have moved to suburban London. See Peter Townsend, *The Extended Family and the Kinship Network in the Family Life of Old People* (London: Routledge and Kegan Paul, 1957).

15 Leopold Rosenmayr and Eva Köckeis, "Propositions for a Sociological Theory of Aging and the Family," *International Social Science Journal,* xv (1963), 410–26.

16 Irving Rosow, *Social Integration of the Aged* (New York: Free Press, 1967), p. 25.

17 Helen Z. Lopata, "Loneliness: Forms and Components," *Social Problems,* xvii (1969), 248–62.

18 E. Shanas, et al., 1968, discuss the distinction between isolation and desolation.

19 Zena Smith Blau, "Old Age: A Study of Change in Status," unpublished Ph.D. dissertation, Columbia University, 1957.

20 E. Shanas, et al., 1968.

21 A recent study of the relations between middle-class children and widowed parents shows that the emotional dependency of the mother after widowhood impairs her relation with her children—which is manifested by them in lessened contact with her. See Bert N. Adams, "The Middle Class Adult and His Widowed or Still Married Mother," *Social Problems,* xvi (1968), 50–59.

22 I borrow Erikson's term, which represents the last "nuclear conflict" in the sequence of developmental tasks involved in achieving and maintaining ego integrity over the entire span of the life cycle. See Erik Erikson, *Childhood and Society* (New York: Norton, 1963), p. 266.

CHAPTER IV

1 Willy Loman, the tragic protagonist of Arthur Miller's drama *Death of a Salesman,* makes the mistake of applying the criteria of friendship to his work relationships. To him, being a "good guy" and "well liked" makes being a salesman valuable and enjoyable; but these are *not* qualities that count for much in the competitive struggle for success in an acquisitive society. Shrewdness and manipulativeness are the earmarks of the successful market personality, not decency or likability.

2 David Schneider, *American Kinship: A Cultural Account* (Englewood Cliffs, N.J.: Prentice-Hall, 1968), p. 53.

3 Within urban societies, people who live in large metropolitan centers have less association with friends than do those in smaller cities. For empirical confirmation of this point, see the comparison of friendship participation of older people in Elmira, N.Y., a medium-sized community, with that of people in the Kips Bay area of New York City, in Zena S. Blau, "Structural Constraints on Friendships in Old Age," *American Sociological Review,* xxvi (1961), 434.

4 Georg Simmel, *The Sociology of Georg Simmel,* trans. Kurt H. Wolf (New York: Free Press, 1950), p. 320.

5 Such relationships are likely to wane after role exits earlier in life as well—for example, when people change jobs, or are divorced, or experience a long illness, or decline in social class, or any other personal crisis that creates a lengthy interruption in contact. People who do not make a distinction between such friendships and those based on bonds of intimacy feel betrayed by such "fair weather" friends.

6 William Harlan, "Isolation and Conduct in Later Life," unpublished Ph.D. dissertation, University of Chicago, 1950, p. 195.

7 These data are from the Elmira study. The Kips Bay data provide additional verification of the results. See Zena S. Blau, "Old Age: A Study of Change in Status," unpublished Ph.D. dissertation, Columbia University, 1957, p. 40.

8 E. Michael Bannister, "Sociodynamics: An Integrative Theorem of Power, Authority, Interfluence, and Love," *American Sociological Review,* xxxiv (June, 1969), 374–93, advances a similar proposition.

9 The power of parents over young children arises, to an important degree, because the children have no other significant social contacts to turn to when parents disapprove of their behavior. They therefore have no alternative except to "shape up" and "be good."

10 The importance of maintaining friendship bonds with contemporaries is an important theme in *King Lear*. Indeed, the climax of the struggle between Lear and his daughters occurs when they seek to banish his "company" from their households. Without loyal friends, Lear would have lost the last vestige of his independence as a person and would have become totally subject to the authority of his children.

11 All too often this distinction is ignored by students of old age. Take, for example, the following statement: "Friends and neighbors play an important part in the lives of many older people, often providing help and services as well as informal contact with the world outside the home. They are, however, generally less important to older people than children and other relatives, serving more as a complement than substitute for kinship association." Mathilda White Riley and Anne Foner, *Aging and Society,* vol. I (New York: Russell Sage Foundation, 1968), p. 561.

12 See Z. S. Blau, 1957, pp. 32–49; Alan C. Kerchoff, "Family Patterns and Morale in Retirement," in Ida Harper Simpson and John C. McKinney, *Social Aspects of Aging* (Durham, N.C.: Duke University Press, 1966), pp. 173–92; and Bernard Kutner, et al., *Five Hundred over Sixty: A Community Survey on Aging* (New York: Russell Sage Foundation, 1956), p. 116.

13 Bert N. Adams, "The Middle Class Adult and His Widowed or Still Married Mother," *Social Problems,* XVI (1968), 58.

14 G. Simmel, 1950, p. 326.

15 Marjorie Fisk Lowenthal and Clayton Haven, "Interaction and Adaptation," *American Sociological Review,* XXXIII (1968), 20–30. Their results are also consistent with mine, revealing that neither extensive social relations nor intimate friendships constitute as effective a restitution for the loss of the work role as they do for the loss of a marital partner.

16 Simmel, in that same passage, asserts that for women, more than for men, it is the sexual relationship that "opens the doors" to intimacy. The weight of empirical evidence, however, suggests that just the opposite is the case. Women place more emphasis on emotional intimacy as a   **258**

condition for entering and sustaining a sexual relationship (see William Simon and John H. Gagnon, "On Psychosexual Development," in David A. Goslin, ed., *Handbook of Socialization Theory and Research* (Chicago: Rand McNally, 1969), pp. 733–52); whereas for men sexual attraction is more likely to be the primary basis for attachment to a woman, and feelings of love and intimacy evolve through erotic attachment. We are talking, of course, about traditional differences between the sexes. The demand for equality among the sexes has perhaps reduced this tendency. More young women today do not consider love a condition for entering a sexual relationship and are more inclined, like men, to view emotional intimacy as a bonus that may develop in a mutually satisfying sexual relationship.

17 At ages fifty-five to sixty-four, the suicide rate for white men is 39.5 per 100,000 population, while for women it is only 10.9. In the sixty-five to seventy-four age group, the rate among men rises to 39.1, compared to 10.4 among women. In the age group seventy-five and older, the rate among men is 50.5, while that of women drops to 6.7. Among married men, the suicide rates rise only very slightly with age, but among widowed and single men, the rise in suicide is very pronounced. Among women, suicide rates decline beyond age forty-five *regardless* of marital status. See National Center for Health Statistics, *Suicide in the United States 1950–1964,* series 20, no. 5, 1967, pp. 16, 32–33.

18 E. Shanas, et al., *Old People in Three Industrial Societies* (New York: Atherton Press, 1968), p. 272.

19 Nathan Hurvitz, "Marital Strain in the Blue-Collar Family," in Arthur Shostak and William Gomberg, eds., *Blue Collar World: Studies of the American Worker* (Englewood Cliffs, N.J.: Prentice-Hall, 1964), pp. 92–110.

20 See Talcott Parsons and Robert F. Bales, *Family, Socialization and Interaction Process* (New York: Free Press, 1955), for a theoretical exposition of sex role differentiation in the modern nuclear family. Socioemotional tasks are seen as the primary responsibility of the wife and mother, and instrumental functions are considered mainly the province of the husband and father.

CHAPTER V

1 Zena S. Blau, "Structural Constraints on Friendships in Old Age," *American Sociological Review,* xxvi (1961), 429–39.

2 The nationwide figures of the proportion of older men and women widowed in 1960 were as follows:

	65–69	70–74	75–79	80–84	85+	Total Age 65+
Men	10.2	16.8	25.3	37.2	52.8	19.1
Women	37.9	50.4	62.2	73.1	81.4	52.1

Source: United States Census, 1960 Census of the Population, Vol. I, Part 1, 424–25.

3 Newly formed friendships, for example, were restricted to persons of the same sex in more than four-fifths of the cases in the Kips Bay study.

4 According to this principle, it could be expected that marriage would have a detrimental effect on the friendship participation of young people who marry earlier than their peers. Conversely, people who marry later than the majority of their age-sex peers could be expected to associate less with their own peers and either to be more isolated or to associate more with people considerably older or younger than themselves, depending on whether or not they have opportunities to meet people of disparate ages. Empirical study is required to determine whether this is in fact the case among young adults.

5 Indications are that, in the upper segments of the working class, women's tendency to participate mainly with their kin is beginning to change, but overall the differences between the social life of middle- and working-class women still remain. See Gerald Handel and Lee Rainwater, "Persistence and Change in Working-Class Life Style," in Arthur Shostak and William Gomberg, eds., Blue Collar World: Studies of the American Worker (Englewood Cliffs, N.J.: Prentice-Hall, 1964), pp. 36–41. See also Robert J. Havighurst, "Life Styles of Middle Aged Persons," Vita Humana, II (1959), 25–34.

6 Retirement is defined as prevalent if more than a third of the respondents in a category are retired; otherwise, it is considered not prevalent. The effects of retirement on friendships are defined as detrimental if the proportion of people with high friendship participation scores is at least 5 percent larger among the employed than among the retired. If the differences are smaller or negative, retirement is not considered to have adverse social effects.

7 It will be recalled that retirement also affects the morale of women in old age less than that of men. See chapter 2.

8 Irving Rosow, *Social Integration of the Aged* (New York: Free Press, 1967), p. 39.

9 Other recent studies also find the morale and social participation of older people to be significantly higher in age-concentrated residential settings than in age-heterogeneous settings. See, for example, Mark Messer, "Engagement with Disengagement," unpublished Ph.D. dissertation, Northwestern University, 1966, and particularly Frances M. Carp, *A Future for the Aged* (Austin: University of Texas Press, 1966). The latter study is unique in that it reports on a group of older people before and after their move into age-concentrated housing. A significant rise in morale, social participation, self-concept, and health occurred among them; whereas a similarly constituted comparison group that continued to live in the community showed none of these favorable changes.

10 See, for example, Gordon F. Streib, "Are the Aged a Minority Group?", in Alvin W. Gouldner and S. M. Miller, eds., *Applied Sociology* (Glencoe, Ill.: Free Press, 1965), chapter 24.

11 Race segregation, in striking contrast, has been an anti-democratic force. Because the resources available to Negroes were separate but *never* equal to those available to whites, their economic opportunities were greatly restricted by residential and school segregation. The diffusion to Negroes of knowledge and skills that constitute a necessary condition for raising their position in the occupational structure thus requires integration. The reason that some militant Negroes have become supporters of racial segregation is that they view the ghetto as a potential collective revolutionary force that would become dissipated if Negroes were to become integrated into all social institutions and have access to the same opportunities as whites.

CHAPTER VI

1 Erik Erikson, *Identity and the Life Cycle: Selected Papers* (New York: International Universities Press, 1959), p. 89.

2 Similar results were obtained in the Kips Bay study and in studies by other investigators. See, for example, Irving Rosow, *Social Integration of the Aged* (New York: Free Press, 1967); and Mark Messer, "Engagement with Disengagement: The Effects of Age Concentration," unpublished Ph.D. dissertation, Northwestern University, 1966.

3 Marcel Proust, *Remembrance of Things Past,* trans. Frederick A. Blossom (New York: Random House, 1927), vol. II, p. 1063.

4 If, instead of controlling age identification, we control the beliefs respondents hold about the attitudes of their significant others, the relationship between age and age identification remains—which indicates that the sequence suggested in the text is the correct one.

5 E. B. White, "Notes and Comments by Author," *New York Times,* July 11, 1969.

6 William Harlan, "Isolation and Conduct in Later Life," unpublished Ph.D dissertation, University of Chicago, 1950.

7 In a similar vein, Lear, in a sharp confrontation with his daughters, rages at the perfidy of his daughters and chooses to chance physical disaster and death as preferable to enduring the pain of betrayal and rejection inflicted by human agents.

> I tax not you, you elements, with unkindness.
> I never gave you kingdom, call'd you children,
> you owe me no subscription. Then let fall
> your horrible pleasure. . . .
> *King Lear,* Act III, Scene 2

8 Under some conditions, of course, widowhood may also have a detrimental effect on an individual's group memberships. For example, the surviving marital partner may drop out of those friendship groups in which the marital couple had participated jointly, or may discontinue membership in "auxiliary" organizations; that is, where participation of the wife is contingent on that of her husband.

9 It will be recalled that extensive friendships or a single intimate friendship helps forestall demoralization after role exit. But these forms of social participation do not exhibit any significant relationship to age identity.

10 Zena S. Blau, "Changes in Status and Age Identification," *American Sociological Review,* xxi (1956), 201.

11 See, for example, F. J. Roethlisberger and William J. Dickson, *Management and the Workers* (Cambridge, Mass.: Harvard University Press, 1930); William F. Whyte, *Street Corner Society* (Chicago: University of Chicago Press, 1943); George C. Homans, *The Human Group* (New York: Harcourt Brace and Company, 1950); and Robert F. Bales, et al., "Channels of Communication in Small Groups," *American Sociological Review,* xvi (August, 1951), 461–68.

12 Younger workers in industry who are currently advocating the establishment of a policy of retirement for workers after thirty years' service

should consider the unintended effects of such a policy. A "thirty years and out" policy would mean that a man who started in industry at eighteen could retire with a pension at age forty-eight. But under present conditions, at least, early retirement could be expected to hasten the psychological onset of old age.

13 Howard S. Becker and Anselm Strauss, "Careers, Personality and Adult Socialization," *American Journal of Sociology,* LXII (1956), 311–20.

14 See Elizabeth Bott, *Family and Social Network* (London: Tavistock Publications, 1957); and Joel Nelson, "Clique Contacts and Family Orientations," *American Sociological Review,* XXI (1966), 663–72.

15 A network of kinship relations preserved a continuity of identity for the individual in traditional societies, and continues to do so in some of the more traditional subgroups in urban industrial societies—for example, in small communities and in the stable, urban black and white working classes. However, recent research on the white working class reports declining kinship association among the more affluent segments of the working class. See Gerald Handel and Lee Rainwater, "Persistence and Change in Working-Class Life Style," in Arthur Shostak and William Gomberg, eds., *Blue Collar World: Studies of the American Worker* (Englewood Cliffs, N.J.: Prentice-Hall, 1964), pp. 36–41. I suspect that this weakening of kinship bonds may be one source of the rising discontent in the white working class. The same problems of identity that beset the urban, kinship-emancipated middle class can be expected to become intensified in the working class as its traditionally greater participation in kinship networks declines.

16 Conrad Arensberg and Solon Kimball, *Family and Community in Ireland* (Gloucester, Mass.: Peter Smith, 1961), p. 174.

CHAPTER VII

1 Twenty-nine percent of these were spouses of respondents, 32 percent were offspring, 18 percent were other close relatives, and 21 percent were friends or acquaintances.

2 For confirmation and elaboration of the point that conceptions of the age of onset of middle age and old age are earlier among the working class, especially men, than among the middle and upper classes, see Bernice L. Neugarten and Warren Peterson, "A Study of the American Age-Grade System," *Proceedings,* 4th Congress of the International Association of Gerontology, Bolzano, Italy, 1957, pp. 1–6.

3 This is not to deny that the individual's self-image also is communicated in various subtle ways and influences his associate's conceptions of him. In all intimate relationships, influence is, to some degree, reciprocal.

4 Leon Festinger, Stanley Schachter, and Kurt Back, *Social Pressures in Informal Groups* (New York: Harper, 1950), p. 168. For an experimental demonstration of this principle in the field of social perception, see Solomon Asch's classic study, "Effects of Group Pressure upon the Modification and Distortion of Judgment," in Eleanor E. Maccoby, Theodore M. Newcomb, and Eugene L. Hartley, eds., *Readings in Social Psychology,* 3d ed. (New York: Holt, Rinehart and Winston, 1958), pp. 174–83.

5 The difference between the proportion of people who consider themselves old among those not defined as old by their associate and those defined as old by the latter constitutes a crude measure of the influence of another's judgment upon a person's self-image.

6 Leon Festinger, Kurt Back, Stanley Schachter, Harold Kelly, and John Thibaut, *Theory and Experiment in Social Communication* (Ann Arbor: Institute for Social Research, University of Michigan, 1950), p. 5.

7 The figures represent the *differences* in the proportion of respondents who consider themselves old among those judged as old compared to those judged as middle-aged by an intimate.

8 Of course, this does not imply that the appraisals of all his associates are equally significant for the individual. It simply means that one associate's appraisal is more likely to be "representative" of the opinions of all significant others in the case of the person with few associates than in the case of the person who has close ties with several people holding a variety of opinions.

9 The finding in chapter 2, that retirement has more pronounced effects on adaptation than has widowhood, as well as the finding that the influence of a single associate is insignificant for people who have more extensive social relations, directs attention to the significance of numbers in conditioning social behavior and social influence. See Carl W. Backman, Paul F. Secord, and Jerry Pierce, "Resistance to Change in the Self-concept as a Function of Consensus Among Significant Others," *Sociometry,* XXVI (1963), 102–11. The authors report an experiment in which they demonstrate that the degree of resistance to change in self-concept is a function of the *number* of an individual's interpersonal relationships supporting his self-definition.

10 See Seymour Martin Lipset, Martin Trow, and James S. Coleman, **264**

Union Democracy (Glencoe, Ill.: Free Press, 1956), chapter 10. (Italics supplied.)

11 See Bernard Berelson, Paul F. Lazarsfeld, and William McPhee, *Voting* (Chicago: University of Chicago Press, 1954), pp. 107–08.

12 Although these relationships become somewhat smaller when the age of individuals being judged is controlled, respondents still are more often in agreement with their associates in respect to age appraisal than in respect to normative orientation.

13 George Herbert Mead, *Mind, Self and Society* (Chicago: University of Chicago Press, 1934), pp. 154–56.

CHAPTER VIII

1 One way to test this proposition would be to take two samples of older employees, matched by age, education, health, occupational status, and attitudes toward their work. One sample of workers should be drawn from a company that has a compulsory retirement policy, the other from a company that permits workers to exercise discretion over the age at which they retire. Information about the age composition of their colleagues would also be needed; or at least questions should be put to both groups concerning the informal social pressures to retire that are imposed on them by co-workers, first-line supervisors, and management. Probably a significantly lower proportion of workers in the discretionary than in the compulsory situation would express a willingness to retire.

2 Samuel Lubell, "Young Workers Harass Oldsters: 'Get Out, Retire!' " *Chicago Daily News,* May 1, 1959.

3 Lewis Carliner, "Labor: The Anti-Youth Establishment," *New Generation,* II (Spring, 1969), 27–31; "Young Worker, Old Workers Cross Eyes," presented at the Annual Meeting of the Society for the Study of Social Problems, Washington, D.C., August, 1970.

4 George Katona, *Private Pensions and Individual Saving,* Monograph no. 40 (Ann Arbor: Survey Research Center, University of Michigan, 1965), p. 15.

5 Mathilda White Riley and Anne Foner, *Aging and Society.* I, *An Inventory of Research Findings* (New York: Russell Sage Foundation, 1968), 442–43.

6 Erdman Palmore, "Retirement Patterns Among Aged Men: Findings of the 1963 Survey of the Aged," *Social Security Bulletin,* XXVII (1964), 3–10.

7 Ethel Shanas, "Health Care and Health Service for the Aged," *Gerontologist,* v (December, 1965).

8 United States Senate Sub-Committee on Aging, "Report on the Aged and Aging," 1960.

9 Mortimer Spiegelman, *Significant Mortality and Morbidity Trends in the United States Since 1900* (Bryn Mawr, Pa.: American College of Underwriters, 1964), p. 8. (Based on the United States Health Survey, 1959, Health Statistics, Series B, No. 11, p. 2.)

10 M. W. Riley and A. Foner, 1968, p. 214. (Taken from National Center for Health Statistics, *Vital and Health Statistics,* Series 10, No. 17, 1965, pp. 26, 216.) It should be pointed out that many new drugs and new therapies for chronic illnesses are allowing more and more people to live "normal" lives—something rare in earlier times. As a result, there has been a steady decline in invalidism among the elderly.

11 James S. Tyhurst, et al., "Mortality, Morbidity and Retirement," *American Journal of Public Health,* xlvii (1957), 1434–44.

12 Wayne E. Thompson and Gordon F. Streib, "Situational Determinants: Health and Economic Deprivation in Retirement," *Journal of Social Issues,* xiv (1958), 18–34.

13 Talcott Parsons, *Social Structure and Personality* (New York: Free Press, 1965), p. 253.

14 See E. Shanas, et al., *Old People in Three Industrial Societies* (New York: Atherton Press, 1968), p. 218; and Irving Rosow, *Social Integration of the Aged* (New York: Free Press, 1967), pp. 156–59.

15 "Personal reasons" is another face-saving euphemism for forced resignation that is widely used in government and business.

16 Gregory Rochlin, M.D., *Griefs and Discontents* (Boston: Little, Brown, 1965), pp. 378–79.

17 This proposition could easily be tested by comparing levels of activity of two groups of similar age who have the same disease (for example, hypertension): those who are married, employed, or socially active, and those who have experienced major role exits and are relatively isolated.

18 Even the decline of sexual capacity in aging men may well be more a function of boredom with the marital partner than of age itself. William H. Masters and Virginia E. Johnson, in *Human Sexual Response* (Boston: Little, Brown, 1966), furnish some evidence that the exercise of sexuality seems to help maintain sexual powers, while abstinence induces **266**

atrophy. In societies where polygamy is accepted, older men (who are also apt to be the most affluent and therefore able to support several wives) continue to propagate children at an advanced age. Indeed, the institutionalization of polygamy may partly, although of course not altogether, reflect a recognition of the older male's need for novelty to sustain his sexual capacity. In contemporary society, "serial monogamy," which appears to be a growing practice among some subgroups of affluent and successful middle-aged and older men, may serve a similar function.

19 Robert Butler, "The Facade of Chronological Age: An Interpretative Summary," in Bernice L. Neugarten, ed., *Middle Age and Aging* (Chicago: University of Chicago Press, 1968).

20 For a discussion of these issues, see K. Warner Schaie, "Age Changes and Age Differences," and Raymond K. Kuhlen, "Age and Intelligence: The Significance of Cultural Change in Longitudinal and Cross-Sectional Findings," in B. L. Neugarten, 1968, pp. 552–57, 558–62.

21 L. Carliner, 1970; Herbert Gans, "Protest and Young Workers," and Robert Schrank, "It Makes No Difference Now," *New Generation,* LII (Fall, 1970).

22 In the Kips Bay study, older employees were asked, "Do you look forward to the time when you will retire, or do you dislike the idea?" Fifty-six percent who enjoyed their work, 49 percent of those who liked it fairly well, and 30 percent of those who did not enjoy it at all disliked the prospect of retirement.

23 See, for example, Herman J. Loether, "The Meaning of Work and Adjustment to Retirement," in Arthur Shostak and William Gomberg, eds., *Blue Collar World: Studies of the American Worker* (Englewood Cliffs, N.J.: Prentice-Hall, 1964), pp. 525–33.

24 Robert Blauner, *Alienation and Freedom* (Chicago: University of Chicago Press, 1964).

25 E. A. Friedman and R. J. Havighurst, *The Meaning of Work and Retirement* (Chicago: University of Chicago Press, 1954), p. 89.

26 A study of the retirement attitudes of coal miners reports a similar finding: namely, that those miners who wished to retire at sixty-five, more often than those who did not wish to retire then, mentioned "friends on the job" as one of the things they expected to miss when they stopped working. See W. Harlan, "The Meanings of Work and Retirement for Coal Miners," in E. A. Friedman and R. J. Havighurst, 1954, p. 93. A number of studies show that blue-collar workers rank

"people" on the job as a more important source of job satisfaction than the work itself. See, for example, Nancy C. Morse and Robert S. Weiss, "The Function and Meaning of Work and the Job," *American Sociological Review,* xx (1955), 191–98.

27 But work alienation without extensive social relations fosters low morale among older employees in industry. It can be understood why older workers who are surrounded by younger workers succumb to social pressure and increasingly choose to retire as soon as they become entitled to pensions. The recent enactment of the right to a partial pension for auto workers who retire after thirty years' work may promote similar pressures on workers to retire in their fifties, paticularly in periods of high unemployment.

28 A study of interpersonal relations among officials in two governmental agencies found that while competence and extent of informal relations with colleagues were each *directly* related to integration into the work group, they were *inversely* related to one another. Colleagues were attracted to the more competent officials, who merely had to behave in a cooperative manner in order to become integrated. Less competent officials, on the other hand, found it necessary to foster extensive social contacts with their co-workers to become integrated. See Peter M. Blau, *The Dynamics of Bureaucracy* (Chicago: University of Chicago Press, 1955), p. 121.

29 In the Kips Bay study, virtually no difference in social participation was found between satisfied employees and retirants who had liked their work (27 percent and 25 percent, respectively, had high participation scores).

30 The incidence of low morale in the group that liked their work was 26 percent among the employed and 44 percent among the retired.

31 Although the percentage difference is not large (44 percent versus 34 percent), it assumes importance because it is the only comparison in which the "satisfied" exhibit *lower* morale than the alienated.

32 The recognition of this discontinuity may be a factor in the unwillingness of many youths today to "put the job first." Because they invest less emotion in their work and put more time and effort into other activities, they may be better prepared than their fathers to deal with retirement.

CHAPTER IX

1 Interview with E. B. White, "Notes and Comments by Author," *New York Times,* July 11, 1969.

2 Erik Erikson, "Identity and the Life Cycle," *Psychological Issues,* I (New York: International Universities Press, 1959), p. 98.

3 David Riesman, "Some Clinical and Cultural Aspects of the Aging Process," *American Journal of Sociology,* LIX (1954), 379–83.

4 Elaine Cumming and William D. Henry, *Growing Old: The Process of Disengagement* (New York: Basic Books, 1961).

5 See, for example, George L. Maddox, "Activity and Morale: A Longitudinal Study of Selected Elderly Subjects," *Social Forces,* XLII (1963), 195–204; Robert J. Havighurst, Bernice L. Neugarten, and Sheldon S. Tobin, "Disengagement, Personality, and Life Satisfaction in the Later Years," in P. Fromm Hansen, ed., *Proceedings of the Sixth International Congress of Gerontology, Copenhagen, 1963* (Copenhagen: Munksgaard, 1964), p. 39.

6 That is not to say that *all* active people are happier than *all* inactive older people. Throughout empirical research one finds "deviant" cases— that is, atypical responses. In research on old age, the "odd" cells consist, first, of individuals who, though they score low on various activity scales, are nevertheless content; and, second, of individuals who, though they score high on various activity scales, are discontented or unhappy. The explanation of such deviant cases is one of the tasks of science, but the first and highest priority of empirical research is to discover and formulate explanations of the relationships between variables that are most frequently observed, and *then* to identify the conditions under which these observed relationships do not occur.

7 A similar phenomenon can be observed among women, another group long subject to the myth that "biology is destiny." Although only a small proportion of women are active in "Women's Lib," this group is voicing the accumulated resentments of countless women everywhere.

8 Erving Goffman, *Stigma: Notes on the Management of Spoiled Identity* (New York: Prentice-Hall, 1963), p. 121.

9 The quotation is from Bertrand Russell, *Autobiography, 1914–1944* (Boston: Little, Brown, 1968), p. 229.

10 A line from *King Lear* that brilliantly conveys the process I describe above is worth quoting: ". . . I have perceived a most faint neglect of late, which I have rather blamed as mine own jealous curiosity than as a very pretense and purpose of unkindness. . . ." William Shakespeare, *King Lear,* Act I, Scene 4.

11 William Harlan, "Isolation and Conduct in Later Life," unpublished Ph.D. dissertation, University of Chicago, 1950, pp. 225, 234.

269

12 The three questions asked in the Elmira and Kips Bay surveys on which the retreatism scale is based are:

"How often do you find yourself daydreaming about the past?"

"Which of these things give you the most satisfaction and comfort today?"

"How often do you find yourself being absent-minded?"

Coefficient of reproducibility .94.

13 Sigmund Freud, *A General Introduction to Psychoanalysis* (Garden City, N.Y.: Garden City Publishing Company, 1943), p. 67.

14 Ibid., p. 327.

15 The four items of the alienation scale used in Elmira and Kips Bay are:

"How much do you regret the chances you missed during your life to do a better job of living?"

"How often do you feel there's just no point in living?"

"Things keep getting worse and worse for me as I get older."

"How much do you plan ahead the things that you will be doing next week or the week after?"

16 W. Harlan, 1950, p. 40.

17 A score based on the interviewer's rating of socio-economic status, on educational level, and on class identification of respondents was used as the index of socio-economic status. A score of "0" places an individual in the low socio-economic status category; "1" and "2" constitute the middle category; and a score of "3" or higher places the person in the higher status group. The terms "socio-economic status" and "class position" will be used interchangeably to describe these positions.

18 The fact that members of the lower class are more likely to be retired and socially isolated than are people of higher socio-economic status only partly accounts for the higher incidence of alienation among them. Even when these factors are simultaneously controlled, alienation continues to be a more frequent pattern in the lower class than elsewhere.

19 Agreement with this statement is directly related to how successful respondents feel they were in "getting ahead." Thus only 36 percent of those who say they have done "very well," but 75 percent of those saying "not so well," agreed with this statement.

20 Robert K. Merton, *Social Theory and Social Structure* (Glencoe, Ill.: Free Press, 1949), p. 139. I might add that "the doctrine of luck" also serves to deflect criticism from the existing social order.

21 Respondents were asked how much they enjoyed ten current activi-
ies now as compared with when they were fifty—for example, being
with friends, recreation outside the home, religion or church work, doing
things alone at home, etc. Retreatists registered "less interest now" on all
en items, in marked contrast to well-adapted older people.

22 W. Harlan, 1950, p. 225.

23 It would require a complex panel design to determine under which
conditions one or the other of these developments would occur.

24 For a more extended discussion of this point, see Brewster Smith,
"Competence and Socialization," in John A. Clausen, ed., *Socialization
and Society* (Boston: Little, Brown, 1968), pp. 270–320.

25 Sigmund Freud, *Beyond the Pleasure Principle,* trans. J. Strachey
(New York: Liveright, 1950), p. 59.

26 Hans Selye, *The Stress of Life* (New York: McGraw-Hill, 1956),
pp. 128–29.

27 David Bakan, *Disease, Pain and Sacrifice* (Chicago: University of
Chicago Press, 1968), pp. 25–28.

28 The following items were used as validating criteria of adaptation
and maladaptation: reports by respondents of frequency of depression;
psychosomatic symptoms, such as nervousness, headaches, and sleepless-
ness; loneliness; self-rating of health; satisfaction with life and anticipation of the future. On all seven items the incidence of complaints follows
the same pattern: the lowest incidence occurs among innovators and
rises somewhat among conformists; it is still higher among retreatists and
highest among the alienated. Indicators of high morale follow the reverse
order—that is, they are highest among innovators and lowest among the
alienated. See Zena S. Blau, "Old Age: A Study of Change in Status,"
unpublished Ph.D. dissertation, Columbia University, 1957, p. 18.

29 Seventeen percent of the Elmira sample (eighty-one respondents)
exhibited this pattern of response; that is, they were all high on the
innovation scale and low on the alienation and retreat scales. The question may arise why the formation of new friendships was not included in
the friendship participation measure. It is true, of course, that people
with higher participation scores are more likely to have new friends than
those who participate less. But the items on new friendships do not
"scale" with the other three items in the friendship participation scale,
which indicated that some dimension other than participation as such is
involved. This fact, as well as our specific interest in the formation of   **271**

new friendships in old age, prompted the decision to omit this item from the participation index.

30 D. Riesman, 1954, p. 382.

31 Of the *employed,* 51 percent with high participation scores and 56 percent with low participation scores displayed the conformist pattern. The corresponding percentage of conformists were 52 percent among married people with high participation scores and 54 percent among married people with low participation scores.

32 Among high participants, 49 percent and 51 percent of the retired and the employed, and 48 percent and 52 percent of the widowed and married, exhibited conformity.

33 The Kips Bay data show that, at each socio-economic level, the native-born are more inclined to conformity than are the foreign-born, who most often display alienation.

34 Consistent with this finding is a more recent study showing that the opportunities to meet and associate with their own age peers afforded by age-concentrated housing projects benefits the morale of working-class older people more than it does those in the middle class. See Irving Rosow, *Social Integration of the Aged* (New York: Free Press, 1967), p. 39.

35 For the retired and widowed, participation serves as an alternative mechanism of adaptation. For the member of the lower class, it is also a compensatory mechanism, but a less effective substitute, since it does not fully counteract the shocks to which the individual in a disadvantaged socio-economic position is subjected. Even lower-class people with extensive social relations more often exhibit alienation than do people in higher social classes.

36 By and large, of course, a person's feeling of integration is determined by the actual degree of acceptance and respect he experiences among associates, but the person who is actually most deprived of such social support may, on occasion, be the one most prone to suppress this fact.

37 The same principle is exemplified by the finding, reported in several studies of small groups, that the more integrated members of a group are less likely than others to confine their participation to members of the in-group and more likely to have relationships with outsiders. See, for example, W. F. Whyte, *Street Corner Society* (Chicago: University of Chicago Press, 1943), pp. 259–60.

38 A more recent study of participants in organizations composed of and directed to old people also indicates that the type of person whom I **272**

designate an "innovator" is most likely to enter organizations catering to the interests and concerns of the old. See Arnold Rose, "Group Consciousness Among the Aging," in Arnold Rose and Warren Peterson, eds., *Older People and Their Social World* (Philadelphia: F. A. Davis, 1965), pp. 19–36.

39 Alienation also reduces the motivation of older people to utilize available social services. Thus in a recent British study the author states: "The highly anomic . . . tend to have a low level of contact with the social services. The anomic group's negative attitudes to 'public officials' might perhaps lead them to avoid the social services; on the other hand, the lack of the services may contribute towards the anomic attitudes." Jeremy Tunstall, *Old and Alone* (London: Routledge and Kegan Paul, 1966), p. 207.

40 In the same article, Wilensky reports that no more than two in a hundred older people join old people's clubs, and only tiny fractions of them participate in voluntary associations other than churches. Harold Wilensky, "Life Cycle, Work Situation and Participation in Formal Associations," in Clark Tibbitts and Wilma Donahue, *Social and Psychological Aspects of Aging* (New York: Columbia University Press, 1963), pp. 921–29.

CHAPTER X

1 *Chicago Daily News,* January 13, 1969.

2 Black women, out of necessity, far more often remain in the labor force throughout their adult lives. There are several reasons for this. Consistently, work opportunities for black females have been greater than for black males; their educational attainment is higher than that of men; and the proportion of never-married, separated, and divorced black women is considerably higher than among whites. But even in intact families, a far higher proportion of black than white women are employed. This is as true in the middle class as in the working class, because even in the black middle class, the average income of males is considerably lower than that of whites; and it would be impossible for them to obtain or sustain a middle-class style of life, higher education for their children, etc., solely on their own earnings. Whatever their reason for remaining in the labor force, the fact that black women do safeguards them from the malaise and suffering that befall many white middle-class women in middle age today.

3 William Simon and John Gagnon, "On Psychosexual Development," in David A. Goslin, ed., *Handbook of Socialization Theory and Research*   273

(Chicago: Rand McNally, 1969), pp. 733–52; and Daniel Offer, *The Psychological World of the Teen-ager* (New York: Basic Books, 1969).

4 Philip Slater, *The Pursuit of Loneliness* (Boston: Beacon Press, 1970), p. 72.

5 David Riesman, "Some Clinical and Cultural Aspects of the Aging Process," *American Journal of Sociology,* LIX (1954), 381.

6 Robert N. Butler, M.D., "Looking Forward to What?", *American Behavioral Scientist,* XIV (September, 1970), 121–28.

7 Ibid., p. 126.

8 *New York Times,* July 21, 1968.

9 Howard S. Becker, "Personal Change in Adult Life," in Bernice L. Neugarten, ed., *Middle Age and Aging* (Chicago: University of Chicago Press, 1968), p. 156.

10 Georg Simmel, *The Sociology of Georg Simmel,* trans. Kurt H. Wolf (New York: Free Press, 1950), pp. 398ff.

11 Ibid., pp. 121–22.

12 Erazim V. Kohak, "Being Young in Postindustrial Society," *Dissent,* February, 1971, p. 34.

13 James Reston, "Letters from China: I," *The New York Times,* July 28, 1971.

CHAPTER XI

1 Willard Waller, in *Old Love and New: Divorce and Readjustment* (Carbondale, Ill.: Southern Illinois University Press, 1967), describes the early phase of post-divorce readjustment as a period of bereavement.

2 A variant of "natural" exit is when one role partner is forced to exit from a role by the action of a higher authority with coercive power over the individual—such as the state, or parents in relation to minor children.

3 A role partner's death, however, may elicit feelings of guilt if the surviving partner has inadvertently caused it to take place, wished for it, or felt anger over the loss; but in such cases it is the invidious *thought,* not the death itself, that engenders guilt.

4 The murder of a role partner may be the result either of a wish to desert him or of a fear of being abandoned—mixed, of course, with strong **274**

sadistic motives not satisfied by inflicting psychic pain on the other. Murder is an extreme form of desertion in which not merely the relationship but the role partner is destroyed.

5 Even during short encounters at social gatherings, for example, a person often feels uncomfortable leaving another guest with whom he has been conversing, until a third party appears to provide restitution, as it were, for the abandonment. The custom requiring the hostess to come to the aid of her guests when they are caught in prolonged encounters serves to allay the mild feelings of guilt and shame elicited by leaving others or being left. By invoking her authority, the hostess relieves her guests of any responsibility for these acts and thereby seeks to facilitate relaxed and enjoyable sociability. Her motive, of course, is not merely altruistic; a "good party" wins points for her in the social game.

6 By the same token, conferral of the right to vote or to operate a motor vehicle, and the privileges reserved for adults, can also be viewed as restitution made by the polity to the individual for relinquishing the carefree role of a child. Youth is accorded certain rights in return for the assumption of the corresponding responsibilities.

7 See, for example, Sigmund Freud, "On Narcissism: An Introduction," in *Collected Papers IV* (London: Hogarth Press, 1948), pp. 30–59; Gregory Rochlin, *Griefs and Discontents* (Boston: Little, Brown, 1965), pp. 377–86; and Alexander R. Broden, "Reaction to Loss in the Aged," in Bernard Schoenberg, Arthur Carr, David Perez, Austin Kutscher, eds., *Loss and Grief: Psychological Management in Medical Practice* (New York: Columbia University Press, 1970), pp. 199–217.

8 Talcott Parsons, to my knowledge, is the first sociologist to treat illness in old age in the context of role theory, and to articulate the positive functions of the sick role for older people. See "Toward a Healthy Maturity," in *Social Structure and Personality* (New York: Free Press, 1965), pp. 252–54.

9 The extent to which banishment perpetuates the very forms of behavior that it purports to treat is a question that has arisen in various realms—mental illness, delinquency and crime, scholastic failure, and, more recently, old age.

10 This function of social groups explains a host of other empirical findings—for example, Bruno Bettelheim's observation that political prisoners were better able than other prisoners to preserve their integrity against the pressure of concentration camp guards to make them servile and obedient to authority. It explains the many studies in the sociology of formal organization that show how industrial work groups operate as **275**

bulwarks of resistance to production norms imposed by management. And it also explains Emile Durkheim's finding that Jews had lower suicide rates than Catholics and Protestants before 1870, when emergence from the ghettos began.

11 The norm of sexual faithfulness in monogamous societies is predicated on this principle. It is intended to insure undiluted commitment to one's marital partner by bestowing legitimacy only on sexual relationships in marriage. When opportunities for sexual gratification in other role contexts exist for men but not for women, without incurring heavy penalties ("the double standard"), men exhibit less commitment to the marriage relationship than do women.

12 The immigrant Jewish mother who occupied a low status position but had lofty occupational ambitions for her children had the sense—or the effrontery, depending on one's perspective—to recognize one important fact: to maintain control over her children until they finished college she had to sustain an undiminished flow of services to them, whether they liked it or not. Often they did not, but they were not given much choice in the matter.

13 Gregory Rochlin, *Griefs and Discontents* (Boston: Little, Brown, 1965), pp. 2–3, 347–49.

14 In cities, the "singles' bar" has developed to meet this need, which in earlier times and smaller communities was mainly served by the church and other groups. It is noteworthy that such bars have an age-graded character. Some cater to young people, while others have a clientele of middle-aged, formerly married people.

15 George Maddox, "Activity and Morale: A Longitudinal Study of Selected Elderly Subjects," *Social Forces,* XLII (1963), 195–204.

16 This generalization does not apply to institutions for the aged into which the feeble, sick, and senile are herded. The regulations and routines of total-care institutions operate to discourage peer relationships among inmates.

INDEX

Acquaintances, 61–62, 167–68
Adjustment, and patterns of response to aging, 148–74
Adolescence, 188, 190, 221, 224–25. *See also* Youth
Age: categories and friendship, 78–80 ff.; and events in family cycle,
   5, 6; identity, 100–132, 218–22 (*see also* Middle age); importance
   of, 229
Agricultural societies, 6
Alienation, 155 ff., 237; work, 142–46
Altruism, 200–202 ff.
"Anticipatory socialization," 241–42
Anti-intellectualism, 195
Augustine, St., 18
Authentic self, 194, 195
Authority over children, loss of, 7
Automobile manufacturers, 249

Back, Kurt, 120
"Bad breaks," alienation and, 158–59, 160
Bakan, David, 162
Bales, Robert Freed, 184
Banishment, 210 ff.
Bars, singles', 276
Becker, Howard S., 111, 197
Behavior (*see also* Patterns of response to aging):
   associates' influence on normative orientation, 125–32
Berelson, Bernard, 125
Bettelheim, Bruno, 275
Blacks (Negroes): racial segregation, 260–61; women employed, 6–7
Butler, Robert N., 187, 190–91

Carliner, Lewis, 136
Chicago Daily News, 153–54
Children, 223–24, 227–28 (*see also* Adolescence; Parenthood; Youth);
   decline in mortality rates, 4; and identity change in elders, 117; and
   role sets, 65; and self, 130
China, 206–7
Civic service, obligatory, 204–5
Class position (socio-economic status) (*see also* specific classes): and
   age identity, 131–32; and friendship, 79, 83–91; and patterns of re-
   sponse to aging, 156 ff., 172, 173
Clique membership, and age identity, 106–7 ff., 220
Coal miners, 267
Coleman, James S., 124

College. *See* Education and school
Columbia University, New Careers Program, 192
Communities (*see also* Politics): and altruism, 200–202 ff.
Concentration camps, 275
Conformity, 163 ff.
Cuaird, 113–14
Cumming, Elaine, 151, 152

Daydreaming, 155–56, 161
Death, 210, 227, 231 (*see also* Widowhood); rate, 4, 137
Death of a Salesman, 256–57
Desertion, and role exit, 210 ff.
"Disengagement," 151–53
Division of labor, 182–84
Divorce, 20, 230–31, 234, 235, 241, 251
Dropouts; dropping out, 229–30. *See also* Innovators and innovation
Durkheim, Emile, 245, 275

Economy, 181; changes in, 9–12
Education and school, 181, 194, 195–99, 202, 203–4, 241; dropouts, 229–30; and mental deterioration, 141; and retirement age, 12; starting, children and, 224; for women, 179–80, 181
Elmira study. *See* specific subjects
Employment (jobs; occupation; work), 176 ff., 234–35 (*see also* Retirement); and age identity, 105, 109, 118, 121; and changes in economy, 9–12; and friendship, 91 (*see also* Friendship); and morale scores, 26, 63, 64, 164–65, 236; and pattern of response (*see* Patterns of response to aging); and social participation scores, 34; work alienation, 142–46
"Empty-nest syndrome," 22, 179, 180
Encounter groups, 194
Entrepreneurs, retirement of, 10
Erikson, Erik, 114, 149–50, 180, 193, 212
Escapism. *See* Retreatism
Excommunication, 210
Expulsion, and role exit, 210 ff.

Factories and factory workers, 10–12, 135. *See also* Union
Faithfulness: parents and children and, 49–50, 56; sexual, 275
"Falling behind," 229
Families, 4–9, 49–50, 60–61, 221 ff. *See also* Children; Marriage; Parenthood; Widowhood
Farewell parties, 214–15

Farmers, retirement of, 10, 250
Fathers. *See* Families; Parenthood
Feminist movement, 180
Festinger, Leon, 120, 121
Freud, Sigmund, 149, 155–56, 162, 245
Friendship, 33–35, 44–46, 55, 57, 59–98, 199, 219 ff., 232, 237, 239, 240 (*see also* Social participation); and identity change, 106–10; and patterns of response to aging, 166–68 ff.; significance of, 59–75; structural constraints, 77–98
Fromm, Erich, 3
Funerals, 214

"Generation gap," 197–98
Gennep, Arnold van, 242
Goffman, Erving, 153
Grandparenthood, 24; working-class grandmothers, 8
Gratitude, children and, 47 ff.
Great Britain: East London, 256; family assistance, 11
Great Depression, 12
Groups, 17 (*see also* Clique membership; Social participation); and identity, 219–20
Guilt, and role exit, 211

Haven, Clayton, 71, 72
Health. *See* Illness and health
Hefner, Hugh, 252
Henry, William D., 151, 152
Higher class (upper class): and age identity, 119; and alienation; retreatism, 156; and retirement communities, 96
Housewives, 64, 182, 221, 252. *See also* Families; Widowhood; Women
Housing (living space; residence), 94–98; parents' separate from children, 7, 8, 50
Husbands. *See* Families; Widowhood; etc.

Identity, 99–132, 150, 212 ff., 218–22 (*see also* Authentic self); changes in, 99–114; influence of intimates on change, 115–32
Illness and health, 133–42, 216–18
Immigrants, 197–98, 235, 275–76
"Immigrants in time," 112, 197–98
Initiation, 242–43
Innovators and innovation, 160, 163–64 ff., 180, 191–93
Integrity; integration, 149–50, 168–69. *See also* Identity
Intelligence: mental deterioration, 141

"Intimacy at a distance," 54
Ireland, 113–14

Japan, family assistance in, 11
Jews and Judaism, 194, 275–76
Jobs. *See* Employment; Retirement

Kennedy, Miriam, 137
King Lear, 40–47, 54, 56, 114, 257, 261, 269
Kinship, 39–40. *See also* Families; Parenthood
Kips Bay study. *See* specific subjects
Köckeis, Eva, 54
Kohak, Erazim, 205–6

Lagos, Nigeria, 248
Lazarsfeld, Paul F., 125
Leisure pursuits, 176–77, 193. *See also* Retirement; Social participation; Widowhood
Life cycle, 176 ff., 223
Life expectancy, 3–4, 137, 176, 178
Lipset, Seymour Martin, 124
Living space. *See* Housing
London, East, 256
Loneliness, 55–57, 161. *See also* Friendship; Morale
Love, 149, 160 (*see also* Friendship); affairs, 234
Lowenthal, Marjorie Fisk, 71, 72
Lower class (*see also* Working class): and age identity, 119; patterns of response to aging, 156, 158–59, 166, 170 ff.; and understanding of self, 194–95
Lubell, Samuel, 135

McPhee, William, 125
Mao Tse-tung, 206
Marriage, 176 ff., 189–90, 226, 228, 234 ff., 241 (*see also* Divorce; Families; Parenthood; Widowhood); age and, 4 ff.; and age identity, 109, 112–13, 118; and morale, 26, 63 ff., 165, 236; and social participation, 34, 63 ff., 72–75, 80 ff.
Marx, Karl, 143
Mead, George Herbert, 129–30
Mead, Margaret, 112, 197
Medicare, 142
"Mellowness," 154
Menopause, 22, 180

Mental deterioration, 141
Merton, Robert K., 159, 241
Middle age, 23–24, 178 ff., 184–94 ff.; and age identity, 100, 102–103, 110, 116, 119 ff., 130, 132, 218 ff.
Middle class, 179; adolescence in, 225; and alienation and retreatism, 156; and housing, 96; parenthood, 8, 23, 24, 229–30; social participation, 66–67, 85 ff., 96; and work alienation, 143–44
Miller, Arthur, 256
"Momism," 183
Morale, 25–36, 55–57, 62 ff., 225–27 (see also Friendship; Social participation); and health, 140; and patterns of response to old age, 148–74; and work alienation, 144 ff.
Mothers. See Families; Parenthood; Women
Murder, 274

Narcissism, 139–40, 217
Negroes. See Blacks
New York Times, 191–93
Normative orientation, associates' influence on, 125–32

Occupation. See Employment; Retirement
Organizations. See Groups
Orphanhood, 210

Parenthood, 4 ff., 22–24, 47–57, 65, 67–70, 176 ff., 184, 225, 227 ff.; divorcees and, 235
Parsons, Talcott, 13, 184; on sickness, 138–39
Patterns of response to aging, 148–74
Peer relationships. See Friendship
Pensions, 215, 216. See also Retirement; Social security
Playboy enterprises, 252
Political prisoners, 275
Politics: and adjustment to age, 170 ff.; discussing, 125; participation of union members, 124–25
Polygamy, 266
Population: increase, 3; sex composition, 4
Printing shops, 124–25
Prisoners, 275
Protestant ethic, 143, 146, 216
Proust, Marcel, 101

Racial segregation, 260–61
Residence. See Housing

Reston, James, 207
Retirement, 13 ff., 24–36, 62 ff., 71 ff., 78, 88–94, 214–17, 219 ff., 236,
    244 (*see also* Friendship; Morale; etc.); and age identity, 104–106,
    108 ff., 118–19, 121, 122; changes in the economy and, 9–12; health
    and, 134–42, 217–18; and patterns of response to aging, 155, 157, 165;
    and training of youth, 205; and work alienation, 142 ff.
Retirement communities, 94, 95
Retreatism, 151, 155 ff.; and social action, 173, 174; and voting, 171
Riesman, David, 150–51, 164, 185
Rites of passage, 242
Rochlin, Gregory, 16, 139–40, 226
Role exit, 14–20, 62–63, 66, 78 ff. (*see also* specific situations); theo-
    retical essay on, 209–45
"Role loss," 243–44
Role restitution, 233–41. *See also* Role sequences
Role reversal, 40. *See also King Lear*
Role sequences, 222–33
Roles (*see also* specific responses, situations): new, for later life, 176–
    208 (*see also* Innovators and innovation)
Rosenmayr, Leopold, 54
Rosow, Irving, 54; on housing, 95–96; and illness, 139
Rossi, Alice, 241
Russell, Bertrand, 149, 153–54

Sabbaticals, 198
Salk, Lee, 137
Schachter, Stanley, 120
Schneider, David, 49, 60
School. *See* Education and school
Self (*see also* Identity); authentic, 194, 195
Self-employment, 9, 134
Selye, Hans, 162
"Senior citizen," 208
Sex differences, 4, 22–23; and friendship, 34–35, 72–75, 78 ff.; and kin-
    ship structure, 39; patterns of response to aging, 157, 165; and retire-
    ment, 29, 157 (*see also* Retirement); and widowhood, 14, 157 (*see
    also* Widowhood)
Sexual relations, 258; capacity in aging men, 266; and faithfulness, 275
Shakespeare, William. *See King Lear*
Shame, and role exit, 211
Shanas, Ethel, 55
Sickness. *See* Illness and health
Significant others, and self-image, 130

Simmel, George, 70–71, 72, 201, 203; on acquaintances, 61; on faithful-
ness, 49; on gratitude, 47
Simon, William, 187
Singles' bars, 276
Slater, Philip, 182, 183
Social action. *See* Altruism; Politics
Social classes. *See* Class position
Social networks, 112–13. *See also* Friendship
Social participation (*see also* Friendship): and patterns of response to
aging), 160–61 ff.; and work alienation, 144–45
Social security, 10, 12, 215, 218
Socio-economic status. *See* Class position
Spectator activities, 186
Stigmatization, 152–53
Strauss, Anselm, 111
Stravinsky, Igor, 25, 149
Streib, Gordon F., 138
Suicide, 73; religious groups and, 275
Swados, Harvey, 185
Sweden, family assistance in, 11

"Tears of happiness," 32
Thomas, W. I., 178
Thomson, Wayne E., 138
Time of Your Life, 111
Traditional societies, 38–40
Tragedy, 186
Trow, Martin, 124
Trust, and alienation, 159–60, 161
"Turning inward," 140
Tynhurst, James S., 137

UAW, 249
Unions, 10–11; and pension eligibility age, 9; chairman's activity and
political participation of members, 124–25; UAW, 249
Upper class. *See* Higher class

Voting, 125, 170 ff.

White, E. B., 103–104, 149
White-collar workers, 136, 144
Widowhood, 13 ff., 24–36, 62 ff., 71 ff., 78–88, 180, 210, 213–14, 219,
220, 231, 232, 236, 243, 244; and age identity, 105, 106, 108 ff., 117 ff.;

and eagerness to remarry, 234; grandmothers in fatherless homes, 8; median age at, 6; and patterns of response to aging, 155, 157, 165

Wilensky, Harold, 173–74

Women, 4 (*see also* Marriage; Parenthood; Sex differences; Widowhood; etc.); employment of; in labor force, 6–7, 14, 93, 179 ff.; new roles for later life, 179–81; unattached, 35

Women's Lib, 269

Work (*see also* Employment; Retirement); alienation, 142–46; in simple societies, 39

Workers. *See* Employment; Factories and factory workers; Retirement; Working class

Working class (*see also* Lower class; Retirement; Unions): adolescence in, 225; and expressions of affection, 74; and housing, 96; and parenthood, 8, 24; and social participation, 84–88 ff., 96

Youth, 178, 184, 202–6 (*see also* Adolescence; Children); dropouts, 229–30

ABOUT THE AUTHOR
Zena Smith Blau was born in New York and received
her Ph.D. in sociology at Columbia University. She
has lectured at Smith, Stanford, and the University of
Illinois, and has been a research associate at the
National Opinion Research Center, University of
Chicago. Her main fields of interest in sociology are
old age, the family, and child rearing, and she has
contributed numerous articles on these subjects to
professional journals.